BOSTON STRONG

BOSTON

CASEY SHERMAN AND DAVE WEDGE

A CITY'S TRIUMPH OVER TRAGEDY

STRONG

Foreword by Mayor Martin J. Walsh

ForeEdge

ForeEdge

An imprint of University Press of New England

www.upne.com

© 2015 Casey Sherman and Dave Wedge

All rights reserved

Manufactured in the United States of America

Designed by Mindy Basinger Hill

Typeset in Albertina MT Pro

For permission to reproduce any of the material in this
book, contact Permissions, University Press of New England,
One Court Street, Suite 250, Lebanon NH 03766;
or visit www.upne.com

Paper ISBN: 978-1-61168-559-6

Ebook ISBN: 978-1-61168-728-6

Library of Congress Control Number: 2014948151

5   4   3   2   1

Frontispiece: A makeshift memorial for marathon bombing victims at Copley Square,
Boston, Massachusetts, on April 30, 2013. © dinhhang / 123RF Stock Photo

For Martin Richard, Lingzi Lu, Krystle Campbell, Sean Collier,

and all of the survivors of the April 2013 terror attacks in Boston.

Each of you inspires this city and this nation every day.

CONTENTS

FOREWORD

Marathon Monday is always one of the most remarkable days in Boston and has been for more than 100 years.

It's a day when people from across the globe turn their eyes to our great city to watch the world's elite runners compete in one of the most unique and challenging road races known to man. For Bostonians, it's a rite of spring as millions emerge from winter hibernation, congregate along the race route to cheer on thousands of runners and celebrate the human spirit.

Terrorists tried to destroy our beloved tradition on April 15, 2013. They failed.

When I became mayor of Boston in January 2014, fulfilling a lifelong dream of mine, one of the first challenges of my administration was to organize and oversee the first anniversary events of the Boston Marathon bombings. It was a monumental task as I was thrust into the position of trying to calm fears of terrorism while leading the city through one of its most somber moments.

The stories that unfold in the pages ahead may at times be difficult to read. The bombings undeniably left a trail of wreckage in our city marked by immeasurable sadness, tragedy, and heartbreak. The nation lost a little more of its innocence that day as well.

But there are also incredible tales of inspiration, hope, kindness, and heroism. What happened in the days and months after those cowardly attacks was nothing short of miraculous and revealed the indomitable spirit of Boston and America.

Authors Casey Sherman and Dave Wedge spent countless hours over several months interviewing first responders, witnesses, survivors, family members of those who lost their lives, and public officials. Their dedication, compassion, and commitment was fueled by a desire to honor the victims and survivors.

Like Wedge and Sherman, I have met many of the survivors and victims' families and shared in their grief. I came away inspired by their strength and bravery. After reading this book, you will too.

So many of them have shared in something so sad. But they chose not to quit and instead turned their tragedy into ways to inspire and help others. They've formed charities. They've supported one another. They've worked hard to rebuild their lives. They've learned how to find a new normal.

Through their loss, grief, and sadness, they've found ways to help others. They've been incredible models of love and kindness.

The city will never forget what happened that dark day—among the darkest in Boston's long history. We will always honor those innocent people hurt and killed at the hands of cowards.

But the marathon will be stronger—as it certainly was on the first anniversary of the bombings. I watched in amazement for hours as runners crossed the finish line on April 20, 2014, and knew that Boston would never be the same. But I also knew we would be better.

This city is resilient. This is our marathon, and no one is going to take it away from us.

Boston is a proud city, a fiercely loyal city. When you hurt one of us, you hurt us all. When one of us gets knocked down, we help them up. We take care of our own.

We will not be held down. We will not be afraid.

We are strong. We are Boston Strong.

Mayor Martin J. Walsh
BOSTON, MASS.

[1]

PATRIOTS' DAY

The battle, Sir, is not to the strong alone;
it is to the vigilant, the active, the brave.
— Patrick Henry

LEXINGTON, MASSACHUSETTS, APRIL 15, 2013, 5:45 A.M.

The cold ground trembled as the drumbeat of war echoed across Lexington Green, where thousands of spectators huddled together against the early morning chill. With their hands tucked into the lined pockets of heavy coats and heads wrapped in the warmth of woolen hats, hoodies, and scally caps, these hearty onlookers had gathered to witness the annual bloodletting ritual that had grown to symbolize the violent birth of the American Revolution. The crowd stood ten rows deep on both sides of the green, some with arms raised in iPhone salutes to capture the spectacle on video to share later on social media channels like YouTube and Facebook. A group of distinguished guests occupied the best vantage point on a raised platform that had been draped in patriotic bunting and set up directly in front of the Jonathan Harrington House at 1 Harrington Road.

Those who had been coming out to the event each Patriots' Day since the tradition had begun in 1969 recognized seventy-nine-year-old Bill Poole, a retired history and science teacher, who was standing in the center of the green with his silver mane tucked under a dark tricorne hat. For thirteen years, Poole had been a member of a local reenactment group known as the Lexington Minute Men, and the battle he was about to recreate was truly in his blood. Poole was a direct descendant of Ebenezer Locke, a farmer from Woburn who, according to some historians, fired the first musket shot against the British Regulars on that tragic April morning in 1775. Poole had played the role of his ancestor in previous reenactments, but this day was different. This day, he had finally been given the opportunity to perform what was considered the event's lead role—that of Captain John Parker.

It was Parker, a forty-six-year-old father of seven and hardened veteran of the French and Indian War, who had assembled a small band of armed colonists on the green 238 years before. "Stand your ground. Don't fire unless fired upon," he told the group of just under seventy militiamen. "But if they want to have a war, let it start here."

Poole recited his line as the British Regulars, draped in red coats and wearing white britches, formed in tight columns nearly a hundred yards away. The pounding of drums was suddenly replaced by an eerie silence as the crowd watched six actors in the roles of British Major John Pitcairn and others advance toward the colonists. "Throw down your arms, ye villains, ye rebels," one actor shouted. "Damn you, disperse!" The warning was met by a rousing "Huzzah!" from the assembled British Regulars—which in turn triggered a volley of giggles from the event's younger spectators, many of whom had climbed the branches of tall oak trees for a better look at the carnage they were about to witness. Whether the result of steely resolve or simple confusion, the colonists refused to move. With precision and with muskets raised, the Regulars advanced toward their foes. In the guise of Captain Parker, Bill Poole—seeing that his militiamen were grossly outnumbered—ordered them to make a hasty retreat. At this moment, the crack of a single musket shot reverberated across the Lexington Green. The battle had begun.

A moment later, brilliant flashes of orange and white exploded from the muzzles of dozens of Red Coat muskets, and on cue the Lexington Minute Men began to fall to this sacred ground. The crowd gasped as the violence reached its climax when a British Regular plunged his bayonet into the chest of a single downed colonist. As the controlled chaos continued, the Lexington Green disappeared under a blanket of gray smoke that masked the faces of dying men, screaming where they lay. The drums of war thumped loudly once more while the British fell back into position. The smoke soon rose off the green, revealing the sacrifice beneath—the bodies of men lying motionless on the grass. Once again, blood had been figuratively spilled, the annual ritual completed.

The crowd dispersed in silence as the reenactors pulled themselves up from the grass. Hours later, the day would offer a more joyous opportunity to honor the spirit of Patriots' Day, a holiday honoring our colonial forefathers that is celebrated by the Commonwealth of Massachusetts. Many of those gathered in Lexington had planned to regroup in the afternoon to root for their beloved Boston Red Sox playing at Fenway Park, and to cheer on friends and loved ones participating in the 117th running of the world-renowned Boston Marathon. The unsuspecting celebrants would be joined by two young men—Black Hat and White Hat—who were planning a blood ritual of their own.

Detective Sergeant Danny Keeler rose before dawn and made his way to the bathroom quietly so as not to wake his longtime girlfriend, Carol, who was still sleeping soundly in their bed. Today was a holiday for most, but not for him or his fellow officers of the Boston Police Department. They had orders to report for duty on this Patriots' Day, better known as Marathon Monday. Keeler had run the marathon once back in 1978 and would never think of running it again. He looked in the bathroom mirror at his aging face, the sprouts of gray growing out of his mustache and along his temple. He was still fit, muscular even, but his body was built for sprinting, not running long distances. It suited him well on the job, where the finish line meant chasing down a suspect before he made his way over a chain-link fence to freedom.

He sighed, rubbed his hand across his square jaw, and thought back to his younger days of chasing thugs and running the marathon. Those days were long behind him, he thought, massaging his knee, which was recently replaced with a titanium joint. His other knee, also needing replacing, throbbed.

When he did run Boston back during the Jimmy Carter administration, Keeler nearly gave up when he reached the halfway point at Wellesley where his legs turned to rubber and his lungs burned. That day, the only thing that kept him pressing on toward the finish line at Boylston Street was the gruff voice of his former Marine Corps drill sergeant resounding in his ear, demanding that he not quit.

Once a leatherneck, always a leatherneck, Keeler thought to himself as he examined his face once more before hitting the shower. He felt that everything he had earned, he owed to the Corps. He'd been an aimless kid when he first walked into the recruiting office back in 1969. Having left home at age sixteen, he had begun living and working as an orderly at the state psychiatric hospital in Mattapan. Still, it was better than staying in the projects where he'd spent his childhood. "It's a *development,*" his mother always said. "Don't call it a project." Although his mother did everything possible to turn their concrete box into a home, it was what it was—a cramped tenement that felt more like a prison. The state psychiatric hospital wasn't much better, but at least it was much bigger. Understanding there was no future in his current path, Keeler joined the Marines as soon as he was old enough. He survived boot camp and underwent jungle combat training at Camp Pendleton in preparation for deployment to Vietnam, but he never made it out of the United States. When his unit reached El Toro, the Marine Corps base in Irvine, California, that was the launch point for operations in Southeast Asia, it received orders to stand down. It was crazy to think this after all these years, but Keeler viewed the fact that he hadn't fought in Vietnam as the greatest of his many regrets in life. And now his own son was serving in Afghanistan.

But today, as on so many other days, Keeler set aside his regrets and planned to plow ahead as he had always done. And this day would be easier than most. Today was Boston's version of an old Chevy commercial—Marathon Monday was quintessential Americana. Working the marathon was unlike working other big sporting events in the city, where drunken college students would use a big win or loss by the Red Sox, Patriots, Bruins, or Celtics as an excuse to turn over cars and light fires in Kenmore Square. The Boston Marathon was different. The marathon brought thousands of families into the city to cheer on moms, dads, sons, daughters, and even total strangers, most of whom were competing only against themselves, and also to cheer on the countless other participants who, over the past two decades, have helped raise more than $127 million for local charities. Danny Keeler and his men would keep an eye out for trouble as the bars and restaurants along the race route would be packed with people, especially after the matinee Red Sox game let out.

After showering, Keeler pulled on a clean shirt, a pair of jeans, and his New Balance running shoes. He grabbed the keys to his unmarked silver Ford Fusion and walked out the door of his home in Quincy and into the morning chill.

Mery Daniel felt the growing itch of spring fever. She'd been cooped up inside her in-laws' apartment in Mattapan for what seemed like a lifetime. First it was the endless winter that piled up foot after foot of thick, wet snow on her stoop, making it impossible to go outside. Even though she now considered herself to be a hearty New Englander, the Haitian native had never gotten quite accustomed to the unpredictably harsh Boston weather. Now it was the studying—hours upon hours of studying that made her brown eyes strain and her temples throb. Mery had been cramming for her medical board exams, and her focus today was understanding and treating cardiomyopathy, a condition in which a damaged heart could not effectively pump blood.

She lifted her eyes from the textbook and peered at her five-year-old daughter, Ciarra Surri, whose blood had been pumping quite well all morning. The young girl was a little tornado of boundless energy as she danced around the apartment with a wide smile that lit up every room she entered. Every time she looked at Ciarra Surri, Mery couldn't help reflecting on her own journey. Her daughter would grow up with opportunities and conveniences that she could only dream about as a little girl living in the central Haitian city of Hinche, about an hour's drive from Port-au-Prince. Mery had been raised by her mother, Gabrielle Fanfan, who juggled the rigors of running a tiny convenience store with the challenges of caring for four children: Mery, her sister, and two brothers. All five lived in a modest, cramped apartment. Their mother had sacrificed comfort for her kids' education. Just about every *gourde* earned at Gabrielle Fanfan's small shop went toward tuition for the private Catholic schools that Mery and her siblings attended. Still, Mery's childhood was a happy one as her family would entertain themselves with Haitian folktales and by taking long walks to a nearby river to bathe. Her native language was Creole, but she learned how to speak English by reading Harlequin romances — much to her mother's chagrin. Salacious reading aside, Gabrielle recognized her daughter's intellectual gifts early on and knew that Mery could go only so far in life with a Haitian education. So, when her daughter turned sixteen, Fanfan sent her to the United States to live with her father, from whom she had separated when Mery was an infant.

Mery's father, Hary, had left Haiti in the 1980s and had settled in Brockton, Massachusetts, with his new wife, Rose. Brockton, a working class city of 100,000 a half-hour south of Boston, had a large Haitian population, so it was an easy transition for Hary, who found work as a bus driver. The change did not come so easily for his daughter, however, when she arrived a decade later. In Haiti, Mery had been accustomed to a small school, but Brockton High School had four thousand students and was the size of a small college. At sixteen years old, she could very easily have gotten lost, both physically and mentally. At first, Mery was first placed into a bilingual program at Brockton High, but she decided that it was not for her. "I wanted full immersion," she recalls. "I wanted to be an American teenager and to do that, I had to be around other American teenagers."

Mery Daniel was a young woman with big plans. Her father was strict, and curfews were put in place to keep Mery focused on her studies. And focused she was. After graduating, she attended the University of Massachusetts–Amherst, where she studied biochemistry and molecular biology. Mery's only visit back to her native Haiti came in 2010, after a catastrophic earthquake killed more than one hundred thousand people and had left the country's major cities in rubble. Mery returned to her homeland as a member of a group of students who distributed food on behalf of the United Nations. "It was the End of Days," Mery recalls with horror. "So many lives were destroyed. People were devastated and desperate." More than five thousand Haitians who had survived the initial earthquake and the violent aftershocks were later pulled from the rubble with bodies so broken that arms and legs had to be amputated just so the victims could live. The images of those survivors with their crudely wrapped stumps at their elbows and knees would never fade from Mery's memory. She believed that God had put her on earth to help her people—to help all people.

Mery Daniel graduated college in 2005 and went on to receive her degree from the Medical University of Lodz, one of the most prestigious medical schools in Poland. Now back in Boston, she was an aspiring doctor, a mother, and a wife to her husband, Richardson, a fellow medical school graduate who works with autistic children. By Marathon Monday, Mery had completed two of her medical board exams, and she was now studying for a third. She had been concentrating too hard for too long, and now her eyes were glazed over. Mery knew that she had to take a break; she had to get out of her apartment for the day. She had attended the Boston Marathon just once before and had relished the experience. It allowed her to be a part of something that was much bigger than herself. The marathon helped her connect with the city she now called her own. Yes, today was a day to put away the textbooks and to celebrate the fact that she was now a true Bostonian. She would attend the marathon and applaud all those runners who epitomized the courage and determination of the human spirit.

"Is this my sixteenth or seventeenth Boston Marathon?" forty-three-year-old Javier Pagan asked himself while finishing his breakfast at Billy's Coffee Shop on Berkeley Street in Boston's South End, just a few blocks from the finish line. The years all blurred together after doing this for so long. Pagan had been a member of the Boston Police Department for nineteen years and had patrolled Boylston Street on race day for nearly all of them. Normally, his only concern was the weather. The last thing he wanted to do was stand out there in the rain all day, which he had done on more than a few soggy Marathon Mondays. In Boston, the weather in mid-April is always a roll of the dice. But today's forecast called for near-perfect conditions: the temperature was expected to hover around fifty degrees under sun-filled skies. It was a day that could bring record-breaking times for the winners—unless some idiot decided to jump the barricade and tackle one of the elite runners as they made their way toward the finish line.

Pagan and his fellow detail officers would be on alert for exactly that. Only three months before, as the Kenyan marathoner Edwin Kipsang Rotich was nearing the finish line of the 10k Kings Race in Cuiaba, Brazil, he had been grabbed and shoved by a spectator. Rotich still went on to win the race while his attacker, a man with a history of psychological problems, was arrested and thrown in jail. As on prior Marathon Mondays, Pagan would be positioned along the finish line, where he would scan the deep crowd for anyone looking to cause trouble. It was considered light duty for Pagan, an officer who had seen much and had overcome more during his journey.

Pagan grew up in Dorchester, a predominantly Irish neighborhood bordering South Boston. Just a year after he and his family had emigrated from Puerto Rico and had moved into their apartment on Stoughton Street, the entire city collapsed under the weight of seething racial tension triggered by the infamous Busing Crisis, when violent protests flared up in white neighborhoods over the enforcement of public school desegregation. The racial hatred of the time directly impacted Pagan and his family. "We'd walk along Stoughton Street and then Columbia Road, and people would throw beer bottles at us and call us *niggers*," he recalls. "My mom didn't really speak English, so she had no clue. We were little and didn't even know what the N-word was. Finally, the haters figured out we were Hispanic, not black, so they began calling us *spics* instead."

Pagan found both solace and strength at his neighborhood church and a priest there who was also a Boston police chaplain. "Father Francis used to bring the K-9 unit to St. Paul's, and we went out on the police boat during the summer," Pagan remembers. "I liked to watch cop shows, and my dream was to be a police officer. But I was a scrawny kid, and I just never knew that I could do the job."

Weighing less than a hundred pounds in high school, Pagan was smaller than his classmates, but he also realized that he was different in another way: he knew that he was gay. He tried to suppress his feelings and hide his orientation from both his friends and his own family—he had faced enough racial taunts to know that by announcing his sexuality, he would be adding kerosene to an angry fire.

Pagan graduated from Boston Technical High School in 1989 and went on to Suffolk University, in the heart of the city. There he began studying theatre arts, but ended up earning a degree in sociology with a minor in criminal law instead. By then his body had finally filled out, and now he had the education to pursue his life's passion. Javier Pagan wanted to be a cop. He entered the police academy, where his brother-in-law served as an instructor. Among his fellow cadets were a man and a woman who were both openly gay. Their honesty and courage opened the door slightly for Pagan, but not enough to give him the strength to come out himself. That would not happen until his first year on the force—and a surprise awaited him when he did. "When I came out," he recalls, "they all said they knew." Pagan found overwhelming support from his family, especially his three older sisters. He also found support within the ranks of the Boston Police Department. First and foremost, he was a cop, just like them. He had been baptized in blood and had seen more than his share of stabbings and shootings on city streets.

But he wasn't expecting anything like that on this day. He wasn't expecting Black Hat and White Hat.

[2]

MURDER IN WALTHAM

WALTHAM, MASSACHUSETTS, SEPTEMBER 11, 2011, SOMETIME AFTER 7:30 P.M.

As millions around the nation somberly observed the tenth anniversary of the September 11, 2001, attacks on America, a Chechen immigrant named Tamerlan Tsarnaev stood inside the second-floor apartment at 12 Harding Avenue in Waltham, Massachusetts, a relatively quiet suburb just eleven miles west of Boston. The apartment belonged to his friend Brendan Mess, a twenty-five-year-old college graduate who had done little with the degree in professional writing he had earned from Champlain College three years before. Mess was a stoner who had supported himself by selling marijuana and possibly other drugs out of his apartment, a place he had been living in for less than a month and had rarely left. Neighbors had noticed a steady stream of visitors coming and going, but those living on Harding Avenue preferred Brendan Mess over the previous renters, who had used the apartment like a frat house, partying until dawn on many occasions. He lived in the second-floor apartment with his girlfriend, Hilda Eltilib, whose name appeared on the rental lease. Recently, Mess had invited another friend to live with them, thirty-one-year-old Erik Weissman, who had just been kicked out of his own apartment in nearby Roslindale after police raided the place and seized a large stash of drugs and cash. Weissman needed a place to crash while he got back on his feet financially, and his buddy Brendan had been willing to help. Both knew the situation was temporary because, although Erik Weissman was also a stoner and low-level pot dealer, he was actively pursuing bigger things. The bespectacled native of Cambridge, Massachusetts, considered himself a businessman first and foremost. Along with two friends, he had founded a small company called *Hitman Glass,* which manufactured Chihuly-inspired ornamental marijuana pipes to take advantage of the rapid de-criminalization of marijuana sweeping through parts of the country. Weissman's partner had just opened a shop on the outskirts of Los Angeles, and Erik was planning to head west once his legal problems were taken care of in Massachusetts. The raid on his Roslindale apartment had followed an arrest in 2008 for marijuana possession with intent to distribute after he had been pulled over by police while carrying a large brown paper bag filled with smaller plastic bags of pot. The decriminalization of pot wasn't happening fast enough for Weissman, who was also a presence within the Boston hip-hop scene—he had even helped finance the second album for a local artist he dubbed *Virtuoso.*

Another friend of Brendan Mess, Raphael "Rafi" Teken, was also in the second-floor apartment that night. Teken had graduated from Brookline High School in 1992 and prestigious Brandeis University, located right in Waltham, in 1998. At age thirty-seven, he was several years older than both Mess and Weissman, but the three men bonded through their shared Jewish heritage and their love of marijuana. Although an athlete in high school, Teken had set aside his passion for swimming and most other sports as he got older. He enjoyed getting high, but according to those who knew him, he had never pushed his lifestyle on others and was considered a trusted friend who wanted to help people. When his cousin was forced out of her home after a devastating fire, Teken worked tirelessly to collect donations for the family. According to their friends, neither Weissman nor Teken was capable of violence. Brendan Mess, however, was considered a skilled mixed martial artist and in 2010 had gotten arrested for assaulting several people at a store in Cambridge. Still, the trio resembled characters from a Seth Rogen comedy more than they did real hardcore gangbangers. No one could have imagined what they were all about to face.

Tamerlan "Tam" Tsarnaev was another friend of Brendan Mess. The two had become close after meeting at a local gym. Both were physical creatures — Tamerlan more so than Mess, who despite his martial arts prowess was deemed by some to be soft. Tamerlan, a Muslim, considered Mess to be his closest Jewish friend. Out of deference to his pal's religious beliefs, Mess even asked his girlfriend, Hilda, to cook only halal meat, permissible to Muslims, when Tamerlan would visit. Hilda was Muslim herself, but not the practicing kind. An African immigrant, she had refused to follow strict Muslim doctrine when she arrived in the United States. Hilda didn't pray much, nor did she wear a traditional hijab to cover her head and chest. She also drank alcohol, which drew concern from Tamerlan when he was around.

"You're not doing the things Muslim women do," Tamerlan had scolded her during one visit.[1] Hilda didn't perceive his words to be threatening, just a difference in philosophy. If there was fire behind Tamerlan's eyes, both Hilda Eltilib and Brendan Mess failed to recognize it — even though Tsarnaev had more than once hinted that he was something other than what he appeared to be. He had even informed Mess that the FBI had placed him on a terrorist watch list only a few weeks before. Brendan relayed the news to Hilda, and both got a chuckle out of the mere thought. Their friend Tam, they believed, was a threat to no one. But Hilda was gone now. After a fight with Brendan, she had jumped on a plane to Florida, where she was visiting a friend to help clear her head. Hilda was due back in Boston on September 12. She and Brendan would give their relationship another chance. He had even promised to pick her up at Logan International Airport.

Tamerlan Tsarnaev arrived at the Waltham apartment on Sunday, September 11, with another man, Ibragim Todashev, a mop-topped fellow Chechen immigrant whose lean, muscular body and long, crooked nose bore both the reward and punishment of years studying mixed martial arts. He had recently won his first match by applying a guillotine choke and forcing his opponent into submission during an MMA bout in Tampa, Florida. Todashev had trained with Tamerlan, and they were known to have prowled Boston's nightclub scene together before Tamerlan had become more devout. That evening, both men talked their way inside Brendan Mess's Waltham apartment. Mess kept a handgun for protection but apparently did not perceive his friend Tamerlan as a threat. Brendan and Tam talked for an uncertain period of time, their voices never raised high enough to alert neighbors to any trouble. Whatever the alleged reason Tamerlan gave Mess for the visit, Tsarnaev had leverage over his friend because only he and Todashev knew what their intent truly was. Suddenly a knife appeared in Tamerlan's hand. With help from Todashev, Tsarnaev attacked Mess, Erik Weissman, and Rafi Teken, slit each of their throats from ear to ear, and left their lifeless bodies in separate rooms but in identical positions—lying on their stomachs with their heads positioned slightly to the right. All were covered with marijuana leaves and stems. The killers left five thousand dollars in cash but took Brendan's gun. The bodies grew cold overnight as the blood of each victim congealed on the floor inside the apartment at 12 Harding Avenue.

The next day, Hilda Eltilib returned to Boston as expected. She called her boyfriend, but there was no answer. Hilda and Brendan had spoken at 7:30 the night before, and he told her that he loved her. She tried calling once more later that evening to say goodnight, but there was no answer. She knew Brendan, Erik, and Rafi were planning to get together to watch the Dallas Cowboys take on the New York Jets on NBC's *Sunday Night Football*, so Hilda simply dismissed the slight as *men being men*. Still, the words "I love you" spoken by Brendan earlier had kept her heart beating faster during her morning flight from Florida. The fact that Brendan still wasn't answering his phone was a big problem—one that just might complicate her homecoming. Hilda grabbed her luggage, swallowed her growing anger, and walked out to the curb to hail a taxicab. She arrived at 12 Harding Avenue just before 2:30 p.m. on Monday, September 12. She paid the driver, grabbed her bags, and entered the building, where she climbed a flight of stairs and stuck her key into the door. Something was wrong. She turned the key and opened the door slowly, possibly hoping that someone would yell, "Surprise!" Instead, there was only silence. Hilda stepped forward into a grisly nightmare. She gazed in horror at the bodies of her boyfriend and the two others. Hilda turned on her heels and ran down the stairs into the street screaming—"There's blood everywhere!"[2]

Tamerlan Tsarnaev did not attend the wake or funeral for his friend Brendan Mess, a possible clue that had been overlooked by Mess's friends and also by investigators. The fact that the murders had occurred on the anniversary of the 9/11 attacks on America had no special significance for police—it was just a random date on the calendar for these particular crimes. A short time later, Tsarnaev made plans to return to his homeland.

Tamerlan's grandfather, Zaindy Tsarnaev, was just eleven years old when he and his family were forced out of their home in Chiri-Yurt, a small Chechen village overlooking the Caucasus Mountains, by Josef Stalin's troops in 1944. The Soviet dictator was exacting his revenge against the Chechens for their collaboration with the Nazis during World War II. The expulsion of the Chechen people was carried out under Operation Lentil. Despite the fact that more than 40,000 Chechens fought for the Red Army, Stalin was outraged over the time and resources needed to quell two nationalist rebellions and by the rumors that Chechen tribesmen had granted German troops safe passage to the oil-rich fields of Azerbaijan. There would be no safe passage for the nearly five hundred thousand Chechens and more than two hundred thousand ethnic Ingush, Kalmyks, Balkars, and Karachays who were forced onto unheated freight cars and shipped off to Siberia and Central Asia. The refugees were crammed into the cars like cattle. No one had room to sit. Thousands, many of them children, died during the grueling two-week trek. Years later, one survivor said that Soviet soldiers would simply toss bodies of the dead out of the cars and onto the snow. When Zaindy Tsarnaev and his family arrived in Tokmok, Kyrgyztan, they had to survive on clover and potato skins left out by local villagers. Countless more refugees died during that harsh winter, when the ground proved too frozen to properly bury the dead. Mourning relatives would dig ditches only half a meter deep, wrap their loved one in an old piece of cloth, and bury them. Most times, their bodies were dragged out of the earth and devoured by starving dogs. Those fortunate enough to survive to the spring were put to work in the town's *kolkhoz* (collective farm). Able-bodied boys like Zaindy Tsarnaev were forced to work on the farm for little or no pay and also ordered to perform a minimum of fifty days each year doing government work such as road construction. Those who shirked their duties were shipped off again—this time to Siberia.

A decade later, in 1957—four years after Stalin's death—the Soviet Union allowed its dispossessed peoples to return to their ancestral lands, but Zaindy Tsarnaev and his family stayed in Tokmok, along with many other Chechens who formed a small, tight-knit community. As an adult,

Zaindy pieced together a living by trolling through town in search of some-thing of value to sell. He usually found his way to the local dump, as others had, and would dig for hours on end through a vast wasteland of garbage in hopes of finding metal wires or a few glass bottles that could later be sold. But the dump could be a dangerous place, and Zaindy Tsarnaev never paid much attention to his own personal safety. Tokmok was home to a Soviet airbase where thousands of fighter pilots were trained during the hottest days of the Cold War, and the dump was sometimes used by the military to discard old equipment. In 1988, during one visit to a dump the villagers had nicknamed The Golden Pit, Zaindy thought he scored a big payday. He uncovered several metal objects from a trash heap, objects he believed were worth more than the bottles he normally found. He tossed them into his rusty car carelessly. The metal objects, which were in reality old Soviet munitions, exploded on impact—smothering the vehicle and Zaindy Tsarnaev with flames.

Ruslan Tsarnaev, a son of Zaindy's, left their homeland and immigrated to the United States in 1995. He changed his last name to Tsarni, the origi-nal Chechen spelling of Tsarnaev, and lived in Washington State before re-turning to Kyrgyzstan a few years later with his wife, Samantha Fuller, the daughter of a former CIA case officer. The couple lived briefly in the city of Bishkek, where Samantha Tsarni worked for Price Waterhouse on privat-ization projects, but the two soon had a falling out and divorced in 1999, after their return to the United States. Ruslan Tsarni remarried and within a few years was earning more than two hundred thousand dollars a year, plus stock options, which allowed him to build a sprawling, two-storied home in the upscale community of Montgomery Village, Maryland. He had earned his success as millions of other new Americans had: by work-ing hard and striving for a better life. This core ethic had been lost on his brother, Anzor, who had come to the United States in 2002 with his wife, Zubeidat, and their youngest son, Dzhokhar. Originally, Ruslan had high hopes for his relatives, especially Dzhokhar's older brother, Tamerlan, who spoke about earning an engineering degree in America. But Tamerlan was a talker and not much of a doer—just like his father, Anzor, and his grandfather, Zaindy. Anzor and Zaindy had been cut from the same cloth. Neither man had a formal or extensive education, unlike Ruslan, who was a trained lawyer. Instead, Anzor found work with his hands, like his father before him. He had been a mechanic back home and dreamed of opening a profitable garage in the United States. After his arrival in the spring of 2002, when he and his wife declared political asylum, Anzor leaned on a fellow Chechen for assistance.

Dr. Khassan Baiev was a celebrated trauma surgeon who had treated thousands of soldiers on both sides of the wars between the Russians and the Chechens. At one time, he had been the only surgeon for nearly eighty thousand people living in Grozny during the height of the conflict. Baiev claimed to have performed eight brain operations and sixty-seven amputations within one forty-eight hour period. Because of his strict adherence to the Hippocratic oath, Baiev was labeled a traitor by both sides and was under constant threat of assassination. In 2002, the surgeon fled to the United States, where he was sponsored for political asylum by the human rights organization Physicians for Human Rights. Baiev later settled with his family in Needham, Massachusetts, a suburb of Boston.

One day, Baiev received a call from his fellow Chechen Anzor Tsarnaev asking for help. "Please, can you help me?" Anzor begged over the phone. "There's no one here to meet us."[3] Baiev opened his home to the Tsarnaev family and allowed them to stay in Needham for one month before helping them transition into a third-floor apartment with Tamerlan, Dzhokhar, and their two daughters, Bella and Ailina, The place was on Norfolk Street in Cambridge, which was a self-declared asylum city for immigrants, both legal and illegal. Anzor and Zubeidat felt the only way to get ahead in their new world was to inflate their status in their old one. The couple told anyone who would listen that they were trained lawyers back home. This was untrue. Anzor's brother, Ruslan, and their three sisters had all earned law degrees, but he had received no such diploma. He also claimed that the reason he had fled was because as a prosecutor, he had tried to break the local mob's stranglehold on his community. In reality, Tsarnaev and an uncle traded in a number of different products, including tobacco. Their business most likely drew the attention of local mobsters, who — according to family lore — responded by cutting off the head of the family pet, a German shepherd, and dumping it on the Tsarnaev's doorstep.

Whether this is true or something the couple concocted after watching a film like *The Godfather*, it fit their narrative of violent persecution. Zubeidat also told a co-worker that Russian mobsters had once kidnapped Anzor and beaten him so severely that they had no choice but to flee to the United States. The glorification of her husband, and thereby herself, was an important element of their relationship from the start. The couple met in the 1980s, she an ethnic Avar, a people who had been in constant conflict with the Chechens for centuries. Zubeidat was both volatile and alluring and had set out to win Anzor's heart despite the disapproval of both families. Her arrival in America was like one extended walk down the red carpet. Zubeidat was very much the epitome of the modern Muslim woman. She paraded around in flowing dresses and high heels and pushed Anzor to dress with style to match her own. While Zubeidat got work as a home healthcare assistant, her husband tried his hand working on cars. Anzor particularly enjoyed working on older cars without computer chips as they reminded him of the Soviet-model automobiles he had worked on in the past. Anzor had no garage, so he bartered for space or did his repairs in the street when the weather was good. Loyal customers would sometimes get invited to the Tsarnaev home for a traditional meal of dumplings and chicken soup. One such customer, a journalist attending nearby Harvard University on a fellowship, was thrilled to receive an invitation to dine with Anzor and his family as he had planned to write about Russia's Islamic insurgency. Alan Cullison remembers climbing up the narrow, cluttered stairway of the Tsarnaev's Norfolk Street home where he was greeted by Anzor, Zubeidat, and the children who offered a demure hello before retreating into the corner of their three-hundred-square-foot apartment. The wife dominated the conversation from the very beginning—grilling Cullison about life in America, especially about the prospect for a good job for their eldest son, Tamerlan, who stood silently with arms folded in the doorway of the tiny kitchen. The conversation flowed in Russian as Cullison ate and answered Zubeidat's rapid-fire questions the best he knew how. The journalist asked Anzor what he thought of Russia's violent oppression of the Chechens, but Anzor and even Tamerlan appeared more concerned about earning money in the United States than in the fighting back home. Zubeidat enjoyed the conversation and was intrigued by Cullison's interest in the plight of Chechen refugees. Following another dinner,

Zubeidat praised Cullison as a "real *dzhigit*" (warrior), while dismissing her own husband with a wave of her hand.[4]

Zubeidat's attitude toward both America and Islam began to slowly shift as she opened herself up to more radical Muslim thinking about the attacks of September 11, 2001, when nineteen al-Qaeda terrorists hijacked four commercial airliners and flew two of them into the World Trade Center towers and a third into the Pentagon. The fourth plane, United Airlines Flight 93 out of Newark, New Jersey, crashed into a field near Shanksville, Pennsylvania. In total, 2,996 Americans were killed and more than 6,000 others injured. The fact that two of the flights, American Airlines Flight 11 and United Airlines Flight 175, had originated in Boston was not lost on Zubeidat Tsarnaev, who had grown to believe that the tragedy was orchestrated by the United States government as a plot to make Americans hate Muslims. Gone soon were the flowing dresses and the high-heeled pumps. Zubeidat now wore the traditional hijab to cover her once spiked, raven hair, a change in appearance that impacted her business. Zubeidat had transitioned from home healthcare aide to aesthetician after attending cosmetology school and had landed a job at Essencia Day Spa in the affluent town of Belmont, Massachusetts. She seemed fit for the job but soon began showing up for work wearing a head scarf and carrying a prayer rug on which she prayed five times a day in the salon. She made her female co-workers and customers uncomfortable and angered her bosses by refusing to work on men after her imam told her that it was sacrilegious to touch a male that had gone through puberty. "She went crazy religious," said spa co-owner Larissa Dubosarky. "I had to let her go. She refused to deal with male clients and wouldn't do waxing."[5]

After her firing, Zubeidat began offering facials out of the living room of their small apartment. Meanwhile, Anzor shifted his focus away from his wife and toward their son Tamerlan, whom he believed was the key to their American dream.

[3]

EASY MONEY

Danny Keeler walked into his office at 650 Harrison Avenue at 7:30 a.m. He had a large hot coffee from Dunkin' Donuts in his hand and a smile on his face. This was *easy money* day. Unlike members of the fire department, all Boston police officers are ordered to work on days like this when large crowds can sometimes get out of hand. Some police officers constantly griped at the fact that they can never watch the Super Bowl, the deciding game of the World Series, or the Boston Marathon with their families—but not Keeler. He welcomed the overtime duty. He and Carol had just purchased a place in Naples, Florida, in a neighborhood that included twelve retired Boston cops, and the extra money would come in handy. Keeler's youngest daughter, Julie, was still in college at UMass-Amherst, and between the high cost of tuition and books, his wallet was always on the lighter side. He huddled quickly with the guys who would be patrolling the finish line with him before gathering outside on the adjacent basketball court with dozens of other officers from District D-4 (Back Bay/South End) and District D-14 (Allston/Brighton). All the names had been culled from the same overtime list. There were others who had simply volunteered for marathon duty from nearby District B-3 (Mattapan) and supervisors from across the city looking to pick up some easy overtime. Boston Police Captain Paul Ivens, who had previously served as commander of the Boston police bomb squad, gave roll call.

"Guys, try to keep the drinking crowds down," Ivens told his men. "If you see any issues, call for help immediately. Grab a quick breakfast, and I want everybody on post by 11 a.m. We're gonna have the wheelchair runners coming in. We're gonna have some of the handicapped guys coming in early. When they come across—be looking at the crowds, don't be looking at them. I don't want any Rosie Ruizes or any of that bullshit."

Until this day, the name Rosie Ruiz signified all that could possibly go wrong with the Boston Marathon. During the eighty-fourth running of the marathon in 1980, Ruiz, a Cuban American, was crowned the winner in the women's category with a record-breaking time of 2:31:56. Questions about her astonishing finish were raised immediately by many at the finish line who noticed that Ruiz wasn't sweating or out of breath. She also appeared a little flabby and out of shape. Hers was not the body of an elite runner. Other elite runners including men's winner "Boston" Billy Rodgers pointed out that Ruiz did not remember some of the key intervals of the race itself. Other runners could simply not remember ever seeing Ruiz anywhere along the 26.2-mile course. Witnesses who did remember seeing Ruiz claimed she had jumped out from a crowd of spectators on Commonwealth Avenue, just half a mile from the finish line. A few months before, Ruiz had run the New York City Marathon and was credited with a time of 2:56:29, which qualified her for Boston. Yet someone from that race came forward, claiming that she had seen Ruiz on a subway headed to the marathon that day. After an investigation, Ruiz was stripped of her win and relegated to a punch line and an embarrassing footnote in Boston Marathon history.

The chances of another Rosie Ruiz situation were slim. Keeler and his men were more concerned that students from any of the nearby colleges would mistake Patriots' Day for St. Patrick's Day and use the day off from school as an excuse for an all-day drinking fest. In 2012, Keeler and his men confronted what he calls "Euro kids with money" who were hanging out the windows of a hotel along the finish line. "I remember going to them and saying, 'Hey, enough's enough. You're throwing shit out the windows down on people, and we're just not gonna have it.'"

Normally, Keeler and his men from District D-4 would communicate by police radio on channel five. But since they were working on the marathon detail, they were ordered to correspond on channel one, where they could get minute-by-minute updates on the status of the lead runners. Once the leaders hit Hereford Street and began their turn onto Boylston Street, officers would normally hear Keeler's voice on the radio. "Okay, guys at the finish line. Heads up, heads up now, they're coming down." It was all very routine and that's exactly how Keeler liked it. Nothing out of the ordinary would happen here. Not today.

As Danny Keeler and his men pulled on their orange vests and made their way to the finish line, their boss, Commissioner Ed Davis, was busy preparing for his seventh Boston Marathon as the city's police commissioner. Davis, a towering figure with a deep, booming voice and the face of a bulldog, had been Boston's top cop since the fall of 2006. To many in the Boston law enforcement community, he was still seen as an outsider. Davis's roots were planted not in Boston, but in the mill city of Lowell, just over thirty miles to the north. Thirty miles seemed more like three thousand miles to many Boston police officers who believed that the city would be better served by a commissioner who had grown up and worked on its streets. But Lowell and Boston shared many of the same challenges. Both were plagued by depressed neighborhoods where drugs led to violence and violence often led to death. Ed Davis started his law enforcement career as a beat cop in Lowell in 1978. He had been born and raised in the city and was known for his fierceness and also his fairness. Criminals often thought better than to tangle with the imposing Davis on the street, and the last thing they wanted was to see his long, stern face at their door. But he wasn't the "lock 'em up and throw away the key" type. Instead, Davis understood early on that a community could only gain positive change from within. The same went for him. He took college courses on weekends at Southern New Hampshire University, where he learned the importance of grassroots organizations and human services when it came to modern policing. He applied those teachings to his life on the street, where on a daily basis he dealt with drug pushers and drug users—including former professional boxing contender Dicky Eklund, whose story was later chronicled in the Oscar-winning film *The Fighter*. The city of Lowell saw something special in its native son and eventually elevated him to police commissioner, in 1994. Over the next five years, Davis and his department oversaw a rapid reduction in Lowell's crime rate—the fastest drop in crime of any city its size or larger in the country.

Davis's success caught the eye of Boston mayor Thomas M. Menino, who needed to replace outgoing police commissioner Kathleen O'Toole after she accepted a job with the Garda Síochána in Ireland. O'Toole's two-year stint running the Boston Police Department had been tumultuous at best. She was forced to accept full responsibility on behalf of the department after a Boston cop named Rochefort Milien shot and killed Emerson College student Victoria Snelgrove as officers tried to quell a disturbance in Kenmore Square after the Boston Red Sox beat the rival New York Yankees in the 2004 American League Championship Series. At the time, Snelgrove was just days away from celebrating her twenty-second birthday. Officer Milien and others on duty that night had been armed with a semiautomatic "less lethal" riot gun called an FN 303, which shoots a spherical projectile that is designed to break up on impact in order to avoid inflicting a critical injury. But the shot fired at Snelgrove struck her face and opened a three-quarter-inch wound behind her eye. The pellet then broke into nine pieces and damaged her brain. Snelgrove was pronounced dead at Brigham and Women's Hospital approximately twelve hours after being shot. A special investigative panel led by former US Attorney Donald K. Stern blasted the Boston Police Department, claiming that poor planning and a breakdown of command contributed to the Snelgrove tragedy. The city of Boston paid five million dollars to the victim's family — the largest wrongful death settlement in Boston's history. Commissioner O'Toole demoted the police superintendent who was in charge that night, suspended two others, including Milien, and wrote official reprimands for two more. Commissioner O'Toole had not signed off on the operations plan for the Red Sox celebration, and Mayor Menino backed his commissioner, pledging his full confidence in her leadership. "Anyone who second guesses her [O'Toole], doesn't understand the quality of this individual," he said at the time.[6]

Still, the buck stopped with the commissioner, and she was strongly encouraged to pursue another job. Once O'Toole was out, Menino[7] could move the department forward. For only the second time in more than three decades, the mayor looked outside the department for a replacement. Menino chose Ed Davis, and the impact the Lowell native had on Boston was almost immediate. During his first three years as commissioner, the number of shootings in Boston plummeted by forty percent and acts of serious crime had dropped eighteen percent. The city had also celebrated three more world championships by the Red Sox, Celtics, and Bruins on Davis' watch.

On April 15, 2013, Commissioner Davis woke up early, made some phone calls to his staff, and left his Hyde Park home around 9 a.m. He headed to Boston Police headquarters at One Schroeder Plaza for the marathon. Although boots-on-the-ground officers like Danny Keeler expected nothing out of the ordinary, it was the job of Davis and others to do the necessary planning for a worst-case scenario. Since the terrorist attacks of September 11, 2001, cities such as Boston had been preparing for a day that they hoped would never come. The marathon, with its thousands of international runners, spectators, and dignitaries—plus the fact that it is nationally televised—has always been considered a soft target by law enforcement authorities. The security planning literally goes on all year. It starts the day after the race and continues until the marathon begins again in Hopkinton a year later. Chief among Davis's responsibilities was to check in regularly with the Boston Regional Intelligence Center (BRIC), a unit that was set up post-9/11 to ensure that law enforcement officials share information about potential threats. Officers in the BRIC receive regular briefings from the FBI, CIA, Homeland Security, state police, and other federal and state agencies about any possible issues that could pose a threat to Boston. The process was followed as usual in the months, weeks, and days leading up to April 15, 2013.

"Everyone looked through what was happening with the world picture and the different intelligence streams that were coming in," Davis says. "There were no known specific threats to this event. But we realize the marathon is a soft target, and there is always a possibility and especially in this event where you have such a focus, an international focus, on the finish line.

"That is when you have the highest visibility of this event," Commissioner Davis continues. "From the perspective of someone involved in a terrorist event, the fewer cameras, the less possibility there is that someone is going to try to target this because their interest is international."

The commissioner and his team went through their checklist and were satisfied with their preparation. Bomb-sniffing dogs had already made regular sweeps down Boylston Street to the finish line that morning. There were more than eight hundred officers on patrol for marathon duty. Metal barricades lined Boylston Street as historically the biggest threat has been the possibility that someone would try to harm a runner or block the race. The barricades also control the flow of the crowd and keep vehicles away from the thousands of spectators, not to mention the VIP grandstand outside the Boston Public Library at the finish line. Around noon, Davis, his wife, Jane, their children, Kaitlyn and Phillip, and some friends all made their way to the VIP grandstand to celebrate their adopted city—a city they had grown to love.

Davis's counterpart at the Massachusetts Emergency Management Agency (MEMA) had already been at his desk since 5 a.m. and was still feeling a little foggy from the wedding he had attended the night before. Kurt Schwartz wasn't too concerned. Although it was his job to plan for both natural and manmade disasters in Massachusetts, Patriots' Day was historically the slowest public safety day of the year. Bald, slender, and bookish, Schwartz was the polar opposite of Ed Davis in just about every way. He had grown up far from Massachusetts in a wealthy suburb of Detroit, Michigan. The product of private schools, Schwartz came east in 1974 to attend Wesleyan University in Middletown, Connecticut. During the summer of his freshman year, Schwartz found himself serving as a seasonal police officer on Martha's Vineyard. He returned to Wesleyan for his sophomore year, took an EMT class, and worked at night for an ambulance company. That training allowed him to return to the Vineyard for the next three years, where he continued working as a summer cop while also serving as one of the island's few emergency medical technicians. At that time, police stations on the Vineyard were equipped only with station wagons, which served as transportation for those arrested and also for those who were injured. "I was horrified because I was working in Connecticut on real ambulances, and I'm down on the Vineyard throwing people in the back of station wagons," Schwartz recalls. It was the excitement and adrenalin of responding to emergency calls that drew him to public service. Like Ed Davis, Kurt

Schwartz dreamed of a career as a police officer. He had been offered a full-time position on Martha's Vineyard, where the police chief told him that he'd be sent off to study at the police academy and would also be in charge of emergency medical services for the town. The offer was a dream come true for Schwartz, who then dropped out of college and in 1977 entered the Boston police academy. He returned to Martha's Vineyard, where he worked as a full-time police officer for the next five years while continuing to collect college credits. He had a bright future ahead of him, but Schwartz made an ill-fated decision that cost him not only his career as a cop, but very nearly also his ability to walk. While on vacation in Aspen, Colorado, in his mid-twenties, Schwartz—who was an accomplished skier—was clowning around on the slopes when he suffered a serious compression injury to his back. "I was jumping off moguls and landed real hard on a mogul field, and the pain just went all over," Schwartz remembers. "My body buckled over, and I landed on my skis and stopped. My whole back went into a spasm." He spent the next four months in the hospital undergoing a series of surgeries. Schwartz eventually recovered but knew that the lingering effects of his injury would not allow him to return to police work. While on medical leave from the police department, he finished his studies at Wesleyan and went on to law school at Boston College, where he continued to work nights on ambulances that were dispatched throughout the city. After law school, he climbed up the criminal justice ladder, from Prosecutor for the Middlesex County District Attorney's Office, to Chief of the Criminal Bureau for the Massachusetts Attorney General, and eventually becoming Undersecretary of Law Enforcement for the Commonwealth. In 2007, Governor Deval Patrick promoted him to Undersecretary for Homeland Security and Emergency Management in the Executive Office of Public Safety and Security (EOPS), where it was his responsibility to coordinate the strategic response of the Massachusetts National Guard and two EOPS agencies, the Department of Fire Services and the Homeland Security division. In emergency situations, Kurt Schwartz served as the governor's most trusted counsel. With no apparent threat looming on marathon day, he figured he would have limited conversations with his boss, who would make a brief appearance at the finish line to crown the women's winner. At 2:15 p.m. on April 15, Schwartz climbed into his vehicle and drove toward

Copley Square with little on his mind except for maintaining crowd control during the city's signature event.

Patrolman Javier Pagan gazed over the barricades on Boylston Street directly in front of Marathon Sports and LensCrafters. He had been ordered by his supervisor to stand at the end of the finish line, facing the crowd. There was a sea of people clogging the sidewalk. All had witnessed men's division winner Lelisa Desisa of Ethiopia and women's division winner Rita Jeptoo of Kenya cross the finish line with times of 2:10:22 and 2:26:25, respectively. Their journeys toward the finish line had begun more than two hours earlier and 26.2 miles southwest in Hopkinton, where an estimated 23,336 runners from across the globe gathered for the start of the race. Before the loud crack of the starting gun, the competitors lowered their heads for a twenty-six-second moment of silence to remember the school children and faculty members killed during the shooting rampage at Sandy Hook Elementary School in Newtown, Connecticut, five months prior. Organizers at the Boston Athletic Association had also dedicated Mile 26, the final mile of the marathon, to the families of the Sandy Hook victims. Several families had been invited by the BAA to sit in the VIP section at the finish line in Copley Square. Javier Pagan could identify—if only partially—with that unspeakable tragedy. His husband, Pedro Richard, was a retired New York City police officer who had responded to the attacks on the World Trade Center towers. The couple met at a gay officers' banquet in 2005 in Worcester, Massachusetts.

Over time, Pedro shared his feelings of loss and pain with Javier, who did his best to comfort him. Pagan could scarcely imagine what it must have been like to have been an officer on patrol in New York the day nineteen hijackers turned passenger planes into missiles. The uncertainty—the panic. How could a cop maintain some level of control in order to help people when the city was under attack? Pagan hoped to God that he would never find out.

Mery Daniel had passed thousands of spectators on her way to her current vantage point in front of Marathon Sports on Boylston Street. She was proud of the fact that she had not spilled her cup of hot chocolate during the long walk from Commonwealth Avenue. Mery's husband, Richardson, had dropped her off earlier that afternoon at the MBTA station between Massachusetts Avenue and Boylston Street. He would take their daughter, Ciarra, to run errands while she got to relax for a few hours. They promised to rendezvous later in the day for an early dinner. Mery began her morning on Newbury Street, the heart of Boston's chic shopping district just one street over from Boylston. There she enjoyed a breakfast of pancakes before walking over to Commonwealth Avenue, where she watched the elite runners pass by on their way to the finish line. The atmosphere was electric and fun, and she could only imagine the excitement felt by those watching their friends and loved ones crossing the finish line. At that point, she decided to leave her spot on Commonwealth Avenue and began walking alone to Boylston Street, where Black Hat and White Hat were waiting.

[4]

SAFE HAVEN

For every hour Anzor Tsarnaev spent fixing beat-up cars in a cold, open space that had been donated to him by the owner of a Cambridge rug company, he spent another two at the nearby Somerville Boxing Gym molding his eldest son, Tamerlan, into a contender and amateur champion. There was little doubt that the young man was talented. His trainers liked the fact that he could play both the violin and piano as it suggested to them a willingness to study and learn. Tamerlan was born with the physical tools also—a physique he had inherited from his father. He was tall and broad shouldered, which gave him a reach advantage over many of his opponents. He could also punch—hard. He fought in a straight-ahead style popular with Russians and eastern Europeans who were beginning to dominate weight classes in the professional ranks. Anzor saw greatness in his son and pushed, prodded, and yelled at Tamerlan until his voice echoed in the young fighter's head. The father would routinely make a spectacle of himself—screaming and flailing his arms if he saw that Tamerlan was not working hard enough or if he thought a sparring partner was getting in a cheap shot. Anzor was such a disruption at times that he would be ordered to stand in the back of the gym and out of ear shot of the other fighters. The stubborn father would not stay at a distance for long, and would soon charge back toward the ring screaming instructions to his son. Anzor Tsarnaev had put his future—his family's future—in the hands of Tamerlan. Glory in the boxing ring would make up for the misery and failure at home.

Anzor and Zubeidat were drifting farther apart as her views became more radicalized. While the father tried to embrace the American Dream, the mother pushed back by insulating herself deeper inside her religion. The couple's other children were virtually hopeless. Their daughters, Bella and Ailina, had inherited Zubeidat's beauty, and that led to trouble. First, Bella had fallen for a Brazilian boy in high school, which did not sit well with her parents. Anzor ordered Tamerlan to scare the teenager away, which he did by slugging him in the jaw. The parents would select a mate for their daughter and believed they had found the ideal suitor on the Internet. His name was Elmirza Khozhugov, and he was a twenty-year-old Muslim originally from Kazakhstan. Anzor announced that Bella and Elmirza would be married, but the daughter fought the idea. Deeply ashamed of the fact that he had lost control over his wife and now his eldest daughter, Anzor attempted to save face by offering Elmirza their other daughter, sixteen-year-old Ailina, as a consolation prize. The teenaged Ailina did not defy her father's wishes as Bella had done. Ailina and Elmirza began dating, and he got her pregnant. The couple was married in 2007 just a few weeks before she delivered their child. Ailina Tsarnaev was now a wife and a mother, and she was still just sixteen years old. With a newborn in tow, the newlyweds moved to Bellingham, Washington, where trouble began almost immediately. Ailina began arguing with her husband about his alleged infidelities, and he responded by beating and choking her. The relationship ended a year later, but not before Tamerlan flew to Washington State to thrash Elmirza for harming his sister. Tamerlan, however, was not above striking a woman himself. He was arrested by Cambridge police in 2009 for slapping his then girlfriend, Nadine Ascencao. Tamerlan admitted to the assault, but the case was eventually dismissed.

Ailina and her one-year-old son moved back into the Tsarnaev's tiny Cambridge apartment, where her sister was now raising a child of her own. Bella had dropped out of high school during her junior year. She traveled to Kazakhstan, got married, and had a baby. Bella's marriage lasted about as long as her sister's had. Both daughters were now back at home, living in cramped quarters and under the watchful eye of their parents. As stern as Anzor could be, he was no match for the domineering Zubeidat, who tried to control every facet of their daughters' lives. Feeling smothered by their mother, the sisters soon moved out of the apartment on Norfolk Street and into a homeless shelter. Trouble followed Ailina, who was later arrested in 2010 for allegedly using a counterfeit bill to pay for a meal at an Applebee's restaurant in Dorchester. Ailina then lied to police about the incident and refused to give up any names of those who had accompanied her to the restaurant that day. The sisters eventually moved to New Jersey, where Bella landed in court, charged with marijuana possession and distribution. She was also arrested in December 2012 after police responded to a domestic disturbance call at her apartment in Fairview, New Jersey.

Marijuana use was an even bigger problem for the youngest Tsarnaev child. Dzhokhar, dubbed "Jahar" by his friends and classmates at Cambridge Rindge & Latin—the high school once attended by Oscar-winning actors Matt Damon and Ben Affleck as well as NBA great Patrick Ewing—was a lazy-eyed stoner who lacked any real ambition, despite scoring good grades and excelling on the wrestling mat. Although he did not share his older brother's imposing build, the smaller and softer Dzhokhar worked just as hard and impressed his coach enough to be selected as captain of the high school team. But though he took such a fevered interest in Tamerlan's athletic career, Anzor was never seen at any of his youngest son's wrestling matches. When Dzhokhar was presented with the team's MVP award during his senior year, none of Dzhokhar's family members attended the ceremony to see him accept the honor. This lack of interest and guidance triggered a rebellion, and the youngest son began smoking pot frequently. If Anzor found a marijuana joint inside Dzhokhar's 1999 green Honda Civic, he would react with a hard slap to the back of his son's head instead of a helpful dose of fatherly advice. But it wasn't as if Dzhokhar's marijuana use had made him an outlier among his peers, especially those in the pot-smoking crowd. Dzhokhar was a typical American teenager who enjoyed a little weed, listened to rap music, and liked fast cars. Of his immediate family, it was Dzhokhar who had assimilated most thoroughly into their adopted homeland.

Tamerlan, the family's great hope, also began to party, much to the dismay of his father. Anzor had invested a great deal of time in his son's boxing career—hundreds of hours spent accompanying Tamerlan during his pre-dawn road work through the streets of Cambridge and hundreds more bouncing from sweaty gym to sweaty gym, filling his son with grand ideas of becoming an Olympic boxer. For Anzor, having his son represent the United States during the Olympics would be the ultimate sign of American success, and that success would have a dollar sign attached to it. The Olympics had been a lucrative launching pad for other boxers such as Sugar Ray Leonard and Oscar De La Hoya, and it would mean large purses right out of the gate for Tamerlan, who would otherwise have to slug his way through the ranks as a club fighter. And Anzor knew that he could market his son well. Tamerlan was ruggedly handsome and flashy. He was prone to performing backflips in the ring, and his flamboyant attire—which alternated between white fur and snakeskin, and military-style boots and khakis—always set him apart from the crowd. Some fighters snickered and called Tamerlan's outfits "Euro-trash," but he could back it up in the ring—which was the only thing that truly mattered. In 2009, Tamerlan won his first New England Golden Gloves championship, which propelled him to the national tournament in Salt Lake City, Utah. Fighting as a heavyweight, the Chechen immigrant wanted to make sure everyone attending would remember his name. A consummate showman, Tamerlan wore a silk scarf and mirrored sunglasses while introducing himself to fellow competitors at the tournament. Inside the ring, his bite matched his bark. He dropped his opponent to the canvas with a thunderous punch, then dominated him for the rest for the bout. Yet when the judges' scorecards were announced, the opponent was declared the winner—over a chorus of *boos* from fans who believed that Tamerlan had clearly won.

A year later, during the 2010 Golden Gloves tournament, Tamerlan tried to intimidate his opponent even before they both stepped into the ring. He approached the fighter and his trainer in the locker room and vowed that he would take them both down. The trainer, outraged by the breach of pugilistic protocol, complained to tournament officials that Tamerlan, who was still a year away from being eligible to apply for US citizenship, should not be allowed to compete.

Tsarnaev won the tournament but lost the war. Golden Gloves of America later announced a change in policy that prohibited all non-citizens from participating in its Tournament of Champions—which meant that Tamerlan could not advance to the US Olympic trials.

Both Tamerlan and Anzor were devastated by the news, and the Tsarnaev family quickly began to unravel. Tamerlan turned his focus from training to the nightclub scene, while his mother clutched more tightly to her Koran. It was while prowling the bars in Boston that Tamerlan caught the eye of his future wife, Katherine Russell.

Russell, an attractive brunette from an upper-middle-class neighborhood in North Kingstown, Rhode Island, arrived in Boston in the fall of 2007 to attend Suffolk University. By all accounts, Russell was a typical college student. She wore jeans, T-shirts, and skirts, and she liked clubbing. Her parents were in the medical field: her father, Warren, graduated from Yale and worked as an emergency room doctor, and her mother, Judith, was a nurse. Katherine and her two younger sisters were raised Christian, but no one remembers them being devoutly religious. Katherine attended public high school in North Kingstown, where she excelled at art. She chose to major in communications at Suffolk University and even had plans to enter the Peace Corps. But her life was dramatically altered when a friend introduced her to Tamerlan at a local club.

Tsarnaev was at a particularly low point in his life. He had no job, his boxing career was floundering, and his academic career showed little promise. Tamerlan had quit attending Bunker Hill Community College, where he had struggled mightily in his accounting classes. He later enrolled at Mass Bay Community College but dropped out after just three weeks. Tamerlan was seeing another woman at the time, so his relationship with Katherine was casual at the beginning. He also had *another* woman in his life—one whose influence began to overshadow his father's.

Zubeidat Tsarnaev grew hysterical when Tamerlan told her that he wanted to move out of their Cambridge apartment for a life on his own. She cried for several days and told him that he was turning his back on his culture and its tradition of a son staying in the family home with his mother until marriage.[8]

Fearing that she had lost her daughters and was now losing her sons, Zubeidat Tsarnaev urged Tamerlan to spend his evenings reading the Koran with her instead of carousing with his American friends. Readings were often followed by research as Tamerlan used the family's only computer to scour Islamic fundamentalist websites in search of nourishment for the ideas his mother had been planting in his head. These sites and others claimed that the attacks of September 11, 2001, had been orchestrated by the United States government in an attempt to turn America against the Muslim world.

Despite her hatred of the West, Zubeidat had depended on government assistance for her very survival. For four years—from October 2002 to November 2004, and again from August 2009 to December 2011—the Tsarnaev family collected Supplemental Nutrition Assistance Program benefits, or food stamps. Anzor Tsarnaev also collected Transitional Aid to Families with Dependent Children benefits, or welfare, during two separate periods in 2003 and 2009.[9] At one point, Zubeidat also chose to steal what she could not take legally from the government. In June 2012, with her marriage to Anzor unraveling, Zubeidat walked into the retailer Lord & Taylor at the Natick Collection, a posh suburban shopping mall just outside Boston, and tried to walk out with $1,624 in women's clothes. She was detained and arrested for shoplifting and two counts of malicious damage to property. Zubeidat's mug shot bore little resemblance to the confident, modern woman who had arrived in America nearly a decade before. Her face appeared weathered. She had heavy bags under each eye, and deep lines formed by worry and resentment etched trails near her mouth.

It seemed that the only bright spot for Tamerlan was his growing relationship with Katherine Russell, or Katie as she was known to friends. But their carefree affair turned problematic when Russell discovered that she was pregnant. Once again Anzor and Zubeidat found themselves at a cultural crossroads as one of their children had found love outside their heritage. Tamerlan did his best to appease his parents by announcing that Katie would convert to Islam and take the name Karima upon marriage. They were wed in June 2010 at the Masjid Al-Qur'aan mosque in Dorchester, Massachusetts. Katie, now Karima, gave birth to a daughter they named Zahira, but she would not be allowed to care for the infant. Instead, she was forced to work to support not only her newborn but also her new husband, who showed no willingness to get a job. Tamerlan stayed home with the baby while Karima worked as many as eighty hours per week as a home health aide. When he was not watching Zahira at the apartment he still shared with his parents, Tamerlan frequented a nearby mosque, socializing with fellow Muslims who shared his radical views. This deep fall into the abyss of Islamic extremism was too much for Anzor, whose influence over his children had been usurped by his wife. He told Zubeidat that he was moving to the Russian republic of Dagestan, which borders Chechnya, and the couple filed for divorce.

It was at this time that both Tamerlan and his mother first drew the attention of authorities, both here and abroad. Intelligence officials in Russia had secretly recorded a telephone conversation between Zubeidat and Tamerlan in which they discussed jihad—which can be interpreted as the physical struggle (war) against all non-Muslims. The Russians brought this information to the FBI, which conducted a brief, three-month investigation into the mother and son. The authorities added Zubeidat's and Tamerlan's names to the widening pool of potential threats in its terrorism database and moved on. The Feds did not understand, nor did they take seriously, the true threat posed by Tamerlan—who at the time was using his Facebook page to promote a Chechen news article that urged all Muslims to take up arms against America. But Tamerlan could not join the war himself until he gained a more intimate knowledge of what it felt like to kill. On September 11, 2011, Tamerlan Tsarnaev and his Chechen companion Ibragim Todashev crossed the threshold of Brendan Mess's Waltham apartment and into madness.

Months later, in January 2012, Tamerlan made plans to return to his native Dagestan to seek out Mahmud Mansur Nidal, a young terrorist who had fallen in with a group of insurgents operating in Dagestan's capital of Makhachkala. Dubbed the Makhachkala Gang by local authorities, Nidal and his men were responsible for several bloody attacks, including a pair of bomb blasts in May 2012 that killed fourteen people at a police checkpoint. In that particular attack, the bombs were detonated fifteen minutes apart. The first explosives were hidden in a red Mitsubishi sedan. The second bomb was concealed in a parked minivan and was triggered shortly after first responders arrived at the scene. According to Russia's National Anti-Terrorism Committee, the combined force of the explosions was equal to nearly two hundred pounds of TNT.[10]

Tamerlan Tsarnaev and Mahmud Mansur Nidal were alleged to have met while Nidal was on the run. "He [Nidal] had been a wanted man for some months before the attack," said Russian investigator Shamil Mutaev in a May 2013 interview with *Time*. "He had gone underground. I don't believe [Tsarnaev] could have been allowed to visit him underground." Mutaev further explained that there would have been a serious vetting process before Tamerlan was allowed to meet with Nidal in hiding. "They [Makhach-kala Gang] do not just invite outsiders over for tea."

According to the Russian newspaper *Novaya Gazeta*, Tsarnaev met with Nidal several times in 2012 while the insurgent was interviewing new recruits. Their clandestine meetings were later discovered by members of the counter-extremism forces of the Interior Ministry Police of Dagestan. Word quickly spread to Russian intelligence officials, who then reached out again to their counterparts in the FBI to obtain more information about Tamerlan Tsarnaev.

JOY ON BOYLSTON STREET

Denise and Bill Richard had a decision to make. How would they spend the crisp spring day with their three children, eleven-year-old Henry, eight-year-old Martin, and seven-year-old Jane? They were an outdoorsy couple who loved hiking and bike riding. Bill had once been a runner, but back problems had forced him to hang up his sneakers. He first met Denise while the two were attending Bridgewater State College in the early 1990s. Bill was studying geochemistry, and Denise was preparing for a career in early-childhood education. They were opposites, but their differences were what attracted them to each other. Bill had grown up in Salem, Massachusetts, where he played high school soccer. Denise was raised by her parents, Bob and Helen O'Brien, on Belfort Street in the Savin Hill section of Dorchester. A self-proclaimed rough-and-tumble "Dot rat," Denise brought her city sensibility with her to Bridgewater State, where she met Bill and his college buddy Larry Marchese. "She was witty, sharp, intuitive, and quick," recalls Marchese, "whereas Bill was an all-around good guy who wore his heart on his sleeve." The couple hit it off and carried their romance beyond college. They shared a condo in Quincy, but Denise felt it was too far from Boston, despite the fact that it was only twelve miles away. So they purchased a condo together on Telegraph Street in South Boston, where they entertained friends each year at the annual St. Patrick's Day parade. One particular point of pride for the couple was the fact that their front door can be seen during a shot in the Oscar-winning film *Good Will Hunting*. Bill and Denise enjoyed movies and television, especially episodes of *Seinfeld*, which was the top-rated comedy at the time. "Bill and I use Seinfeld references in just about every conversation," Marchese says. In fact, Bill reminded Larry of Jerry Seinfeld. "They're both very neat and orderly. Bill is very funny himself, but he doesn't need to get a laugh at someone else's expense. He doesn't break balls."

Bill Richard also prided himself on his ability to cook. He always served up large spreads for family and friends on holidays and at New England Patriots games, to which he and Larry held season tickets. "Bill's chili always drew raves at our tailgate parties," Marchese recalls. "His secret ingredient was replacing traditional chili beans with Boston baked beans." Bill was also the type of guy who would take home the turkey carcass from Thanksgiving dinner and boil it for homemade soup.

The couple married in the fall of 1995 at St. William's Church, just down the block from Denise's childhood home. Her parents had moved to Florida after her father, Bob, retired from his job at Gillette. However, Denise could not see herself living anywhere but her home turf. When the real estate market skyrocketed in the late 1990s, the Richards cashed in on their South Boston condo and moved across the highway to Dorchester. It was a move that confounded their friends. "They bought the most run-down, nasty shithole in Dorchester," Marchese remembers, smiling. "It was so bad that the local guide for historic homes called the place 'ugly beyond words.'" The house on Carruth Street had been split into several apartments, which meant that the stairs no longer went the right way, and it was so dilapidated that several dead rats were found inside the walls during renovation. Undeterred, Bill and Denise worked on the Victorian for more than a year with contractors and eventually transformed it into a beautiful home—a home where they could raise a family. Arriving in 1998 was a son they named Henry, followed by his brother, Martin, and later, their sister, Jane. Their friend Larry Marchese and his wife, Nina, moved further south to Braintree to raise a family of their own, but they never missed a Christmas Eve celebration at the Richards' Carruth Street home. "Christmas Eve is a blast. It's an open house; neighbors and friends. Both sides of the family are there," Marchese says. "The place is packed. All night long Bill is getting ready to sing 'The Twelve Days of Christmas.' Everyone gets assigned a day, and you sing your brains out." Marchese says that young Martin was especially fond of this holiday tradition.

Not only had Bill and Denise seen the potential in their home, they also saw the potential in their neighborhood, which had been plagued by drugs. One nearby house had been a constant nuisance for residents and local police. It was owned by an elderly woman whose son was suspected of dealing drugs out of the home. When the woman could no longer afford to live there, Bill and a neighbor bought it and restored it to a single-family home.

"That's when neighbors began to zero in and respect Bill as a 'family first, community first' kind of person," Marchese says.

It was at that point that Bill Richard began to get involved in community causes. When a woman was raped at the nearby Ashmont Street MBTA station, Bill complained that the area was too dark and therefore too dangerous for residents. He helped form a task force that successfully lobbied Mayor Tom Menino for a much-needed renovation. He later became the president of St. Mark's Area Main Street, a civic organization whose mission was to revive one of Dorchester's once-prominent business districts. As Bill focused on creating a better environment for his young family, Denise became a stay-at-home mom, shepherding the kids to school, where she worked part-time in the library, and driving them to soccer practice. The couple never appeared to be motivated by money. They had just enough to live on and drove around Dorchester in a Ford and a used Volvo. They did own a small summer home on a lake in New Hampshire, but Bill and Denise calculated their true wealth in terms of their three healthy kids, their abundance of good friends, and the positive impact they made on their community.

On the morning of April 15, 2013, Bill and Denise Richard contemplated whether to jump in the car and go for a ride to a local hiking trail, or whether to take their kids into the city to watch the Boston Marathon. They had been going to the marathon for several years, and their children always loved the experience. The couple weighed a day of hiking against the once-a-year spectacle, and the Boston Marathon won. Bill and Denise grabbed Henry, Martin, and Jane and jumped on the MBTA headed toward the finish line on Boylston Street.

Heather Abbott always looked forward to spring. Not only because it signified a break from the icy Rhode Island winters but also because it signaled the pending arrival of summer. And summer in a beach town like Newport means lots of friends, family, and visitors. And for Heather, the official beginning of spring each year was ushered in by the Boston Marathon. Every April for the past several years, she would make the pilgrimage up to Boston to spend the day reconnecting with good friends she'd spent the previous summer partying with in Newport.

Newport, with its majestic mansions, cobblestone streets, and breathtaking ocean-side cliffs, transforms each summer from a sleepy New England burg into a bustling resort town — a playground for wealthy singles from Boston, Providence, and New York. It's not uncommon for groups of city-bound single people in their 20s, 30s, and even 40s to join together and rent luxurious condos for the summer so they have somewhere to unwind each weekend.

Heather, a single, thirty-eight-year-old human resources manager at Raytheon, grew up in nearby Lincoln, Rhode Island, the only child of Rosemary and Dale Abbott. Rosemary retired from Mass Mutual in 2013, while her husband Dale, a retired salesman, continued to work in the mailroom at the Citizens Bank part-time. The couple has been married for forty years and raised Heather on a quiet cul-de-sac in the suburban town. Her parents still live in the comfortable house on Rosewood Drive where Heather grew up. Pretty and athletic, she took tap, jazz, and ballet lessons as a child. As a teenager, she taught dancing to little girls at a school called Dance Rhode Island. Heather wanted to go to school at the University of North Carolina, but her parents thought the idea of their only daughter moving away for college was absurd.

"'Are you crazy? What if you get sick? What if something happens? How are we going to get you?" her mom told her. "You need to go somewhere close to home."

She trusted their advice and enrolled at Stonehill College in Easton, Massachusetts, where she studied accounting. The school was nice and she made some good friends, but she didn't love the small, private Catholic college — largely because her then boyfriend was back home in Pawtucket, Rhode Island. Still, she excelled academically and tutored struggling high school math students just down Route 138 in the hardscrabble city of Brockton. She graduated from Stonehill in 1996 and moved back home to

Rosewood Drive in order to save money as she started her first job at a Providence accounting firm. She soon left that job and took a human resources position at a small industrial design firm, also in Providence. She attended night classes at Providence College and got her MBA, which then landed her a job that had her traveling all around the Northeast—from Burlington, Vermont, and Augusta, Maine, to Wilkes-Barre and Scranton, Pennsylvania. By then she was living on her own in North Providence, and she hit the road every Monday. On the weekends, she barely even unpacked, leaving her suitcase at the foot of her bed. Eventually she became sick of the traveling, so she took a labor relations manager position at Roger Williams University, then, in 2007, she went to work for Raytheon, where she handled sexual harassment, discrimination, and other employee complaints. She was originally drawn to Newport for the summer social scene, but she grew to love the seaside community year-round. She loved taking runs along the storied Cliff Walk and paddleboarding on Third Beach. She loved having post-beach cocktails with friends at the Atlantic Beach Club and hosting small dinner parties for friends visiting from out of town.

She spent a few summers renting beach houses with friends and fell in love with the city. She eventually rented a quaint, colonial-style townhouse in the heart of Newport, across the street from some of the city's most striking mansions. The winters can be long in Newport as wild New England nor'easters whip up winds that bring sleet, freezing rain, and piles of snow. She doesn't have many visitors in January, February, and March, but once the sun starts poking out its head in April, her phone rings a little more as friends are eager to visit. By June, her social calendar is generally booked.

On April 15, 2013, Heather woke up early, showered, blow-dried and brushed her long, blonde hair, and got dressed for a day of fun in Boston. She planned to meet several Rhode Island friends with whom she rented a Newport house each summer and whom she hadn't seen in months. As on every Marathon Monday, they would take the trip to Boston by train, go to the Red Sox game, then watch the race from the Boylston Street finish line. Heather set out and, along with her friends Jessica, Jason, Michelle and Al, drove to the MBTA commuter rail station in Providence. There they met another friend and took the train up to South Station in Boston.

It was a sunny, mild day, and the group was excited. They laughed at old jokes from the previous summer. They caught up on the latest news with each other. They checked their various devices for text messages. The plan was to meet at Fenway Park and then at Forum, a café near the finish line and their traditional gathering spot,

First pitch at Fenway was at 11 a.m., and the foe was the Tampa Bay Rays, a former expansion team that had become an American League East powerhouse and top nemesis of the Sox. While Boston is generally a fairly conservative city—many of the Puritan blue laws are still on the books, including one banning happy hour—Marathon Monday is one occasion that the city really lets loose. Along with St. Patrick's Day, it is one of the few days that thousands gleefully play hooky and hit the city's many pubs and bars at uncommonly early hours. Following tradition, Heather and her friends rolled into a Kenmore Square pub to have a pre-game morning cocktail. Afterward, with the sun glistening in the pale blue sky above, the group walked from Kenmore to Fenway and through the turnstiles into the hallowed ballpark. They grabbed some draft beers and made their way to their lower box seats, smiling, laughing, and joking the whole time. It was Jackie Robinson Day, and the hometown team paid tribute to the former Brooklyn Dodger who broke pro baseball's color barrier.

The game was a defensive battle, and Heather and the others grew bored and decided to leave early. They stopped in at a Lansdowne Street hotspot called Game On! for a drink before walking from Fenway toward Boylston Street, where they would congregate at Forum. The crowds were thick as the group negotiated blocked intersections and packed sidewalks lined with metal barricades. Being from Rhode Island, Heather wasn't exactly sure of the best route and got lost on her way. By the time the group made it to Forum, the Rays had tied the game at two, and outfielder Mike Napoli hit a walk-off double to bring home Dustin Pedroia, giving the Sox a dramatic 3–2 win.

Forum was crowded, and four of Heather's friends were already inside. There was a short line to get in as the doorman checked IDs. Out on the sidewalk patio, former New England Patriot offensive lineman Joe Andruzzi—a cancer survivor—was throwing a fundraiser for his charity foundation. Lots of local celebrities, politicians, and socialites were in and out of the event all day, including another former New England Patriot, Matt Chatham, and his wife.

Michelle L'Heureux has never been a runner. Her mother, Linda, had been a runner and always pushed Michelle to run, too. As kids, Michelle and her sister, Danielle, would spend many weekends watching their mom run in local road races. Slender, tall, and athletic, Michelle is built exactly like her mom, but she never got the running bug. In fact, she'd tell friends, "I'd rather eat half a dozen donuts on the couch than run a quarter mile."

She is not lazy. On the contrary, Michelle is a self-described "cardio junkie." She just does everything *but* run.

Michelle hits the gym five or six days a week, taking spinning classes and working out on the elliptical or the treadmill. She also walks roughly twenty-five to thirty miles a week with her dogs, Romeo and Louis. Romeo, a tiny, silky terrier with golden-brown hair, and Louis, a Great Dane–Black Lab mix, are her family, and they give her motivation when she's feeling lazy. Michelle was raised in rural Auburn, Maine, with her parents and her younger sister, Danielle. Their modest single-family home was on the outskirts of Auburn near the Lewiston line, an area of Maine known to locals as Frenchville or Little Canada for its predominantly French-Canadian population. Sherwood Drive is in a quiet, suburban neighborhood on the edge of both the countryside of Maine and the dense, urban city of Lewiston. The elementary school that Danielle and Michelle attended is at the end of the street.

Growing up, their dad, Paul, kept Michelle especially busy. She was a cheerleader and she skied at Lost Valley ski area in Auburn. Every Christmas, Michelle and Danielle would open their stockings and find a season pass to the nearby mountain, which had just two ski lifts and a handful of small trails. But what Michelle loved most was riding horses. From the age of eight, Michelle had begged her parents to pay for riding lessons. She eventually broke them down, and they bought Michelle her own horse for her thirteenth birthday. This was no easy purchase for a family living on a fireman's salary, but Paul L'Heureux saw it as a shrewd investment for his daughter's future. Plus, he believed that riding would keep her active and away from teens who were headed in the opposite direction, into trouble. Michelle rode American Saddlebreds and owned and cared for three horses during her teenage years. Her favorite, a horse she named Libby, was also her best friend. She showed in Maine and all over New England. In Maine, she won the year-end equitation awards for her age group, which qualified her for the New England Horseman's Council in Good Hands finals—the region's top horse show.

Michelle kept her horses at Walnut Hill Stables in Cape Elizabeth, a rolling farm town along Maine's rocky coast. The stables were about half an hour from Auburn, but that did not stop Michelle from riding six days a week. A typical day for her meant arriving at Edward Little High School before dawn, followed by a full day of course work, then cheerleading practice with the Red Eddies pep squad. Michelle would then go home, have a quick dinner with her parents and Danielle, and jump in her dad's car for the ride to Walnut Hill. Michelle would do her homework while father Paul drove. They would finally return home just in time for a little sleep before starting it all over again the next day.

Michelle loved every minute of it. Her dad had been right. Riding did keep Michelle busy and away from the high school party scene. In fact, she did not try alcohol until she went away to college at William Woods University in Fulton, Missouri. The school's riding program was among the top in the country, and Michelle continued to perform at shows, including the prestigious American Royal. After college, she moved back East and settled in Boston, where city life made it difficult to pursue her lifelong passion. Yet she eventually embraced the urban elements of Boston and morphed into a self-described city girl. Boston was perfect because it wasn't too big. Michelle shied away from large-scale events because she didn't like the crowds, which is why she had never gone to Copley Square to see her boyfriend, Brian Chartier, cross the finish line. Brian had run the Boston Marathon several times, but each time she stayed as far from the finish line as possible. Instead, she would typically head out to Newton and wave to Brian from Commonwealth Avenue near Boston College and the arduous Heartbreak Hill—the stretch between miles 20 and 21 where, over the decades, many runners have made their last stand. Bustling with partying college students, it was an exciting place to watch the race, but not as frenzied or crowded as the finish line at Copley Square. On April 15, 2013, Michelle made the decision — a life-changing one, as it turns out — to head to the finish line for the first time to watch Brian. A client relations manager for John Hancock Insurance, the major sponsor of the marathon, Michelle took the day off and planned to meet up with friends, have a few cocktails, and watch Brian finish his tenth Boston Marathon. Brian was a workforce manager at Hancock when the couple met and started dating in 2002. Brian was not your typical jock or long-distance runner. He was an average and affable guy who had always been a calming force for Michelle. She often kidded him about his terrible sense of direction and was quietly relieved to know there was little chance that he'd find his way off course during a race this size.

"Tomorrow will be Brian's 10th marathon and he is ready to go!" Michelle posted on her Facebook page on April 14. "I am very proud of him!! Even though I think you have to be a little nuts to run that much — hehe. I am also very excited to see two of my favorite friends run their first marathon! It will be a very fun day for them, and I cannot wait to celebrate with them! Best of luck and much love!"

She was brimming with excitement. The night before, Michelle made signs to cheer on Brian and another friend. The morning of the marathon, she woke up early as usual and went to the gym. After her workout, she went back to her apartment just over the Neponset Bridge in Quincy and took her dogs, Louis and Romeo, for a long walk along Wollaston Beach, letting them have plenty of fresh air because she knew she'd be gone all afternoon and evening. She finished up the signs, showered, and watched the race coverage on TV. As she was getting ready, she got a call from Brian, who was in Hopkinton getting ready to start his race.

"We'll be standing on the Newbury Street side on Boylston near the finish line," Michelle told him.

"Okay. I'll see you later. I love you," Brian replied and hung up. He put his phone in his backpack, which was loaded onto a bus to be driven to the finish line for him to retrieve after the race. Michelle finished getting dressed. She put on skinny jeans and flat shoes. She decided to take the dogs out for one last time before she left. It was a chilly morning. She had her purse all packed up and was ready to go. She stood outside watching the dogs and had a parting thought: *Maybe I should put my boots on.* Michelle changed out of her flats and put on a pair of black, heavy-duty North Face boots. They were much warmer. She drove from her house down the street to the North Quincy MBTA stop. She hopped on a Red Line train and took it to Park Street, where she got off and met her friend Nicole Morin. They hugged, smiled, and chatted about work and friends as they walked to another friend's apartment on Beacon Street. They poured a couple of mimosas to celebrate Patriots' Day and Marathon Monday before they walked as a group to the finish line.

[6]

DAGESTAN

By the early spring of 2012, Russia's FSB (the successor of the KGB) already had information in its possession about the potential terrorist threat posed by Tamerlan Tsarnaev, thanks to a 2010 interrogation of a Canadian boxer named William Plotnikov. Plotnikov and Tsarnaev appeared to be mirror images of one another. Plotnikov had immigrated to Toronto from Megion, Russia, an oil-rich city in western Siberia, in 2005 when he was fifteen years old. Like Tsarnaev, Plotnikov had studied boxing and had used the sport to help his transition into his adopted homeland. Known as Willy to his family and friends, the tall, lanky Russian was not born into the Muslim faith but instead converted from Christianity in 2009, four years after arriving in Canada—roughly the same time his father, Vitaly, had a spiritual awakening of his own and became a Jehovah's Witness. Vitaly Plotnikov had emigrated west to ensure that his son was granted an opportunity for a solid education and to keep the boy out of the clutches of Russian gang leaders who had historically preyed on young athletes. Vitaly, a former athlete himself, had taught his son how to box while the man worked for an oil company in western Siberia. When the family moved to Canada, Vitaly could only secure menial work such as stocking shelves at a local supermarket. Like Anzor Tsarnaev, Vitaly Plotnikov saw potential pugilistic greatness in his son and urged William to join a local boxing program. The coach there realized quickly that Plotnikov had the talent and smarts to go far and believed there was Olympic glory in the teenager's future.

Plotnikov fought in tournaments around Ontario, where he eventually won two regional championships. As Tamerlan Tsarnaev struggled to adjust to life in Cambridge, Massachusetts, Plotnikov experienced similar growing pains in Toronto. He couldn't connect with Canadians his age because they dressed and spoke differently. The Russian expatriates that William knew drank too much and drugged too much, so Plotnikov began looking elsewhere for companionship, which he later found inside a Toronto mosque. He connected with a mullah with radical views and soon began reading the Koran and praying five times a day.

In September 2010, Vitaly Plotnikov returned home from vacation in Florida to find a note on the counter from William, saying that he had gone to France to observe Ramadan. From there, the converted Muslim traveled to Moscow and eventually Dagestan. His parents never saw him in person again. It would be several months before William made any contact with them at all. Russia's respected independent newspaper *Novaya Gazeta*, touted for its investigative reporting, reported that William Plotnikov was detained by FSB counter-terrorism agents in early 2011 and identified as an "adherent of radical Islam."[11] During the interrogation, Plotnikov was forced to give names of other radical Muslims he knew and communicated with, both in person and online. One of the names extracted during the detention was that of Tamerlan Tsarnaev. It is not known whether Plotnikov had ever met Tsarnaev or whether they had maintained a virtual relationship. Tsarnaev once visited a relative in Toronto, but there is no evidence to suggest he met with Plotnikov. Their passions for boxing and jihad certainly overlapped, and Russia's FSB took the connection seriously enough to alert their American counterparts in the FBI. The Feds reported back that agents had interviewed Tamerlan Tsarnaev in Cambridge and found no links to terrorist activity. "We began investigating Tsarnaev and placed him on record after his name came up in the [Plotnikov] investigation in Dagestan," an official from Russia's Center for Combating Terrorism (CEPE) told *Novaya Gazeta* in 2013. "We pay special attention to foreign nationals or Russians who recently converted to Islam. They are extremely ideological and psychologically vulnerable. They can be convinced to do anything, even a suicide bombing."[12]

Once Plotnikov was released from FSB custody, he burrowed himself into the wooded hills of Utamysh, an insurgent stronghold of three thousand people close to Dagestan's capital, Makhachkala.

The only time Plotnikov corresponded with his father, Vitaly, he did so through a Russian social networking site, VKontakte. During those online conversations, William told his father that he no longer had use for material goods as "they won't bring rewards on Judgment Day that without doubt will come."[13] The young Muslim, now twenty-three, also chided his father for posting photos of William's mother in a bathing suit on the beach. That particular online conversation got heated over Vitaly's earnest warning to his son to resist fanaticism.

"Do you really call me a fanatic just because I have cast aside the false constitution of man and instead took up the law of the Lord?" William wrote on July 23, 2011.[14]

It would be the last contact William Plotnikov would have with his father.

As darkness fell on July 13, 2012, Russian forces raided a farm outside Utamysh, catching the Dagestani mujahideen by surprise, and lit up the night sky with artillery fire. At least seven rebel fighters were killed during the long, overnight battle, including the bearded young man known to villagers as the Canadian. After the smoke had cleared, survivors carried the body of William Plotnikov into the village, where his body was washed and then buried under a stone carved with a crescent moon and star. Weeds were allowed to grow wild over the gravesite in adherence to local beliefs that the flora helps the dead atone for their sins. Before his death, Plotnikov shot a video inside his cramped camp in the forest outside Utamysh. On tape, William and his fellow rebels shared details of their nightly dinner ritual and showed off their weapons. A cheery Plotnikov then compared Russia's President Vladimir Putin and President Barack Obama to "pigs and monkeys."

"We will kill you," Plotnikov smiled. "We will make plans against you."[15]

Tamerlan Tsarnaev had visited Dagestan at the very same time as Plotnikov's immersion into the mujahideen. Just days after the young insurgent's death, Tamerlan fled the region and headed back to the United

States. The decision was an urgent one, revealed by the fact that Tamerlan had not waited to pick up his new Russian passport, which—according to his parents—was the reason for their son's visit to his homeland.

The killing of Plotnikov also coincided with the death of Tsarnaev's other likely mentor, Mahmud Mansur Nidal, which occurred just two months before in May 2012. Nidal and his so-called Makhachkala Gang had just orchestrated the two suicide bombings in which fourteen people were killed. The bombs were set off within minutes of each other to kill not only innocent people but also those first responders who had arrived on the scene to help. On May 18, 2012, counter-terrorism troops surrounded the house where Nidal was staying. An expert was called in to negotiate the teen terrorist's surrender, but Nidal had other plans. In a tense standoff that lasted several hours, Nidal negotiated the release of his mother, wife, infant son, and two friends. During this time, about 150 Nidal supporters showed up and threatened the masked Russian troops, while others stormed the police station where Nidal's friend Abdurakham Magomedov had been taken for questioning. The next morning, with talks of surrender breaking down, Nidal threw a grenade out of a window toward a military vehicle. The blast was loud but caused no injuries. Masked Russian commandos responded immediately and opened fire on the home. Nidal was killed and the house was torched to the ground.

Shamil Mutaev, the Russian law enforcement officer who had attempted to negotiate Nidal's surrender, does not believe the insurgent would have risked capture by meeting with Tamerlan Tsarnaev. Yet a source from the CEPE told *Novaya Gazeta* that the men had been seen together "on multiple occasions." Tamerlan's actions following the raid on Nidal's home are also curious. The CEPE source told *Novaya Gazeta* that Tamerlan immediately left his father's home where he was staying and moved in with other relatives, and that he was rarely seen in public from that point on. When Tsarnaev's father, Anzor, informed Russian authorities of Tamerlan's abrupt departure following the July death of William Plotnikov, they refused to believe him. Counter-terrorism agents checked passenger lists on foreign flights and staked out bus terminals and train stations in hopes of spotting the so-called American. "It appears that Tamerlan Tsarnaev came to Dagestan aiming to join the insurgents but was unsuccessful. It's a difficult process," the CEPE source told *Novaya Gazeta*. "First you make contact with the liaison, then there's a quarantine period—the insurgents check out each person before allowing them to join. After his contacts, Nidal and Plotnikov, were killed, Tsarnaev got cold feet and fled."[16]

When the FSB learned that Tamerlan had made his way back to the United States, they informed both the FBI and CIA, but their requests for a follow-up inquiry went unanswered.

There is also confirmation that Tsarnaev made contact with a third man while in Dagestan—a distant cousin, Magomed Kartashov, who is considered to be one of the region's most influential Islamists. A former cop and wrestler, Kartashov is the founding leader of a group called Union of the Just, which routinely denounces US policies and whose members have been imprisoned for abetting terrorist activities. In an interview with *Time*, an associate of Kartashov recalled meeting Tamerlan Tsarnaev at a cookout along the Shura-Ozen River near Makhachkala, Dagestan, in late June or early July of 2012, at the tail end of his visit. "Folks were saying that he [Tamerlan] was a champion of boxing in America," the unidentified man told *Time*.[17] The man claims that Tsarnaev had a narrow view of the violence occurring in Dagestan, and that he had referred to it as a "holy war." Others tried to correct him by pointing out the fact that much of the fighting was amongst the Muslims themselves. The group eventually changed Tamerlan's mind as he soon began to talk about "holy war" in more of a global context, with America being the ultimate enemy.

When he arrived back in Massachusetts in July 2012, Tamerlan Tsarnaev was a different man. His Euro-trash days were long gone, and now he sported a dark beard and dedicated the majority of his time to his prayers. He was also a man on fire, known for making loud outbursts inside his Cambridge mosque, especially when the imam granted followers the right to celebrate truly American holidays like Independence Day and Thanksgiving. He was asked to leave the mosque on at least one occasion when he called the imam a "hypocrite." Tsarnaev's scorn was not only relegated to his mosque. He also confronted a shopkeeper at the Al-Hoda market on Prospect Street in Cambridge for his decision to sell halal turkeys for Thanksgiving. As Tamerlan continued to spiral out of control, his mother, Zubeidat—who had been his anchor, his greatest supporter, and the most influential person in his life—decided to move back to Russia. She said the reason was to care for a sick brother, but it was most likely to avoid prosecution for the shoplifting case. Tamerlan, his wife, Katie, and their child were now the only ones left in the Norfolk Street apartment, and it appeared that they would have to move out soon because they could not afford the landlady's rent increase. With outside pressure continuing to build, Tamerlan lost himself inside his computer: he opened a YouTube account as a platform to post incendiary messages promoting jihad against the West. Tamerlan was also drawn to the digital al-Qaeda magazine *Inspire*. Written and produced by al-Qaeda operatives in Yemen, *Inspire* urges its readers to conduct lone-wolf attacks on the West by setting forest fires, ramming motor vehicles into large crowds, and by building homemade bombs. In the first issue of the English-language magazine, Tamerlan read and reread an article called "How to Make a Bomb in the Kitchen of Your Mom." The graphic accompanying the story showed the skyline of New York City. "If you are sincere in your intentions to serve the religion of Allah," the article reads, "then all you have to do is enter your kitchen and make an explosive device that would damage the enemy if you put your trust in Allah and then use this explosive device properly."[18] The article recommends that the use of a pressurized cooker is "the most effective method." The writer, who developed the article under the nom de plume The AQ Chief, takes the reader step-by-step through the bomb-making process and even offers a few safety precautions:

1. Put you [*sic*] trust in Allah and pray for the success of your mission. This is the most important rule.
2. Wear gloves throughout the preparation of the explosive to avoid leaving fingerprints.
3. This is an explosive device so take care during preparation and handling.

With his mother now gone, Tamerlan had no one else to share his beliefs or plans with, so he began nurturing a relationship with his younger brother Dzhokhar, who had idolized him since day one. The pair read the Koran together and scoured websites like *Inspire* and others to provide them both with the training and motivation for what was to come. Dzhokhar Tsarnaev had graduated from Cambridge Rindge & Latin and was now attending the University of Massachusetts-Dartmouth, where he had earned a scholarship with the hope of one day becoming an engineer. Unlike his brother, Dzhokhar did not wear his religion on his sleeve. However, he used to warn friends against taking God's name in vain, and he did manage to give up his beloved pot smoking for his Ramadan fast. On the rare occasions when Dzhokhar debated US foreign policy with his friends, he told them that he believed some acts of terrorism were justified because the US was "dropping bombs all the time."[19]

A good student in high school, Dzhokhar rarely applied himself in his college courses, which he found too easy. "Using my high school essays for my English class #itsthateasy," he once tweeted. "You know what I like to do? Answer my own questions cuz no one else can."

He longed for life back in Cambridge and returned home every chance he could. Since most of his friends were also away at college and his parents had fled the country, Dzhokhar spent more and more time with his older brother, who ordered him to pray five times a day. Tamerlan was now filling the void left by of Anzor's absence. Although Anzor had showed very little interest in his youngest son, Dzhokhar missed his father desperately. "I can see my face in dad's pictures as a youngin [sic]," he tweeted in 2012. "He even had a ridiculous amount of hair as me." The one aspect of his life that he continued to keep hidden from his family, especially his older brother, was his drug use and his lucrative role as a pot dealer. Dzhokhar was known to keep large Tupperware containers of marijuana in the mini fridge of his dorm room and had several regular customers. He pocketed more than one thousand dollars per week and sometimes carried a gun to protect his cash and his stash. Dzhokhar did not use the money for school purposes—he owed about twenty thousand dollars to UMass because his financial aid package had been suspended due to his rapidly declining grades. Instead, he spent his windfall on trips to New York City and parties with friends.

On September 11, 2012, Dzhokhar Tsarnaev became a naturalized United States citizen after completing a US civics and English test, being interviewed by a federal immigration officer, and passing a criminal background check. With 2,500 immigrants packed into the TD Garden sports arena, Dzhokhar stood up with his right hand raised. "I hereby declare, on oath, that I absolutely and entirely renounce and abjure all allegiance and fidelity to any foreign prince, potentate, state or sovereignty," he declared. "That I will support and defend the Constitution and laws of the United States of America against all enemies, foreign and domestic; that I will bare true faith and allegiance to the same. . . ."

Dzhokhar Tsarnaev received his citizenship on the eleventh anniversary of the 9/11 attacks and the first anniversary of the bloodbath inside the apartment in Watertown.

Over the next several months, the brothers Tsarnaev carefully hatched their plan. Following instructions found on the Internet and perhaps lessons taught by insurgents like Mahmud Mansur Nidal in Dagestan, Tamerlan and Dzhokhar used their Cambridge apartment as a base camp and possible laboratory for making bombs. In early February 2013, Tamerlan drove over the Massachusetts border to Seabrook, New Hampshire, where fireworks are legal, and spent two hundred dollars on two "Lock and Load" kits, which included forty-eight shells from Phantom Fireworks. Each shell was designed with two explosive powders. Back in 2010, an aspiring terrorist name Faisal Shahzad purchased fireworks from the company's sister store in Pennsylvania to help construct a pressure cooker bomb he later planted inside a Nissan Pathfinder in New York's Times Square.

Fortunately, that attempt was foiled by a pair of street vendors who spotted smoke coming from the vehicle. The bomb was lit, but it had failed to explode.

Tamerlan and Dzhokar Tsarnaev would work long hours to make sure that mistake did not happen twice.

CALM BEFORE THE STORM

On a normal Marathon Monday, the city's longest-serving mayor, Thomas M. Menino, would be at the finish line to crown the men's winner. It was a duty he had performed for nineteen previous years and one that he looked forward to annually. The eyes of the sporting world are on Boston every Marathon Monday as the Red Sox play one of their first home games of the season and later the world's finest long-distance runners seek to make history on one of the nation's oldest and most challenging marathon courses. The race is filled with pageantry, pomp, and circumstance, and the finish line is a gathering spot for the city's power brokers — from politicians and the media to business leaders and local sports celebrities. It's an annual rite of passage in spring that Menino embraces with all his heart.

Like the city he represents, Tom Menino was forever the underdog. The son of a factory foreman from the tough Boston neighborhood of Hyde Park, his early life showed no signs of his later success. After graduating from high school in 1960, Menino found work as a door-to-door salesman for Metropolitan Life Insurance. He wasn't flashy. He was squarely built and spoke with a thick tongue that gave some people the impression that he was slow. Menino was smart, though — smart enough to build a consensus within every group he connected with. His power was both subtle and disarming. Menino took a few college courses at night but soon gave it up, reminding his father that Harry Truman had never gone to college. Menino would eventually earn a bachelors degree from the University of Massachusetts-Boston, but in the interim, he slowly climbed his way up the steep ladder of local politics. In 1983, he was elected to the Boston City Council, where he would serve the people of District 5 (Hyde Park) for nearly a decade. Menino gobbled up committee appointments and eventually became chairman of the Boston City Council's Finance Committee (later renamed the City Council Ways and Means Committee), and later rose to become City Council president. His home life was quiet and secure. Menino had been married to the same woman, the former Angela Feletra, since 1966, and the couple raised two children in Hyde Park. Described as more of a sturdy blocker-and-tackler type than a flashy quarterback, few outside Menino's family gave him any chance of aspiring to higher office. He had flirted with the idea of running for Congress in 1992 but decided not to when the district he had his eye on dissolved. The decision to wait proved fortuitous. A year later, President Bill Clinton selected popular Boston mayor Ray Flynn, an avid runner and son of South Boston, to become the United States' Ambassador to the Holy See. Flynn, who had once had presidential dreams of his own, accepted the position to the Vatican, which made Tom Menino acting mayor of the city of Boston. Some viewed Menino as merely a caretaker of the office once held by political legends such as Kevin White and the so-called "Rascal King" James Michael Curley. Surely Menino, with his cringe-worthy vocal delivery and sluggish gait, would be no match in the general election against the likes of James Brett, a smooth-talking state politician; Mickey Roache, a former commissioner of the Boston Police Department; or Christopher Lydon, an acerbic television personality and host of the city's PBS newscast. But Menino's campaign commercials, which poked fun at his style, won over the city's voters. "I'm no fancy talkah," he said, smiling into the camera. But what he was—was a doer. In the 1993 election, Tom Menino beat out seven other challengers, and he never lost another election. In fact, no candidates have ever managed to even come close. As mayor, Tom Menino consolidated his power and ran the city of Boston with nearly complete autonomy. During his administration, he reduced gun violence in the city, which at one point had rivaled both Washington, DC, and Detroit. He helped bring the Democratic National Convention to Boston in 2004 and also opened up the South Boston waterfront to commercialization, which has been effectively shifting the heart of the city closer to the water ever since. Despite his success, Menino continued to get skewered in the press for his malapropisms—he once called Boston's lack of parking spaces "an Alcatraz" around his neck. His reign was marked as much by steady leadership and progressive urban mechanics as it was goofy missteps. Screwing up the names of Boston sports figures like Adam Vinatieri, Jason Varitek, and Rajon Rondo would likely have sunk lesser politicians. For many, though, these mistakes became endearing over time, and supporters and critics alike felt that Tom Menino possessed a mayor-for-life type of power in the city.

But on race day 2013, the seventy-year-old mayor was in the hospital, recovering from a host of ailments, including a compression fracture he suffered in his back. The injury was the latest setback for the aging mayor, who in 2013 was diagnosed with Type II diabetes and also suffered a broken leg. He has had an impressive history of injuries and surgeries. In 1997, he was twice hospitalized for kidney stones. In 2003, a cancerous tumor was removed from his back. In 2004, he was diagnosed with Crohn's disease. In 2008, he had arthroscopic surgery to repair his knee, which he injured when he nearly fell while carrying the Red Sox's World Series trophy. In 2010, he was hospitalized for an infection after he scraped his elbow while on vacation in Italy. Menino also had two more knee surgeries, a surgery to repair drooping eyelids, and he had to wear a walking boot for weeks in 2012 after breaking his toe. In October 2012, the mayor was back in the hospital yet again for a respiratory infection and a blood clot. He spent nearly two months in Brigham and Women's Hospital, where he sustained a compression fracture in his back from lying in bed. In February 2013, he was living at the city-owned Parkman House, rather than his Hyde Park home, because the stately mansion was handicapped accessible with elevators and ramps, unlike his modest single-family house. He was walking with a cane but still managed to make it to some public events. Speculation swirled as to whether the mayor had had a stroke—rumors that were stoked by a TV appearance while he was in the hospital during which he spoke slowly and slurred his words even more than usual. Aides attributed the speech difficulty to medication and denied the mayor had suffered a stroke or any other more serious ailment than what was described. In March 2014, just three months after leaving office, he was diagnosed with an advanced form of cancer that spread to his liver and lymph nodes.

The mayor's health problems had Boston's political scene abuzz in early 2013 as politicians and pundits wondered whether Menino would seek an unprecedented sixth term. City Councilor John Connolly called the mayor's bluff and decided not to wait, announcing in February that he was in the mayor's race—whether Menino ran for reelection or not.

On March 28, 2013—just two weeks before the marathon—Menino announced that he would not run again.

"It's a very difficult decision," a humbled Menino said. "It's a hard decision—the hardest in my career, the hardest of my life.... There have been a lot of unsolicited calls, people saying, 'You have to stay.' How do you say no to that? But I have to do what's best for Boston and for me."

"I love this job," he added. "For 20 years, I've challenged the people and the people have challenged me. They've always been by my side on good days and bad days. We've made decisions that were not always popular, but they always trusted me."

He formally made the announcement in an impassioned speech at Faneuil Hall with his family by his side. It was an emotional decision, one that he said he made because he was unable to resume a "Menino schedule."

The former Hyde Park city councilor prided himself on making it to dozens of public events every week. Visiting everywhere from senior centers, schools, and libraries to parks and new businesses, throughout his twenty-year tenure the mayor was a fixture in Boston's neighborhoods—so much so that urban lore has it that half of Boston's population claims they met him while he was mayor. When he realized he couldn't keep up his usual pace—or endure a grueling summer of campaigning against an opponent thirty years his junior—the writing was on the wall, and he stepped aside. His announcement rocked Boston's political world and immediately set off a frenzy among wannabe mayors. Menino vowed to stay out of the race and resumed his work at city hall, unknowing that the biggest task of his storied political career was looming just days away.

On April 12, 2013, Menino was still recovering from his back fracture and long rehab and was easing back into a more full work schedule when a freak accident landed him back in the hospital. Just three days before the marathon, Menino was walking into an event at the Lee School in Dorchester when he awkwardly twisted his ankle and fell to the ground.

He was brought to city hall where he iced it, but the pain throbbed and soon his ankle swelled up like a balloon.

The mayor went back to Brigham and Women's Hospital, where it was confirmed that he had fractured his fibula and needed surgery. The procedure was performed on Saturday, April 13, when doctors repaired the fracture with screws and a metal plate. On Marathon Day the venerable mayor was once again bedridden, recovering from yet another surgery.

For Boston City Councilor Mike Ross, who had announced just four days before the marathon that he was running for mayor, the event was his first big chance to get out and greet thousands of potential voters, fundraisers, and movers and shakers. A handsome, single forty-year-old, Ross is the son of a Holocaust survivor and was hoping to become the city's first Jewish mayor.

Besides the political ramifications of the party circuit, Ross loves the marathon. It finishes in his Back Bay district; plus, he himself is a big runner who organized a weekly runners' group along the Charles River so that women who wanted to run that route would not have to run it alone.

That morning, he and an aide headed to the Mandarin Oriental hotel, where he ran into fellow councilors Stephen J. Murphy and Bill Linehan. He then made his way to an event at the Lenox Hotel.

"I have to get to every marathon event that's possible," Ross told his aide, knowing the importance of making a strong start in the mayoral race, which would eventually field a dozen candidates.

He then stopped by an event at the Charlesmark Hotel that was being attended by a woman he was seeing at the time. He took pictures with supporters in front of the hotel, which he posted to his Instagram account. From there, he went into Marathon Sports to check out some new sneakers by Boston-based company New Balance. The place was filled. There was a line at the counter. People waited for clerks to get them their size. Tourists scooped up T-shirts, jackets, and other items emblazoned with the Boston Athletic Association marathon logo. The councilor was eager to try on the new running shoes, but his aide was tugging at his sleeve, telling him they had to get to another party. A female sales clerk came over to the councilor.

"Can I help you?" she asked.

"No, I'll come back," he replied.

Massachusetts Governor Deval Patrick was looking forward to some down time. Today was Marathon Monday, and his only official duty was to crown winners at the finish line at Copley Square. After that, the rest of the afternoon was his to putter around his home in Milton. The governor's wife, Diane, a partner at the prestigious law firm Ropes & Gray, was in New York City for the day on business. Their daughters were now off on their own. Sarah lived in California, while her sister, Katherine, lived in Boston's South End. Governor Patrick's family had often been public news. First, it was announced back in 2007 that Diane Patrick was receiving treatment for "exhaustion and depression." A year later, Katherine announced to the world she was gay. Through it all, the governor stood in loving support of his family, even as the pressures of his office continued to build. Elected in 2006 as the first African American governor of the Commonwealth of Massachusetts and re-elected in 2009, the Milton Academy and Harvard graduate and native of Chicago's rough South Side had developed a particularly thick skin during his years in politics. When he arrived in office, he was criticized for lavish spending on office drapes and his lease of a new Cadillac. He was criticized by the media for not holding news conferences to announce every new initiative. Compared to Mayor Menino, he was not viewed publicly as a man of the people—although he was an effective campaigner when he had to be. But the two shared a similar trait in the ability to roll up their sleeves and get the job done—whatever it was.

2013 had been a particularly difficult time for the governor. The state's crime lab was a mess thanks to chemist Annie Dookhan's criminal mishandling of evidence. Her crime had now placed thousands of successful prosecutions in jeopardy. Patrick's second in command, Lieutenant Governor Tim Murray, was currently under investigation for crashing a state-owned vehicle while driving one hundred miles per hour without a seatbelt. Murray was fined $555 for the accident but did not face any significant charges. Still, many did not believe Murray's claim that he had simply fallen asleep at the wheel during his pre-dawn drive, and there was wide speculation about what had really happened. With both scandals hovering above the Massachusetts State House, Governor Patrick could take some comfort in the fact that—for one day, at least—the spotlight would not be on his administration. Appropriately, the media would instead be focused on the Boston Marathon winners and those countless others who were crossing the finish line for one cause or another. Governor Patrick visited Mayor Menino in the hospital that morning.

"The mayor was devastated that he couldn't go to the finish line," Governor Patrick recalls. "This was his last marathon as mayor, and I could tell that he hated to miss it."

Normally, Menino attends the race and gives a speech at a pre-marathon pasta dinner on City Hall Plaza the night before. This year, with the mayor ailing, Governor Patrick would have to spend a little more time at the finish line shaking hands with sponsors and spectators alike. He was dressed casually in a pair of tan khakis and matching tan baseball cap. The sun was out but had done little to warm the chilly April air, so the governor wore a thick vest under his grey sport coat. The women's winner, Rita Jeptoo, crossed the finish line a full thirty-three seconds faster than her main rival, Meseret Hailu of Ethiopia.

"Today I was running like 2006," Jeptoo said at the finish line. "I was ready when I came to Boston." In 2006, the Kenyan won the race by ten seconds.

The men's winner, Lelisa Desisa of Ethiopia, had finished the marathon 16 minutes earlier.

Tradition dictates that the governor place the crown of laurel leaves on the women's winner, and Patrick did just that as Jeptoo grinned for the cheering crowd. With Mayor Menino in the hospital, Patrick also crowned Desisa. The two winners then stood together with their warm-up jackets on, each with a hand on the Boston Marathon trophy. More photos were taken, and the roar of the crowd grew louder. Despite the throngs of people now gathered on both sides of Boylston Street, Officer Javier Pagan felt he could relax a little bit. The most stressful part of the day was now over.

The winners had crossed the finish line unmolested by a drunken reveler. The crowd had been mild mannered so far. As Pagan scanned their faces, he saw spectators smiling, chit-chatting, and monitoring the progress of their husbands, wives, sons, daughters, and friends. After the winners were crowned, Pagan moved further down Boylston Street and away from the finish line a little in order to get out of view of people trying to snap that all-important finish-line photo of their loved ones. Governor Patrick stood on the shady side of Boylston Street, greeting school children who had the day off and shaking hands with well-wishers. After a few more minutes, he alerted his driver that it was time to leave. It was now just after 1 p.m. The governor looked forward to easing into his other role—husband.

"I needed to run some errands and maybe squeeze in a workout," he recalls. "I also needed to get those pansies in their pots."

8

TERROR STRIKES

On the morning of April 15, Tamerlan Tsarnaev was clean shaven. Gone was the thick black beard he had grown while in Dagestan the year before. He put on a white V-neck T-shirt, tan pants, and a black baseball cap with white trim. He no longer looked the part of a terrorist—and that was exactly the point. Tamerlan once again had that Euro-trash look that had caused him to be ridiculed in the boxing gym. He donned a thick, dark-hooded coat and a pair of sunglasses to cover his dark eyes. Today, he would appear to be just another Bostonian taking in the relative warmth of spring and the city's most cherished sporting event. His brother opted for a dark V-neck tee, a beige hoodie, dark pants, and a white baseball cap, which he wore backward over his tousled hair. He looked like a college boy who had woken up too late for class. But of course that was the old Dhzokhar. Today he would prove to be something entirely different. The brothers carefully loaded two homemade pressure cooker bombs into nylon backpacks and lifted the straps over their shoulders to feel the weight. The bags were heavily loaded, but the nylon material was strong—and so were the Tsarnaev brothers. Each would have no problem carrying the heavy backpacks to their final destinations. The bombs themselves had been built within the pressure cookers as the online instructions had suggested. The devices were filled with ball bearings, zippers, nails, and black powder—which had been taken from the fireworks Tamerlan had purchased in New Hampshire. Each bomb carried an improvised fuse made from a string of Christmas lights. They would be set off by remote control detonators fashioned from model car parts.[20] The most recent successful detonation of a pressure cooker bomb occurred in Pakistan in 2010, when insurgents attacked members of World Vision, a US-based Christian group that was operating out of the northwest part of the country. Six Pakistani workers were killed when the pressure cooker bomb was detonated remotely. Tamerlan and Dhzokhar had assembled their crude bombs while they cared for Tamerlan's infant daughter, Zahira. The baby's mother Katie, or Karima as she was now called, worked long hours to pay for food and to keep the family from getting thrown out onto the street. What she may not have known is that some of her weekly income was getting siphoned off by Tamerlan to purchase the materials he would need to kill.

By early afternoon, the brothers had made their way to Boylston Street. The first surveillance picture of the pair, time-stamped at 2:37 p.m., shows Tamerlan and Dhzokhar on nearby Gloucester Street. Tamerlan is wearing his backpack over both shoulders, military style. The dark glasses hide his sinister eyes. Dhzokhar is carrying his backpack slung low over his shoulder, student style. The brothers stopped in front of Whiskey's Smokehouse at 855 Boylston Street, where they chatted briefly with eyes scanning the crowd. They soon parted ways. Tamerlan took up position just outside Marathon Sports at 671 Boylston, where the crowd stood four to five people deep. Multinational flags waved in the breeze as runners from several countries crossed the finish line with arms raised in personal triumph while loved ones cheered from the sidewalk and from the grandstand across the street. Dhzokhar walked further down the street away from the finish line, looking for a suitable target. He strolled by Forum at 755 Boylston Street when something suddenly caught his eye. It was a family—an all-American family. There was a mom, a dad, two boys, and a little girl. In Dhzokhar's mind, it was perfect. He paced back and forth, looking for the ideal spot to drop his backpack. Once he found it, he called his brother.

Martin Richard was having a great day. He had the day off from school, and his parents had just bought them all ice cream. He had competed in the BAA's relay race on Saturday as part of the marathon weekend festivities. The marathon was fun, but it was no match for the excitement Martin felt when he saw his favorite team, the Boston Bruins, play at the Garden. Bruin's center Patrice Bergeron had been the boy's favorite player, but Martin figured that *his* only way to make it to the pros was as a goaltender. Martin practiced constantly in goalie pads that were bigger than his little body. Like most boys his age, Martin dreamed big and hoped to one day be good enough to wear the spoked B in the center of a black jersey before an adoring Boston Garden crowd.

Also standing outside Forum was Heather Abbott and her friend Roseann Sdoia, a forty-five-year-old North End property manager whom Heather knew from Newport. Roseann—or Ro, to her friends—and Heather had many mutual friends and usually met up at Forum on marathon day to catch up. Heather was hoping to see Roseann there because Heather was considering moving to Boston's North End. If there was one person who could help Heather make such a move, it was Roseann, who knew the tight-knit neighborhood's real estate market as well as anyone. It was time to go inside, so Heather handed the bouncer her driver's license and began walking in.

Across the street, lifestyle writer Megan Johnson was working the crowd at the VIP party at the Mandarin Oriental hotel. Johnson had cut her teeth covering the celebrity scene in Boston as part of the *Boston Herald*'s "Inside Track" gossip column. Each year, she'd hit the party circuit on marathon day to see what the mucky-mucks were up to, and perhaps catch a scoop on a drunken pro athlete, politician, or reality TV star. She had recently departed the *Herald* and had turned to writing for *People* magazine, among other publications—so on April 15, 2013, she was off the clock for the first time in years. She woke up that morning thrilled to not be working and thought to herself how excited she was to enjoy a free day—one of the most fun, wholesome events Boston offers. It was her tenth time going to the marathon, but the first she wasn't covering. As she left her North End apartment, she soaked in the sunshine and watched a small parade make its way down Hanover Street. She then headed to the party at the Mandarin Oriental, which is located right at the finish line on Boylston Street. She arrived there around noon and found the party in full swing. The ballroom was packed with people, who stood by the floor-to-ceiling windows to watch the runners come by. The competitive runners had already come and gone, and many of the VIPs and politicians were making their way into the party after watching the winners from the grandstands outside the hotel. Megan and her friend took a selfie right by the windows around 1 p.m. They smiled, innocently enjoying the day, like the thousands of others blissfully unaware of the terror that was being organized below. The crowd included a who's who of Boston's fashion, political, and business worlds. Marilyn Riseman, a fixture on the city's fashion and social scene, mingled with fellow elites, as did PBS television host Emily Rooney, daughter of the late *60 Minutes* legend Andy Rooney. Public relations guru George Regan was also there, talking up clients and networking. The party is the hotel's signature annual event—a gift back to its loyal clients and the city as a whole. The magnificent glass windows give the best indoor view of the marathon finish line in the city. Coupled with the open bar and elegant buffet, it's one of Boston's hottest parties every year—a place to see and be seen.

Michelle L'Heureux had been following her boyfriend Brian's progress on her phone through the Boston Athletic Association's runners' app, which lets friends and family track their loved ones through the BAA's website. Each runner's bib includes a small computer chip that sends a signal to the site, allowing followers to see where exactly on the course a runner is located at any given moment. Michelle was also tracking two other friends who were running. Around 1:45 p.m., Michelle and her friends arrived at Marathon Sports, right near the finish line. It was sunny, the weather was mild, they had a few cocktails in them, and everyone in their group was in a free-spirited, fun mood. It was a great use of a vacation day, Michelle thought as she scanned the colorful, sun-splashed crowd.

"I'm so glad we stood at the finish line," Michelle said to her friend Nicole. "Why have I never done this before? This is so fun!"

Also standing with them were Michelle's close friend Caroline Reinsch and her boyfriend Christian Williams. Just a few feet away from Nicole was twenty-seven-year-old Jeff Bauman, who was standing with a group of friends to watch his girlfriend, Erin Hurley, run the race.

As Brian neared the finish line, Michelle and her group yelled to him. He saw them and slowed down. They were all screaming at him.

Michelle blew him a kiss.

He kept running, and Michelle watched him head down Boylston Street toward the finish line. She was so happy for him. Michelle took a picture with Nicole, each holding signs. In the background of the photo, you can see the LensCrafters store next to Marathon Sports. She posted the picture on Facebook with a message that read, "Brian just finished!!! Yay!! 3 hours and 41 minutes!!!"

Nicole decided she was going to meet some friends at the Cactus Club, a popular Boylston Street watering hole a few blocks away.

"I'm going to see my friend at the Cactus Club. I'll be back," Nicole said. They talked about whether Michelle would go meet her at the bar, or if they would just meet back at Marathon Sports. Michelle had to wait for Brian, who was headed to shower at his gym in the Berkeley Building near the John Hancock tower.

"Just text us," Michelle told Nicole.

Nicole headed off but texted her only a few minutes later. "Line too long at Cactus Club. On my way back," she wrote.

"We're in the same spot," Michelle replied.

Meanwhile, Brian ran to the bus and got his backpack. He pulled out his phone, switched it on, and called Michelle.

"I've got my bag. I'm going to go shower," he said. "Then I'll come meet you guys. I know where you are because I saw you."

"Love you," Michelle responded.

At approximately 2:48 p.m., Tamerlan Tsarnaev received a call from brother Dzhokhar on a prepaid, throwaway cell phone. It was a quick conversation lasting only a few seconds. The call ended, and both men walked casually away—this time without their backpacks.

Moments later, the finish line of the Boston Marathon was rocked by a thunderous explosion. Plumes of white smoke swirled high into the air, masking the agonizing screams below. It was similar to the battle recreated on the Lexington Green several hours before, only this time it was real—and catastrophic. Runners on Boylston Street were knocked down as the ground trembled under their feet.

Michelle L'Herheux's boyfriend was walking toward the Berkeley Building when the first bomb went off. "That didn't sound right," Brian said to a man next to him. But he didn't think it was something bad. He thought it was perhaps a dump truck banging or some other construction-related noise.

Her friend Nicole, who was walking back toward her group, saw the explosion. She saw a big puff of smoke and heard screaming. She knew her friends were right there. Stunned, she hardly had a moment to think, when behind her was another loud *boom*, this one at Forum. She didn't know where to go, so she ran down Fairfield Street in search of safety, uncertain if there were more explosions to come.

Inside the first blast site, Michelle was in the middle of the most horrific nightmare imaginable.

She heard an excruciatingly loud explosion and looked up in front of her and saw a lamppost shaking from the blast. The image of the lamppost swaying is burned into her brain as an enduring image that haunts Michelle to this day.

She doesn't remember falling to the ground, and pictures from the scene show that she never fell down. She does, however, remember pushing herself up from the ground with her hands, possibly because she had been partially knocked over at some point.

Oh my God, this is a terrorist attack, she thought to herself immediately.

She shielded her head with her arms and ducked down. She couldn't hear anything. It was complete, dead silence. She looked past the lamppost toward the VIP bleachers and saw people running, screaming, crying, falling. But still, there was silence.

She saw smoke all around her, accompanied by a "disgusting" smell. She turned around—it felt like it took her twenty seconds just to turn around—and the whole scene appeared in slow motion.

As she turned, her hearing slowly came back, and she heard anguished, terrified screams and desperate yells. She witnessed total chaos. She started taking snapshots in her mind—snapshots that remain seared into her memory. She saw a foot in a sneaker on the ground right next to her own left foot. About three feet in front of her, she saw Jeff Bauman, sitting on the ground, both legs gone and blood pouring out of him.

That's not real, Michelle told herself.

She saw another woman, later identified as Krystle Campbell, eviscerated in a pool of blood.

That's not real, she said to herself again.

And she saw her friend Christian, covered in blood. Her other friend Caroline, who was unaware that she was two weeks pregnant, had already run away from the scene. She sustained serious wounds to her right thigh, while Christian's leg and hand were shredded by shrapnel. *That's not real*, she repeated.

She saw blood everywhere. It didn't look real. It looked like she was in the middle of a movie scene.

She surveyed the carnage and thought to herself, *I can't be standing in this and not be hurt.*

But she couldn't feel anything. She looked down at her calves and didn't see anything amiss. But then she looked down at the left side of her leg and saw that all of the flesh on the inside of her knee was gone. There was blood running down inside her boot. It looked awful, but she couldn't feel any pain at all. She looked around at the mounds of tissue, limbs, and debris on the ground and wondered if some of it was pieces of her leg.

She thought she ran a block away from the scene, but in actuality, she ran only a few feet and stumbled through the shattered front windows of Marathon Sports.

She ambled up to the counter and said: "Please help me! Please help me!" The store's manager, Shane O'Hare, looked at her with horror on his face. Michelle looked down and saw her arm was torn apart as well. She saw a flap of flesh hanging from her left arm and the muscle sagging out. She saw a lot of blood and wondered what other parts of her might be hurt.

"Help me! Help me!" she screamed.

Suddenly, she felt herself being picked up by several people and lowered to the floor. One of them elevated her leg onto a chair. She saw people ripping T-shirts into strips. A man ripped off his belt and cranked it around her shoulder.

"I'm so sorry I have to do this. It's for your own good," the man said.

In addition to Shane O'Hare, the people who helped Michelle were Lauren Blanda, who worked at City Sports on Boylston; Marathon Sports employee Joe McMenamy; and Andrew Daley, a former Marathon Sports employee who was working as a sales rep for Adidas the day of the race.

Joe held Michelle's arm as she was being treated on the floor of the store. Michelle looked up into his eyes.

"Don't leave me," she said.

"I'm not going anywhere," Joe replied.

Mery Daniel did not feel the blast, but she heard it. At first, she thought it was a problem with an electrical speaker. Mery also didn't realize that she was lying on the ground. She opened her eyes and looked to the left, where she saw another woman lying on the sidewalk with blood trailing down her arm. She was traumatized and confused. Mery then looked down at her own body and saw blood pouring out everywhere. She too felt as if she were in a movie. *This can't be real*, she told herself. She could hear others screaming over the loud ringing in her ears. Her nostrils were filled with the pungent odor of burning flesh. As a medical student, Mery knew that many of her major arteries were destroyed. She looked over and saw smoldering limbs strewn about. She thought immediately of her daughter, Ciarra, and thanked God that she had not brought the child here—to hell. But would her child grow up without a mother? Mery gazed helplessly at her broken and bleeding body. *Am I gonna die?* At that moment, she heard another blast.

9

FIRE AT FORUM

While shocked onlookers were trying to make sense of what they had just seen and heard outside Marathon Sports, Bill Richard knew exactly what was happening. At first many believed they had witnessed a transformer explosion or a pyrotechnic display gone awry. Bill Richard knew it was a bomb. He also believed that his family would be safer on the street than standing on the sidewalk. At that moment, Bill was standing on the edge of Boylston Street against the barricade. He jumped the fence and reached immediately for the closest family member—his eleven-year-old son, Henry. Bill lifted the boy safely over the barricade and placed Henry beside him on the street. He then stretched his arms across the barricade once more and was knocked back by a wave of searing metal and intense heat. Broken nails, ball bearings, and chunks of the pressure cooker shot out like a hundred speeding missiles through the crowd outside Forum. The backpack had been placed directly behind eight-year-old Martin, and the boy took the brunt of the impact. Like the scene unfolding a block down the street, smoke and chaos filled the air outside Forum. Bill Richard stood on Boylston Street and saw what was left of his beautiful family. Martin was lying on the ground—alive, but just barely. He managed a whisper.

"How is Jane?" he said faintly.

Martin Richard then closed his eyes and died. A first responder—a firefighter from Lynn, Massachusetts—ran over and tried CPR on the little boy, but the chest compressions were of no use. He was gone.

Eleven-year-old Henry, however, didn't have a scratch on him under his singed clothes. The boy was always quick to elude his mother when she

tried to clean his ears, and doctors would later say that the wax buildup actually saved Henry's hearing. That was not the case for Bill Richard, whose
eardrums were blown out by the explosion. He suffered ninety percent
hearing loss in one ear and fifty percent in the other. Still, he and Henry
were the least injured of the family. Bill fought the ringing in his ears and
tried to stay focused on getting his loved ones help. He grabbed his daughter, Jane, and held her on his hip. The bottom half of the little girl's left leg
was missing. Jane was not severely bleeding — at first. Soon, the blood began to flow, and Jane was laid down on the street as first responders applied
a makeshift tourniquet to her wound. The frightened little girl looked all
around, wondering what had just happened. She needed her mom, but Denise was severely injured herself and couldn't rush immediately to her side.
At that moment, another woman stepped in and offered comfort.

Tracy Munro was at the marathon to cheer on her uncle and others she
knew who were running. Her young daughter, Stella, had created a big sign
that read *Go Uncle Robby!* for Tracy to wave at the finish line. She had scored
tickets to a private event at Abe & Louie's restaurant, where she had enjoyed lunch and drinks with friends while waiting for her uncle to cross the
finish line. Tracy was never big on crowds and had never gone to Boylston
Street during the marathon before. This being her first time, she marveled
at the excitement and the sheer thrill of being there. At 2:45 p.m., she left
the restaurant and moved down the street toward Forum, where she and
her cousins pulled out their cowbells and began cheering on the runners
as they made their last strides toward the finish line. A group of soldiers
from the Massachusetts National Guard jogged past her in full camouflage
gear, wearing forty-pound backpacks. The troops called themselves the
Tough Ruckers and ran the marathon to honor their fallen comrades who
had been killed in Iraq and Afghanistan. As they crossed the finish line,
there was a deafening boom.

"Oh cool," Munro said. "They're firing cannons to salute the soldiers."

Moments later — a second explosion.

"Brown, billowing smoke just shot up in the air," she recalls.

Still, Munro could not fathom that Boston was under attack. At first, she
thought that the explosions were caused by a train collision or derailment
on the tracks that ran underground along Boylston Street. Suddenly, a wave
of spectators descended upon her. Her chest pounded and her eyes darted

in all directions. She had to run or get crushed by the stampede. Munro dropped her handbag and ran down the sidewalk toward Fairfield Street, where she turned the corner and stopped with her back against the wall as hundreds of panicked spectators ran past. Munro took a few moments to gain her composure, and she realized that people had been hurt and that people needed help. She held her breath, found her will, and ran back in the direction of the smoke and stench of burning body parts and blood. Munro returned to Forum and was ill-equipped for what she witnessed.

"I saw severed limbs everywhere," she remembers. "People were screaming, their pants literally on fire."

Munro's mind was racing, but everything was moving in slow motion in front of her. She spotted her handbag, which contained her cell phone, and knelt down to retrieve it. On her knees, she saw a child lying before her on the sidewalk. She immediately thought of her young daughter, Stella, and her parental instincts kicked into gear. As a man tried to apply a tourniquet to the child's leg, Munro placed the child's head in her lap. Staring down, she could not tell whether it was a boy or a girl. The child's hair had been burned off. The child continued to look all around with terrified eyes.

"Look at me, baby," Munro said soothingly. "They're taking care of you. What's your name?"

"Jane," the girl replied softly.

"How old are you?"

"Seven."

Munro relayed the information to the first responders. "It's a girl. Her name is Jane!"

"I just stared into her eyes," Munro recalls. "She wasn't alone. I wanted her poor mother to know that a mom was taking care of her. Something aligned for me to be there at that moment."

Munro helped firefighters place the little girl into the ambulance. She saw Bill and Henry Richard, and her heart sank. "I realized that they had gone there as a family. Again, I thought of my Stella."

Munro returned to the sidewalk and tended to more victims. She took off her scarf and offered it as a tourniquet; she carried buckets of ice out of the restaurant to treat the wounded. She then noticed another child lying on the sidewalk. At this point, there was no one tending to his injuries.

"Why aren't we helping him?" she screamed. She peered into Martin Richard's lifeless eyes and learned the crushing answer.

Soon, someone would cover Martin Richard's body with a sheet. This angered his mother, Denise, who was conscious—despite the fact that a projectile had pierced her right eye.

"Don't cover his face!" she yelled.

Lingzi Lu had been standing close to Martin Richard. The twenty-three-year-old Boston University graduate student had fallen in love with the city during her short time in Boston. A product of China's one-child policy, Lu was raised in the northeastern city of Shenyang with a passion for music and a mind for math. She attended Shenyang's Northeast Yucai School before moving on to the Beijing Institute of Technology. Her parents urged her to apply to graduate school in the United States, and she was accepted to the statistics program at BU. After arriving in Boston in the fall of 2012, Lu created a photo gallery on her Facebook page. The title for the album: "New Beginning at BU."

The young woman with soft eyes and an engaging smile made friends easily with other Asian students, and had planned to spend the day with a small group of friends at the marathon—a spectacle she had never seen or experienced before. Lu's spirits were high as she had just received word that she'd aced a big exam. She and her friends had found their way to Forum, and within minutes—Lu was gone. Dhzokhar Tsarnaev had claimed a second victim with his backpack bomb. Projectiles from the pressure cooker tore through the young woman's lower body, killing her almost instantly. There should have been more deaths outside Forum, but much of the blast had been contained or halted by a large postal box that was bolted into the ground just a few feet away from Lingzi Lu and Martin Richard.

As Heather Abbott approached the entrance of Forum she was startled by an incredibly loud *boom*, followed by a cloud of smoke more than a block away. She turned, saw people running away from the noise, and knew immediately that something bad was happening. But before she could react, the second pressure cooker bomb exploded just a few feet away from her on the sidewalk. She was blown off her feet and catapulted through the front door and into the restaurant. There were others blown through the glass and into the restaurant, too.

Smoke filled the air. It was dark. People screamed. Others ran. She landed on the floor and opened her eyes, wondering what the hell was going on.

Heather thought to herself about the people running, *How do they know where to go? How do they know there's not another one?* She was paralyzed with fear, but that quickly gave way to excruciating pain in her left foot. It felt like it was on fire.

She tried to get up but couldn't. Her foot was useless. She started crawling toward the back of the eatery and screamed out for help. She thought to herself that no one was going to come help her because everyone was literally running for their own lives. She was crawling on the floor just a few steps away from the patio, infected with fear and uncertainty. She thought she was going to die right there on the floor of Forum.

But then a woman appeared next to her. She took her hand and touched her head. It was Erin Chatham, wife of former New England Patriot player Matt Chatham. She looked down at Heather's destroyed foot and started to cry.

"What's your name?" Erin asked her.

"Heather," she replied.

Erin and another woman grabbed her by the shoulders and began dragging her away from the doorway.

"Matt!" Erin yelled, tears in her eyes. "Come quick!"

The hulking, bald-headed ex-linebacker emerged and picked Heather up off the floor.

"Hail Mary, full of grace, the Lord is with thee," Erin said, reciting the Catholic prayer. "Blessed art thou amongst women, and blessed is the fruit of thy womb, Jesus...."

Matt Chatham carried her toward the rear of the restaurant and into a stairwell.

"Holy Mary, Mother of God, pray for us sinners, now and at the hour of our death," Erin concluded. Others were running into the stairwell too.

Heather couldn't look down at her foot. She knew it was seriously damaged, if not gone completely. She saw a trail of blood behind them.

Matt carried Heather down the stairs and outside into a back alley. Heather's friend Jason was there.

"That's my friend. Give her to me," Jason said.

"No, she's really hurt," Matt replied.

Dazed but somehow fully aware of her surroundings, Heather looked down at the ground. She saw drops of blood. She knew it was hers. Her friend Jessica was there, too. Jessica was crying. Matt put Heather down on the ground. Jessica, Jason, and some others gathered around her. Jessica laid her head on Heather's head, tears streaming down her face.

"I'm not going to leave you, Heather," Jessica sobbed. "I won't leave you."

Another friend held Heather's head in his trembling hands. He looked at Heather's foot.

"Oh my God," was the response.

A surgeon and a nurse who happened to be at Forum came over. They used a belt to cinch a tourniquet tightly above Heather's knee. It likely saved her life.

She was in severe pain and kept wondering to herself where the ambulance was.

Why is it taking so long? she wondered. She thought of her parents back in Rhode Island.

The ambulance couldn't get near the alley, so Matt Chatham carried her back through the restaurant to the front sidewalk where the bomb went off.

Heather tried not to look, but she couldn't help but see the blood. And the limbs—the bodies. She knew people were dead.

Something very bad has happened, she thought to herself. *What is going on?*

She held back tears and kept focused on staying awake. She just wanted to get to the emergency room.

"What's your name?" Erin Chatham asked her again. She kept asking Heather her name and where she was from to keep her talking—to keep her from slipping into unconsciousness.

Across the street at the Mandarin Oriental's VIP party, the mood had gone from joy and frivolity to utter panic. Just half an hour before, the party was slowing down as many of the suited CEOs, politicians, and philanthropists had finished their glad-handing and were off to other events. About two dozen remained in the spacious ballroom, enjoying the last remnants of the swanky buffet and—of course—gossiping. The innocent mingling was soon interrupted by a hellacious *bang!*

"What the hell was that?" Megan Johnson asked aloud. No one seemed very concerned.

Roughly twelve seconds later, a second explosion—infinitely louder—erupted just across the street. The guttural, bowel-shaking *boom* rocked the building. The giant windows, where just seconds earlier patrons had been watching runners go by, were now literally jiggling and waving from the impact of the blast. *They look like pieces of rubber,* Megan thought.

Those sitting near the windows started walking away at a quick pace toward the back of the room and out the rear exit that filtered into the Prudential Center.

"What's going on?" Megan asked one visibly shaken passerby.

Someone uttered the word *bomb.*

"No way," Megan said.

She had assumed—as many did that day—that the VIP stands had collapsed or maybe a transformer had blown.

Two minutes after the explosion, the Mandarin staff came into the room and started ushering everyone out into the glass vestibule that connects the hotel with the Prudential Tower and its adjacent mall. That's when people started realizing that something was horribly wrong.

Corralled into the glass walkway, scared and confused, people tried using their cell phones, but there was no service. Megan looked down from the walkway and saw a young girl sprawled out on the street in front of Max Brenner Chocolate Bar, a restaurant across the street. She was wearing a blue T-shirt and khaki-colored shorts and had blonde hair that was laid out underneath her head. Her legs were bent at the knee and pointed to the side. It looked like she was sleeping in the middle of the street.

The only thing that seemed abnormal was a small red splash under her head, which Megan quickly realized was blood. She thought to herself that she must have been a jumper who had hurled herself off the building across the street. But everyone kept saying, to no one in particular, "It's a bomb. A bomb."

The street below was chaos. There were tons of people running in every direction as police tried to gain control of the panicked situation. There were runners sitting on the side of the street, some nursing minor injuries and others huddled with their families.

A group of people stood looking at the young woman lying on the cement. She was surrounded by police and EMTs.

Cops with bomb-sniffing dogs soon showed up. Discarded bags were everywhere. Police started hustling people away from the scene, fearful one of the bags could contain another explosive. The area in front of Max Brenner and Forum, where just moments earlier people had been enjoying cocktails and lunch, was now filled with police vans, bomb squad officers, EMTs, firefighters, and ambulances.

Megan saw several children crying but was struck by how many adults were clearly horrified by what they were witnessing. Some had their hands clenched into fists and were shaking and crying.

Megan jumped on Twitter. Her hands were shaking hard as she started to type into her phone.

"What is happening???" she tweeted.

Within seconds news started flowing into her feed. People were replying to her tweet that two bombs had gone off. Her journalistic instincts kicked in, and she started snapping pictures and video of the scene and tweeted them out.

"Two explosions at the marathon, I see one severely injured body," she tweeted.

A group of EMTs stood around an unidentified blonde woman in a circle. Megan wondered why they weren't working on her. Why weren't they helping her?

Within a few minutes, an ambulance backed into Megan's view and she saw the woman loaded onto a gurney and put into the vehicle. It drove away.

When the bombs went off, public relations executive Geri Denterlein, who was managing the guest list at the VIP party, was on an escalator in the attached Prudential Center, heading back to her office. She had just left the Mandarin and never heard the explosions, but as she reached the bottom of the escalator, a swarm of people ran toward her, some screaming and all looking terrified.

Oh my God, what's going on? she thought.

Her phone began buzzing with calls from the media looking for information. Geri poked her head into Haru, a sushi restaurant on Boylston Street. The TV was on, and there was live coverage of the explosions.

Confused and uncertain, she tried to head back to the Mandarin, but by then the entrance was sealed with yellow police tape and cops were evacuating the hotel. She headed to the Harvard Club on Commonwealth Avenue and set up shop, working the phones with hotel managers, executives, and the press.

At 3:10 p.m., a voice came over the loudspeaker in the Prudential Center.

"Can I have your attention, please. Public Safety is reporting . . . criminal activity on Boylston Street," the voice said.

Boston City Councilor Mike Ross had just left Marathon Sports and turned the corner onto Exeter Street when the first bomb went off.

His ears were ringing. He turned toward the sound and saw a sea of humanity racing toward him. There were so many people that the councilor instinctively just ran with the crowd away from Boylston Street.

A block or so away, he saw a cab. But it was a red cab from the town of Brookline. Being a city councilor, he knew the rules in Boston were strict that out-of-town cabs are not allowed to pick up passengers in Boston proper. He thought about this for a split second, but then realized the gravity of the situation.

This was a dire emergency. So he grabbed as many people as he could and shoved them into the cab and jumped in himself. He told the driver to just drive away from Boylston Street.

He thought about his friend at the Charlesmark. His ears rang. He told the driver to take the group to his house in Mission Hill. There, the group exited the cab, all of them stunned and confused about what was going on.

The councilor was safe but quickly realized that whatever had happened on Boylston Street had happened in his district. He knew he had to get to work.

He started getting calls from constituents, clergy, business owners, friends in the neighborhood. There were so many questions: Where do we go? What happens to our business? Have people died?

Ross realized that the neighborhood needed a safe place to go for comfort, assistance, answers, love, community. He called Boston Police Superintendent Danny Linskey and asked him if there was a way to open the historic Trinity Church in Copley Square as a resource center for residents and businesses.

"Impossible," Linskey told him. It was in the secure zone.

The pastor of First Church Boston on Marlboro Street offered the cathedral to the community.

"People were freaking out, and they needed somewhere to go," Ross says.

Michelle L'Heureux tried to remain calm while her caregivers wrapped her leg and arm in gauze. She heard others in the store screaming in pain.

Michelle still clutched her phone in a death grip with her right hand. She handed the device to first responder Lauren Blanda.

"Can you punch in 'dad'?" Michelle said. Michelle thought there was a chance she wouldn't make it, or at least would be losing a limb, and wanted desperately to hear the calming voice of her father, Paul, a retired firefighter in Auburn, Maine.

Lauren handed the phone to Michelle.

"Dad, a bomb went off. I'm really, really hurt," she said.

The father's heart started pounding. Michelle would forever be his little girl. His little girl needed his help.

"Michelle, you're going to be OK. You're in good hands. I need you to stay calm and I need you to stay awake," he said. "Stay awake. I'll find out where you'll be. I love you, doll."

"I love you, Dad."

A runner who appeared to be a doctor showed up and asked her how she was doing. The man was checking on the injured, helping to prioritize treatment and transport for the EMTs and firefighters scrambling to deal with all the wounded.

Michelle hung up with her father. An EMT came over and cut off her scarf and jacket.

"Stay with her," the EMT told the group. "We'll be back for her. There's someone a little worse. We'll be right back."

Just then, a fire alarm went off at Marathon Sports. Someone ran in and screamed, "Everyone out!"

Michelle thought there was a fire or another explosion. Andrew Daley, another caregiver, was sitting on the floor next to her.

"I can't feel my hand," Michelle said, her anxiety level rising.

"It's from the belt. You're OK. Your hand is OK," he assured her.

The EMTs returned and picked her up. One of them accidentally grabbed her wounded arm. She winced and screamed in agony.

They put her in a wheelchair and quickly wheeled her out of the store, through the shattered glass and debris. The EMTs ran as they pushed the chair over the sidewalk, past the carnage. Michelle kept her head down, trying desperately not to see anything more gruesome than she had already witnessed.

There was a bandage around her heel, and a woman ran alongside the wheelchair, keeping her leg elevated as they rushed down Boylston to the medical tent, where one of the EMTs called out her wounds.

"Two open blast fractures," the EMT shouted. Thankfully, that information turned out to be erroneous—somehow Michelle had suffered no broken bones.

A blonde female EMT started cutting off all her clothes. They cut off her pants, her underwear and snipped right through the front of her bra.

In a moment of levity, Michelle shouted at the woman doing the cutting, "That's a new bra!" She managed to chuckle a bit.

"At least you have a sense of humor," the EMT said.

She put an IV in Michelle's arm, poured iodine all down the left side of her body, and wrapped her in gauze. A tag was put on her right hand with a number telling the EMTs that she was a priority transport. It was an agonizing wait as Michelle lay there, waiting to be taken to an unknown hospital to be treated for wounds she knew were serious—if not life threatening.

While she was being treated, Michelle managed to fire off a text to a friend. "All cut up," was all she could manage to type. The message got to a friend, who forwarded it to others. The message was interpreted, however, to mean that Michelle had only minor cuts and scrapes, so many of her friends were unaware just how severely injured she was.

Relatives and friends saw her pre-bombing Facebook post and feared the worst, since Michelle hadn't posted anything after the explosions. They started calling and texting. Sitting on a gurney, waiting to be transported, Michelle made a quick call to her cousin.

"I'm really hurt. I'm in the medical tent. Call the rest of the family and tell them," she said. "Dad already knows."

Her pregnant friend, Caroline, was on a gurney to her left, shaking.

Is this really happening right now? was the thought that went through Michelle's head.

Michelle knew she was going to need surgery. She was scared. The only time in her life that she'd had surgery was when she was eight years old and had her tonsils out.

"Am I going to lose my leg?" she asked an EMT.

"You're going to be OK," was the ambiguous response.

She was loaded into an ambulance and driven to Faulkner Hospital. During the ride, she texted Brian that she would be at Faulkner. He told her he loved her.

A young blonde woman was in the ambulance with her, along with a young, African American male EMT. The woman, whose name Michelle has never learned, had cuts, and her clothes were ripped. She was crying.

"Honey, you're going to be OK," Michelle said. She felt bad for the girl. She was so young, vulnerable, and so scared.

Pain started to rush into Michelle's leg and arm. Her leg was bouncing and hitting the bed as the ambulance hit potholes in the streets. They went over a huge one, and Michelle's leg bounced. Her wound shook like a bowl of Jell-O. Excruciating pain shot through Michelle's body.

Her sense of humor surfaced again.

"Fucking Massachusetts potholes!" she shouted. The EMT started laughing.

[10]

UNDER SIEGE

Danny Keeler had spent much of the early afternoon walking up and down Boylston Street popping in and out of various bars and restaurants, including Abe & Louie's and McGreevy's, to monitor crowd control.

"What's your head count?" he'd ask the doorman. "Make sure you keep it at fifty and below. If we come back and it's like that, you won't have any problems with us."

Keeler was walking alone across Gloucester Street when he heard and saw the first explosion. His initial reaction was similar to others who had witnessed the blast.

"I thought a transformer had let loose," Keeler recalls.

Almost a year earlier, the Back Bay section of Boston had been plunged into darkness when a 115,000-volt transformer exploded at a garage on Dalton Street, close to the finish line.

Keeler immediately began running toward the smoke and noise emanating from Marathon Sports. The area was still choked with people. If it was a transformer explosion, someone was likely hurt. His time in the US Marines and his years on the police force had trained Keeler to be instinctive. He had also been trained to run in the direction of trouble — not away from it.

"In thirteen years in homicide, I've been involved in a lot of shootings. I've seen a lot of chaos," Keeler says. "But I firmly believe that God put me there that day."

He had reached Fairfield Street when suddenly he heard another devastating blast—this time coming from behind him. He turned around immediately and could see another large cloud of smoke, followed by the sound of ear-piercing screams.

This ain't no transformer fire, he thought to himself. *We're getting bombed.*

Since he was closer to the second explosion, Keeler decided to double back down Boylston Street to the scene at Forum. There was panic everywhere. People were turning over tables outside restaurants and running in every direction. Keeler tried to wade through the waves of fleeing spectators, but it was impossible. He jumped off the sidewalk and approached the middle of the street when he got his first glimpse of true devastation.

"I saw a leg lying on the street. It was on fire."

The charred body part looked like a log that had been tossed atop a fire pit.

Keeler grabbed his radio. "This is Delta 984. I've got multiple bombs at the finish line. I need some help down here."

He requested that Ring Road, adjacent to Boylston Street, be closed off immediately.

"Ring Road's gonna be our evac route. I need you to shut it down at Huntington [Avenue] for MOP [Mobile Operations], I want that clear. I need the lanes cut clear for the fire department."

Keeler's first thought was to get the victims away from the scene and to the hospital as quickly as possible.

Three officers ran up to Keeler looking for guidance—looking for orders.

"Danny, what do you need from me?" asked Boston Police Captain Frank Armstrong.

"I need you to keep these lanes clear [near the bombing scene]," Keeler told him. "Don't have the fire department come in here and drop their trucks anywhere. Keep these lanes clear."

Keeler ordered the others to gain control of the bombing scenes in front of Forum and Marathon Sports. Meanwhile, other Boston police officers at and around the finish line began calling into dispatch asking for additional help.

"The only one I want to hear from is 984," the police dispatcher ordered. "984's got the channel."

At that moment, Detective Sergeant Danny Keeler took command of the biggest crime scene in the history of the city.

Javier Pagan had never had to fire his service weapon in his nineteen years on the job. He had drawn it many times, usually while working the midnight-to-eight shift while searching buildings or chasing someone in an alley. But he had never before felt that his life was in danger and that he might need to use it to kill someone—until now.

Just before 3 p.m., he was standing near the announcers' booth watching the steady flow of runners cross the finish line. All of a sudden he heard *boom!*

Pagan was about ten feet away from the blast. He put his hand on his weapon and started running toward the explosion. Just then, he heard a second loud blast. He drew his gun. He was surrounded by fellow cops.

"Holy shit," Javier said aloud. He clutched his weapon. His mind raced. His heart rate leaped. He was standing in the middle of Boylston Street, chaos unfolding around him, next to fellow officers Rachel McGuire and Kevin McGill. A photographer snapped a photo of the three of them, in between the two blasts. Rachel has her gun drawn, while Kevin is toting his radio. Javier has his hand on his weapon as he readies to draw it. All three have sunglasses on and stern looks on their faces. A runner knocked down by the blast is lying on the cement in front of them. Debris litters the pavement. The iconic picture would later land on the cover of *Sports Illustrated*.

Smoke filled the air. People were screaming. For Javier, the scene was surreal. Everything was moving in slow motion. He felt like he was watching a movie, and was having a hard time coming to grips with the reality that he was in the middle of a terror attack. He thought back to his training.

"Where there's one bomb, there's two bombs," he remembered. "The first is usually set to do harm while the second is set to kill first responders. It's a classic terror tactic."

He also remembered that the event was being televised, and his mind quickly thought of his family members turning on the TV or the radio, knowing he was at the finish line.

On the sidewalk where the first blast erupted, two rows of fences were lying on the ground. People were under them. He joined the group pulling the fences and barricades apart.

During his career, he had seen plenty of people stabbed or shot, but he had never seen people with missing limbs. He did this day.

Pagan and others grabbed the first barricades outside Marathon Sports and yanked them all the way across the street to the other side. Medical professionals were arriving.

But there were hundreds of people in the bleachers. They began running for their lives and many discarded bags. Pagan, like every cop down there that day, thought every bag he saw was another bomb.

His captain yelled to him, "There's a bag underneath the bleachers!"

Dozens of people raced inside the Boston Public Library just behind the bleachers to escape the carnage outside. He ran over to the glass doors to the library and saw a security guard.

"Lock the door and get everyone to the other side of the security checkpoint just in case this is a bomb!" Pagan shouted to the stunned guard.

There were still runners stuck in the street between where the two bombs went off. Pagan returned to the street and helped direct stranded runners away from the bombing site. His adrenaline pumped. He watched in shock as victim after victim was pulled from the wreckage, most bleeding. Some had limbs missing. Some had their clothes shredded by debris while others looked like they were burned. Pagan was certain people were dead. Judging by the destruction, he thought the number was going to be in the dozens.

Officer Andrew Crosby was less experienced than Javier Pagan, but he had still seen a lot during his seven years on the force—and also during his own childhood in South Boston. The son of a police officer himself, Crosby works out of District D-4 (Back Bay/South End) under Danny Keeler. Boylston Street is his normal daily beat. After grabbing a quick lunch, he had been ordered to relieve another officer on front of Forum at around 1 p.m. He watched as tired runners crossed the finish line one after the next. Crosby was amazed by their resilience.

"People were bleeding [from running]," he recalls. "It just looked awful. It's just fun to watch."

Crosby took up position near the mailbox outside Forum. Someone approached him and asked for the easiest way to cross Boylston Street, since the barricades had made it nearly impossible to do so.

"Well you can take the T down and cross underneath Mass Ave and try that way," Crosby advised.

Seconds later, the first bomb exploded.

"I look and I saw smoke coming up down the street. I remember looking at my partner and he started moving toward the direction of the blast."

Crosby joined his partner, Chris Kenefick, when suddenly he saw a bright flash off to his left. The flash was followed by a big fireball. People started running. Crosby tried to maintain order, but it was impossible.

"I saw a guy lying in the middle of the street. He was a spectator and got blown into the middle of the street," Crosby remembers.

The man looked up at Crosby. "Am I going to die?"

"You don't have a foot," the officer replied. "Let me go get some help."

Crosby turned around and walked to the barricade and saw carnage everywhere. He turned back and the injured spectator was gone.

"Someone must have scooped him up," Crosby says.

He then took the pocket knife off his belt. He cut through the straps of the barricades outside Forum and started ripping them down. While all this was happening, runners were still turning onto Boylston Street and heading toward the finish line.

"Get out of here, get out of here," Crosby ordered them. He then received an order on the radio: "Start clearing buildings."

Crosby had never been more afraid in his life. "I didn't know how many bombs there were," he recalls. "I remember thinking, 'This is it. This is how I'm going to go.'"

Crosby's boss, Police Commissioner Ed Davis, had watched the marathon for about an hour with Governor Patrick and other VIP's before heading back to his house in Hyde Park, where he dropped off his wife and joined a conference call with Vice President Joe Biden and top cops from other big cities to discuss a controversial gun bill making its way through Congress.

Both Davis and Mayor Menino were at the forefront of a national gun reform package backed by Biden and President Obama. Davis took the call in his bedroom. It lasted forty-five minutes.

As soon as he hung up with the vice president, Davis's phone rang. It was Dan Linskey.

"Hey boss, I don't know what we've got, there are two explosions at the finish line."

"What kind of explosions?" Davis asked.

"I don't think they're electrical in nature," Linskey replied.

Davis has had extensive international training regarding the use of IEDs (improvised explosive devices), bombs, and other methods of terrorist attacks. After the subway bombings in London in 2005, which killed fifty-two people and injured more than seven hundred more, Davis spent time with Scotland Yard officials and studied the attack—all the while thinking of the uncanny similarities between that city's mass transit system and Boston's MBTA subways. Immediately, the fact that there were two explosions had Davis concerned that it could be a coordinated attack like so many he's seen internationally. "I was hoping it was a manhole explosion, but I didn't like the sound of it," Davis later recalled.

"Are you there?" Davis asked Linskey.

"No, I'm in Kenmore Square. I'm racing up there now. Making my way up there now."

Davis could hear sirens in the background and police radios blaring. He didn't have his portable radio with him, so he asked Linskey, "What are they saying on the radio?"

"It's Danny Keeler. I can't understand him," Linskey replied.

Davis knew the detective sergeant well. He also knew Keeler was a Marine and was alarmed by the fact that something could rattle the veteran cop. This had to be serious.

"Keeler's calling for all the ambulances in the city, and he says he's got multiple amputations," Linskey said.

It was then that Davis knew Boston had been attacked. And knowing that such attacks often occur in threes, his attention immediately turned toward protecting his officers and the public from a possible third bomb.

Danny Keeler had already dispatched the bomb squad, and officers were boldly checking each and every one of the hundreds of bags discarded on bloody Boylston Street by terrified bystanders.

The commissioner's next call was to Rick DesLauriers, Special Agent in Charge of Boston's FBI office. He called for the FBI's bomb squad, also known as the Explosive Ordnance Disposal (EOD) team, as well as all SWAT units.

"Alright, I'm on my way," said DesLauriers, who was at the FBI's headquarters at Government Plaza across from Boston City Hall.

"We are going to set up a command post at Ring Road, see me at Ring Road," Davis told him.

Davis ended the call, grabbed his service weapon, and headed for the door of his home.

"What's going on?" asked his wife.

"We may have been attacked," he said in full stride. "Turn on the TV and I'll call you when I can."

The tires on Davis's vehicle screeched as he pulled out of his driveway. He dialed Massachusetts State Police Colonel Timothy Alben and asked him to send all available units, especially the bomb squads and SWAT teams, to Boylston Street. The commissioner switched the radio in his SUV to a special frequency used for mass-casualty events. He heard multiple calls for ambulances. Radio chaos. Not quite panic, but as close to it as he'd seen in his decorated career.

His next call was to Mayor Menino in the hospital.

"Mr. Mayor, we've got a situation," Davis told him. "There were two explosions at the marathon finish line."

"Jesus, does it sound like a bomb?" the mayor asked.

"It's not looking good, Mayor, but I'm not certain until I get there," Davis said. "They were reporting multiple amputations, and that's an indication that it was antipersonnel in nature. I'll get back to you as soon as I can."

"Good luck," the mayor said.

Menino had been informed of the situation before the call from Ed Davis. Just before 3 p.m. that afternoon, one of the mayor's security officers came in and told him, "A bomb just blew up at the marathon."

"Get more, get more information," the mayor told the cop. He then addressed his staff. "Let's not get nervous. Everyone calm down."

After talking with Davis on the phone, Menino sent his Chief of Staff Mitchell Weiss out to the command post near the finish line to get a read on exactly what was going on.

Governor Patrick was making his way down Route 3 toward his home in Milton when he got a call from his daughter Katherine, who was living in the South End and could hear the commotion.

"Dad, there were two big booms and everybody is running," she explained frantically. "Was it a cannon? I think there's smoke."

The governor told his daughter to stay calm and yelled up to his state police driver. "Trooper, is there something going on?"

At that moment, the governor received another call, this time from Kurt Schwartz. He had been in the medical tent when the bombs went off. Schwartz had always been a calming voice in any storm. Yet, the governor could sense a hint of panic in his voice now.

"Something has gone off down here," Schwartz informed his boss. "There are body parts everywhere. It's a mess."

Governor Patrick hung up the phone and shouted at his driver. "Get me downtown!"

Commissioner Davis was already speeding down Huntington Avenue with his siren wailing and lights flashing. The first sign of trouble came about a mile from the finish line at the intersection of Huntington and Ruggles streets, where Davis spotted a young couple and a few girls crying hysterically. It looked like they had just gotten off the T, and they were looking at themselves, apparently to see if they were injured.

Not a good sign if there are people impacted by the incident this far from the scene, he told himself.

He made it to Ring Road, stopped short of Boylston Street, got out and jogged toward Forum, the site of the second explosion. There, on the bloodstained pavement in front of the restaurant, Davis saw the bodies of Martin Richard and Lingzi Lu. Davis had no idea who they were at the time, but he knew they were dead. He saw severely hurt spectators, many soaked in blood and with tourniquets tied tight around injuries, being loaded into police wagons to be rushed to the hospital.

Transporting victims in anything other than an ambulance is normally against every city protocol. But in this case, there was no alternative. Every ambulance was busy, and time was of the essence—many victims could have easily bled out and died right there on the street. Doctors would later say that dozens of lives were saved by the quick actions of first responders, volunteers, and citizens, specifically citing the fact that victims were raced to the hospital as fast as humanly possible by whatever means necessary. There were even reports that pedicab drivers raced doctors from the hospitals to the wounded, and brought the wounded to the hospitals.

The commissioner surveyed the scene. He saw broken windows. He saw blood pooling on the sidewalk. He walked on the street, stepping on nails and shards of metal. He recognized it as shrapnel and realized that these were, in fact, antipersonnel devices specifically designed to kill.

Davis kept running to the first bomb scene in front of Marathon Sports. He saw that the blast had taken out windows three stories up. A LensCrafters store had had its windows shattered. There were smoldering body parts strewn along the sidewalk. He ran into Christopher Connolly, BPD's top bomb expert. Boylston Street was littered with backpacks and handbags. Any one of them could contain a third explosive device.

They happen in threes, Davis reminded himself.

It was like a scene from the Oscar-winning film *The Hurt Locker*. The difference was that Connolly and his bomb cops weren't wearing any protective gear as they began checking every bag and item left in the area. They held their breath and flinched as they opened each bag. Using a technique known as slash and tag, they used knives to cut open the bags, visually inspected them all to make sure they weren't packed with explosives, and tagged them to denote that they had been checked and were and safe.

Davis quickly realized that the two attacks were coordinated and were the work of terrorists. From his extensive international training, he knew the double bombing had all the characteristics of Islamic extremism. Even though no one was certain who had set off the bombs or why, Davis knew that their coordination and obvious purpose—to maximize both injuries and death, without regard for women or children—was clear evidence of a planned attack by trained international terrorists, possibly even al-Qaeda.

They got us, he thought to himself, and called the mayor back.

"It looks like a terrorist attack," he told Menino. "I'm not sure when I'll be able to call you back. I'll get back to you as soon as I can, but it might be a while."

The commissioner went through a mental checklist of everything that had to be done. First, he thought back to what he had learned in London in 2005. Because of what he had seen and what his bomb experts had found and told him about, he knew these were pressure cooker bombs very similar to the ones used in the London attacks. But unlike the London bombs, these ones were made with gunpowder. The London explosives used a peroxide-like accelerant.

The first order of business was to clear the casualties. Next was to secure the scene and make it safe for investigators. Wary that there could be more undetonated bombs, Davis ordered his detectives to be careful but diligent. He also knew that video surveillance had been the key to the London bombing probe and that it would also be crucial here.

Danny Keeler knew it, too. "I need you to get all the cameras for me. I want you to go up and down the street both sides, identify where the cameras are, what we have, and list them for later," Keeler told detective Earl Perkins. Perkins was not used to taking such orders. He had been demoted from deputy superintendent to detective sergeant in 2009, without any official reason given by Ed Davis. Still, he was an officer with tremendous pride, and he understood that a job had to be done.

Cops on the street asked people if they had any cell phone videos or pictures of the explosions or the aftermath. Bystanders handed them over freely. Keeler sent Perkins and other detectives from building to building to look for cameras and to get building managers to turn over any available video.

"I wanna see what happened before the bombings, not after," he told Perkins. "If the video cameras are there, we're gonna get it. Don't let anybody fuck with you, and don't take no for an answer."

Both Keeler and Perkins knew time was of the essence, as many surveillance systems wipe out footage after twenty-four hours.

11

SAVING LIVES

Michelle L'Heureux was driven to Faulkner Hospital and rushed into the pre-operation unit in the emergency room, where she was given a morphine drip. The pain slipped away as X-rays were taken of her injuries. The doctors couldn't believe she had no broken bones. They gave her a tetanus shot. A nurse asked Michelle if she could get her anything.

"I really want my mom," Michelle said, breaking into tears.

"Can I get her for you?" the nurse replied.

"No, you can't. She's passed away." Michelle was now sobbing, thinking about her mother, Linda, who died in 2005 of throat cancer. She was just fifty and had never smoked. Linda's mother, Dorothy—Michelle's *mémère* (grandmother)—had passed away just two months before the marathon, at age eighty. They were the two strongest women in Michelle's life, and she desperately wanted them at this moment.

"Do you want the chaplain?" the nurse said.

"Yes."

Michelle sensed controlled panic and an element of fear in the hospital. Doctors and nurses reacted with urgency and professionalism, but many had looks of terror and disbelief on their faces. It was clear that these people were witnessing something none of them had ever dealt with before. A few minutes passed, and a female chaplain arrived. The woman took both of Michelle's hands into her own.

"My mom died, and my *mémère* just passed away and I'm very scared right now. Can you just pray with me that the both of them are with me through this?" Michelle said.

The chaplain prayed with Michelle that her mother and grandmother would watch over her throughout this ordeal. Michelle cried. But the prayer gave her strength, and she felt that she had no option but to be courageous and get through it.

A doctor came in, put an oxygen mask over her face, and said: "You're going to be OK."

On Boylston Street, Mery Daniel was slipping in and out of consciousness. She was drifting away. *Am I gonna die? When I am gonna die?*—she asked herself with eyes half closed. The image of her daughter, Ciarra, entered her mind.

"I was thinking of my baby," she recalls. "I kept thinking, *Oh my God. I am glad I didn't bring her.*"

Unlike most of those wounded outside Marathon Sports, Mery wasn't taken to the medical tent. Her injuries were so severe, first responders placed her in the first available ambulance. The attendants asked her name, and she told them.

"Are you with other people?" One of the EMTs asked, trying to keep Mery alert and awake. She shook her head no. There was frantic debate between the ambulance driver and the EMTs about which hospital to take her to: Boston Medical Center or Massachusetts General Hospital. They quickly decided on Mass General, and Mery could feel the ambulance begin to pull away from Boylston Street.

"One of my legs, I had a tourniquet on it. I thought I was dying. I couldn't believe the irony that as a medical school graduate, I was also a victim," she says. "I should have been among those helping the wounded and not lying on a stretcher like I was."

Despite severe injuries to her legs, Mery was not screaming in pain. In fact, she couldn't feel anything. She was getting very cold and knew that was a sign that she was losing too much blood. Mery passed out and awoke inside Mass General—in fact, she was the first bombing victim taken there. Awaiting her in the ER was a crowd of doctors and nurses, who immediately began ripping her clothes off to get a visual on her injuries. Doctors shouted codes, calling for different departments to get involved. They brought Mery straight into an operating room. She looked down at her right leg, which was covered in blood.

"Save my leg, save my leg," she begged the doctors. Mery fought to stay awake. She didn't want to drift off, for fear that she would never wake up again. A nurse slipped an anesthesia mask over her face, and Mery could fight no more. She fell asleep while the doctors got busy trying to save her life.

When the ambulances arrived at Forum, the EMTs rushed over and took Heather Abbott from Matt Chatham and the group that had helped her. They placed her on a stretcher and wheeled her past the carnage and into an ambulance. They wouldn't let anyone go with her because they needed the room for other victims. There was no handbook for how to handle this one. The EMTs, cops, firefighters, and volunteers were literally packing as many injured people as they could fit into each ambulance.

Heather saw another patient in the ambulance with an oxygen mask.

"I'm going to put an IV in your arm," the male EMT told her.

"My right arm is better than my left arm," Heather responded instinctively, remembering that when giving blood, she had been told that the veins were bigger in her right arm.

"Will you call my parents?" she asked the EMT. Heather's phone was long gone. She had no idea where it was. The only phone number she had memorized was her parents' home number.

Heather remembered that she had not talked to her mother that day and wasn't even sure if her mother knew that she had gone to the marathon.

The EMT made the call. Her mother, Rosemary, was home—thankfully.

"I'm with your daughter," the EMT spoke sternly. "I'm taking her to the hospital. She was injured. You need to get to Brigham and Women's as soon as possible."

"What? Who is this? What are you talking about?" Rosemary asked.

"I can't talk. Just get to Brigham and Women's as soon as possible," he said, ending the call.

It was then that Heather realized she didn't have her pocketbook or her wallet, either. The items were back at Forum among the destruction and blood.

The ambulance arrived at the Brigham, and Heather was rushed into the emergency room. The EMT cut off her clothes. "I have to take these and give them to the FBI," he told her.

From the second she heard the first explosion, Heather had thought of the attacks on 9/11. *The smoke, the people running, the panic.* She knew right away in her mind that it was a terror attack. The EMT mentioning the FBI was only further confirmation. She was brought directly into surgery. A mask was placed over her head, and she went out.

A team of surgeons examined Heather's injuries. Her left heel was completely blown off. What was left of her foot was shattered. There were broken bones and torn blood vessels. Still, doctors felt they could save it. They took a vein from her right leg and attached it to the foot to get the blood flowing. They wrapped it tightly, preserving the flesh and bone as best they could and making sure that all the veins and arteries were sealed off.

The scene at the hospital was frenetic. The scene back on Boylston Street resembled a war zone.

Boston firefighter Elson Monteiro, who was assigned to the corner of Boylston and Hereford streets, ran toward Boylston when the first bomb went off. He then heard the second explosion even closer to his location, so he turned and headed back toward Forum, telling civilians to run the other way, away from the bombs.

He arrived at Forum and started to work on Martin Richard, who had a large amount of shrapnel in his chest.

"In my mind, from visual inspection, [he] was dead," Monteiro wrote in an after-action report.

Martin's mom, Denise Richard, stood over Monteiro's shoulder and told the firefighter the boy was her son. Denise Richard was visibly injured, the firefighter noted. She was taken from the scene by EMTs, and Monteiro moved on to another patient, a man whose clothing was still on fire. Monteiro and some bystanders helped the man remove his burning clothes. The firefighter then moved over to a man whose foot was missing. Monteiro helped secure a belt around the man's upper leg to keep him from bleeding out.

Fellow firefighters arrived with backboards and started removing the most severely injured. Monteiro stayed with the man whose foot was gone and helped put him on a backboard. Firefighters carried the man to three different ambulances, but all were full. They finally put him into the back of a police van with two other severely injured patients. One firefighter held the belt tight around the man's leg and rode with him to the hospital.[21]

Firefighter Phillip Skrabut of Engine 17, District 7 in Dorchester, was assigned to work between Dartmouth and Exeter streets, near the finish line at Boylston Street. He was about five hundred feet behind the finish line walking toward the grandstands when the first bomb went off.

"I saw the blast and then saw a crowd of people fall to the ground," Skrabut wrote in a report.[22]

When he heard the second explosion, he ran up the sidewalk under the grandstand toward Exeter Street, then crossed the street to the bombing site. Police and marathon volunteers were already tearing the barriers away, so Skrabut jumped onto the sidewalk, where he found at least a dozen severely injured people on the ground.

"I went to the closest victim to me," he said. He came across a high school student, Sydney Corcoran of Lowell, Massachusetts, who had been watching the marathon with her mother, Celeste, and father, Kevin. The raven-haired teenager was lying on the ground, conscious and crying. She had a massive shrapnel wound to her right thigh with arterial bleeding.

Another firefighter handed Skrabut an orange scarf, which he tied above the wound as a tourniquet. He also applied direct pressure to try to stop the bleeding. A spectator who said he was a Marine came over and asked how he could help.

"I had him place his hands where mine were and told him to squeeze as hard as he could," Skrabut wrote. "If not for him, I would have had to stay and hold pressure on her leg," Skrabut wrote. "His actions no doubt kept her from bleeding to death."

He then moved to another victim, a middle-aged man who was conscious and was trying to get up. He appeared to have a broken right leg and multiple shrapnel wounds to the face and body, but no life-threatening injuries. "Calm down, sir, and try to breathe normally," Skrabut told him. "Lay still until help arrives."

He then turned to a woman in her late 20s or early 30s. She had a severely deformed lower left leg with a blast wound and an open leg fracture. Her right foot was twisted inward, and her ankle joint was exposed. It was a horrific injury. He grabbed her left leg above and below the wounds and held her. A marathon runner arrived.

"I believe he had a medical background because he immediately took control of patient care, calling off her injuries very systematically and calmly," Skrabut wrote.

It was the firefighter who then began taking directions from the civilian. The marathoner asked him for gauze, so Skrabut gave him a roll from his medical pouch.

"Straighten her left leg and wrap the wound," the marathoner told Skrabut. He then did the same with her right ankle and foot. The marathoner then instructed the firefighter to lift her legs, and he wrapped her hips and legs together so she could be moved. She was put on a backboard, and Boston EMS came over with a stretcher and took her away.

The firefighter never got the name of the marathoner.

"But I am grateful for him to say the least," he said.

Just before the bomb blasts, firefighter Doug Menard, a veteran of the Iraq war, was on roving patrol on the block bordered by Dartmouth, Boylston, and Exeter streets. He was on Exeter Street just past Marathon Sports heading toward Dartmouth Street when the first bomb went off. He was about fifteen seconds away from the scene when the explosion occurred.

"The blast was enough to feel like someone kicked out the back of my knees, however I was able to catch my balance," Menard wrote in a report.[23] "I turned immediately and saw a rush of running wounded coming toward me through the smoke. I seemed to be the closest person to ground zero who didn't have a scratch on me."

Before he processed what was happening, he heard the second *boom!*

"D110 at the finish line. Multiple wounded. Secondary devices. Watch out," Menard barked through the radio. He saw roughly twenty people with severe lower leg wounds on the pavement. As he surveyed the scene, he mentally "black tagged" one female—Krystle Campbell—who appeared "gray" and "didn't look like she was going to make it."

Campbell was a twenty-nine-year-old golden-haired native of Medford, Massachusetts, a suburb of Boston. She had been a top employee of celebrity chef Jasper White in his Summer Shack restaurants, sometimes working seventy to eighty hours per week managing the catering side of the business, which was quite extensive. She was the all-American girl who loved her friends and family. Krystle had taken care of her sick grandmother for nearly two years, and on the day of the marathon she was just a few weeks shy of her thirtieth birthday.

As Menard stood near Krystle, a mother grabbed his leg.

"She was covering her teenage daughter's leg," Menard wrote. He looked down at the girl's leg and saw it was severed just below the knee. He found a cravat in his medical pouch and tied a tourniquet.

"The blood stopped and I moved on, even though the girl and her mother pleaded for me to stay," he wrote. Everyone needed help.

A man next to them was on fire. He had smoke rising from his shoulders and his clothes were ablaze. Menard patted out the flames and checked him for wounds. He had deep cuts -shrapnel wounds to his back. His tattered shirt kept smoking from the "hot shrapnel" in his back.

A Boston cop arrived to help and kept patting out the smoking garments while Menard moved on to other wounded. He went back to Krystle Campbell, where another woman, who turned out to be her friend Karen Rand, was holding her hand. Karen and Krystle had come to the marathon to watch Karen's boyfriend finish the road race. Menard noted that Karen's lower leg was "blown apart."

He didn't have another cravat, but a runner sprinted over and handed the firefighter his running belt. Menard and the runner tied a tourniquet around her leg. A marathon volunteer handed him multiple rolls of gauze, which could also be used for tourniquets. Despite their efforts, Karen later lost the leg.

An EMT asked Menard to help cut off a patient's clothing. As he assisted the medic, someone yelled for help inside Marathon Sports. He ran through the shattered front window of the store and found five injured people. Michelle L'Heureux was among them.

There were civilian doctors working on a woman in the doorway. Menard grabbed a gauze roll and put a tourniquet on the woman's leg. The firefighter and a couple of civilians helped him drag the woman out of the store and onto the sidewalk so that EMTs could take her to the hospital. He then ran toward another firefighter who was working on a man with serious injuries. Menard helped his fellow firefighter put the man on a backboard, and they carried him to the medical tent in Copley Square.

He rushed back to the scene, but by then all the wounded had been evacuated. In the last comment in his report, Menard notes that he then heard a radio broadcast about a possible third device.[24]

Another Boston firefighter, Mike Foley, was busy saving lives in front of Forum. After the second blast, he hopped the barricade and came upon a man whose clothes were on fire. He also saw a child and a woman—later identified as Martin Richard and Lingzi Lu—lying on the ground. They were dead. Foley saw a severed foot on the ground next to the curb and felt nauseous. "The ground was dark—scorched from the explosion and covered with blood and tissue," he recalls.[25]

He came across a man with amputations, who was trying to sit up. Foley grabbed a strap from an EMT and fashioned a tourniquet to the man's right thigh. He waved over a cop.

"Run to the engine and grab me a Stokes basket," he hollered. A Stokes basket is a metal and plastic stretcher used to move patients. They lifted the man onto the basket and slid him into a waiting ambulance.

Foley ran back to the scene and helped an EMT load another severely injured patient onto a backboard, then carried him to an ambulance that had more room. He rushed back and helped EMTs load yet another patient into a police van. He gave another survivor oxygen and helped place her into the same police van.

He then helped direct trucks and ambulances to and from the scene before he was ordered to head back to Engine 33's headquarters on Boylston Street to "take cover from a possible third device."

Firefighter Adalberto Rodriguez thanked God that he had made the decision earlier that day to carry his medical bag. Patrolling the area between Hereford and Fairfield streets, he was keeping an eye out for dehydrated runners and spectators in need of assistance. He'd helped a few dehydrated folks that morning, as well as a couple of people with "flu-like symptoms," but it was an otherwise uneventful day. That would soon change as he would be thrust into the chaos and tasked with helping rescue one of the most vulnerable of the marathon-day victims.

After the blasts, Rodriguez sprinted toward Forum, where he saw people tearing down metal partitions to get to the wounded. He helped a man with shrapnel in his legs. Rodriguez cut the man's pants off and cleaned and wrapped his wounds. He was then directed to a little girl who'd lost her left leg—it was Jane Richard. The stunned firefighter held pressure on the arteries above the girl's injury. He helped put her on a gurney, and the girl was taken away in an ambulance. His attention turned to the girl's father, Bill Richard, who was holding his son Martin in his arms, wailing.

"Don't let him die, don't let him die!" the father cried.

Rodriguez's heart ached at the sound of Bill Richard's screams. He bent down and examined Martin's injuries and was certain the boy was already gone. Still, he tried to calm the anguished dad as best he could, but Bill Richard was inconsolable.

Another boy suffering from severe leg lacerations was lying next to Martin. Rodriguez assumed it was the boy's brother. But it wasn't. It was eleven-year-old Aaron Hern, a California boy who had been standing next to Martin at the time of the explosion. The same shrapnel that tore through Aaron's leg had killed Martin. Tourniquets were tied around Aaron's leg, and the boy was led to an ambulance. Rodriguez moved onto another victim.

His third patient was an adult male "with shrapnel all over his entire body." The man had severe injuries to his left leg. Rodriguez quickly wrapped the man's wounds to slow the bleeding and helped get him into a police van.[26]

He ran back to the scene and saw EMTs giving CPR to a woman who lay motionless on the sidewalk. He later learned the woman was BU graduate student Lingzi Lu. Several people were tying tourniquets around her wounds, desperately trying to save the young Chinese woman. But Lu's injuries were far too severe. She was bleeding out rapidly. Seconds later, she was dead.

Up the street, Boston firefighter James Plourde was climbing through the wreckage toward a candy store, Sugar Heaven, where dazed spectators had taken refuge.

"If you can walk, get out," he yelled into the store. A few people darted past him into the street.

There was a young woman inside with a deep laceration that appeared to be a partial amputation. Plourde and a spectator tied off the wound with a tourniquet. He then carried the young girl to safety. Her name was Victoria McGrath, a twenty-year-old Northeastern University student who was at the marathon with friends. Victoria's leg was saved, and pictures of the firefighter carrying the blood-covered young woman went viral as a symbol of the heroism of the day.

In the middle of Boylston Street, Plourde surveyed the gruesome scene. "There were bodies and blood as far as I could see on the sidewalk," he wrote in a report.[27]

There was an older man on the ground with three people kneeling around him. There were two men with below-the-knee amputations, and no one was tending to them. He knelt down and tried to apply pressure to a woman's severe lower leg injury. He took out his knife and cut a jacket he found on the sidewalk to make a tourniquet.

"This one's still on fire!" a woman yelled, referring to a man smoldering on the sidewalk. Plourde moved on to him and saw more people with apparent amputations.

"Everyone gets a tourniquet!" he shouted to other first responders. People handed the firefighters belts.

Carlos Arredondo was not a firefighter. Rather, he was one of dozens of volunteers and spectators who, without thought, put the needs of others ahead of their own on Boylston Street that day. The fifty-three-year-old native of Costa Rica was working the finish line with his friend John Mixon of Ogunquit, Maine. The pair were there to hand out American flags to spectators and to cheer on runners from Mixon's organization, Race for the Fallen Maine. The group had five marathoners running the race to honor soldiers from Maine who have been killed while serving overseas. Carlos's son Alexander of Bangor, Maine, and Randolph, Massachusetts, was one of the fallen. The twenty-year-old Marine was killed in action in August 2004 during an intense firefight in the Iraqi city of Najaf, about one hundred miles south of Baghdad. Carlos was at his home in Florida when a Marine van pulled up to his home.

"I'm looking for the family of Alexander Arredondo," one of the Marines said as he approached the front door.[28]

"I am the family," Carlos replied, his voice trembling.

The Marines then gave Carlos the news no parent should ever hear. The distraught father responded by running into his back yard and sitting motionless on the grass for several minutes. He called his other son, Brian, and then phoned his wife, Melida. Carlos was both surprised and angry that the Marines had not yet left his property and were still milling about on his front lawn. At that very moment, he snapped. He told the Marines to leave, then grabbed a hammer and began smashing the windows of their van. Carlos then grabbed a propane torch and a can of gasoline.

"Sir, don't do that," one of the Marines pleaded.

Carlos paid no attention. He climbed in the van, smashed more windows and then doused his body with gasoline and ignited the torch.

"I just feel the explosion," he said in an interview with the *Wall Street Journal* in 2005. "It threw me out of the van and immediately I feel the flames all over me. I feel the sensation of burning. The sensation I was on fire."[29]

At that moment, a Marine grabbed Carlos by the pants and pulled him out of the burning van. A TV crew had arrived at the scene minutes earlier to capture video of the vehicle ablaze and Carlos's twitching body being taken away by stretcher. His son Brian watched the drama on television from his mother's home in Bangor. Carlos spent weeks in a hospital burn unit, racking up more than fifty thousand dollars in medical bills. But his personal torture was not yet over. In December 2011, Carlos's only surviving son, Brian, took his own life. The twenty-four-year-old had been battling depression since Alexander's death in 2004. The tragic news rocked Carlos and his wife, Melida—but instead of inflicting more pain on himself, Carlos immersed himself in the peace movement. He and Melida traveled the country, protesting the wars in Iraq and Afghanistan and calling attention to the plight of families trying to cope with the loss of loved ones struck down—both on the battlefield and beyond.

Both Carlos and John Mixon were across the street from Marathon Sports when the first explosion occurred. The power of the blast knocked Mixon, a ruggedly built Vietnam vet, right out of the grandstand bleachers. The two friends immediately ran toward the smoke, and Mixon began tearing apart the barricades with his hands. Carlos leapt over the barricade and landed on his feet in a pile of burning limbs. He attended to two women who were bleeding and screaming on the ground. One victim was covered in heavy debris. Carlos lifted the rubble off of her, which allowed her to breathe. He then turned his attention back to the barricade, helping to pull it down so that other first responders could reach the victims. Carlos and Mixon noticed a man lying on the ground with both legs in makeshift tourniquets. It was Jeff Bauman. Bauman was being cared for by Dr. Allan Panter, a fifty-seven-year-old emergency room director from Gainesville, Georgia, who had traveled to Boston to watch his wife, Theresa, run the race. Panter had just worked on Krystle Campbell. The doctor had advised another first responder on the proper way to check her pulse—which was there, but faint.

"I reached down and swung her back around so that her head was at my feet," Panter recalls.[30] "I gave her a couple mouth to mouth breaths, started screaming for an ambu bag, because I'm more in ER mode—I want tools to work with. And that's when the Boston volunteers started pouring in."

Someone handed Panter an ambu bag, which acts as a manual resuscitator, and he continued his attempt to save Campbell's life. He and others got the woman on a stretcher and rushed her to the nearby medical tent. She died on arrival.

Panter returned to the scene and worked feverishly on Jeff Bauman, whose legs bad been blown off in the blast.

"Help me, help me," Bauman moaned.

Jeff looked down at his body and saw that he was covered in blood and that his legs were missing. Panter applied his makeshift tourniquets with precision. Carlos Arredondo appeared at Panter's side, and together they lifted Bauman into a wheelchair. Carlos and two marathon volunteers ran Bauman and the wheelchair away from the scene. Associated Press photographer Charles Krupa captured that moment in a photograph that became the most iconic image from that tragic day, for two reasons. The catastrophic injuries to Bauman's legs—his right leg has been blown off at the knee, and his left is a distortion of raw, burning flesh and charred bone—reveal the gruesome horror of the attack. And Arredondo—who is wearing his customary cowboy hat as he rushes Bauman to safety—exemplifies the selfless heroism demonstrated by ordinary citizens on that calamitous April afternoon.

Once Bauman arrived at the ambulance, Carlos tried to climb inside. He did not want to leave the young man's side. The EMTs had to push him out of the vehicle.

"You can't be in here," one EMT yelled.

In Jeff Bauman, Carlos saw his two deceased sons. He could not be there to help his boys in their times of need, but he would do everything he could now for the young bombing victim.

"Where, where you take this man?" Carlos asked.

"BMC, Boston Medical Center," the EMT told him as they closed the ambulance door.

Once most of the injured people had been evacuated from the area, Carlos's friend John Mixon began thinking about his daughter, a student at nearby Emerson College. He reached her apartment and was relieved to find that she was safe. John then changed his shirt, which had been covered in the blood of so many victims, and got cleaned up. Refreshed but still shaken by what he'd seen, Mixon was in for another shock. The FBI was calling his cell phone. They were looking for his friend, Carlos Arredondo.

12

TAKING COMMAND

Just as the explosions were being reported over radios and scanners at the police and fire departments, word spread of another emergency. The John F. Kennedy Library in Dorchester was on fire. The presidential library, a popular tourist spot right along Boston Harbor, was open that day, but there were no reports of injuries. The sky above the library was shrouded in thick, black smoke. Fire engines raced to the scene. Word of the fire only heightened the citywide panic and fueled the notion that Boston was under attack at multiple locations. The library was evacuated, but the smoke cleared quickly. Firefighters then walked onto the roof of one side of the library, where a large opening was covered in black soot from an explosion or fire. There was little information available at first, and there were conflicting reports as to whether the fire was related to the bombings.

While firefighters hosed down the charred library, Boylston Street was filled with frightened and confused people. Harried cops strung up yellow crime scene tape on cross streets as runners wrapped in foil blankets made their way out of the bomb scene—some crying, all with looks of shock and confusion across their weary faces. Panicked relatives of runners and spectators, many in tears, peppered officers with questions about how to find their loved ones.

TV cameramen ran with reporters by their side, seeking out witnesses to interview and racing to find officials to get the most up-to-date information on what exactly was happening. With no cell phone service in the Boylston Street area, reporters, cops, politicians, and citizens alike were largely in the dark regarding the full scope of the emergency they were now facing. People were being directed to safe locations, and police maintained control of the scene, but no one—including those at the top of the chain of command—truly had any idea what was really going on.

Was it a coordinated attack? Were there more bombs? Was this al-Qaeda? Or was it a homegrown terrorist in the vein of Oklahoma City bomber Timothy McVeigh?

A popular early, knee-jerk theory was the latter, with many citing the fact that the bombing occurred on April 15, tax day—just as the federal government was in the midst of a budget-driven shutdown.

Don Nelson, a veteran photographer for Boston's NBC-affiliated TV station WHDH, was working at the finish line when the explosions rocked the city. His camera rolled and caught the explosions and bloody aftermath. His footage has been widely disseminated since the attacks and provides some of the best documentation of the explosions and their gruesome aftermath.

"The first one blew," Nelson said at the scene. "Nobody in the street got hurt, none of the runners. One guy [a runner] went down. Smoke went straight up in the air. About fifteen seconds later, the second bomb went off. I ran down and I saw one guy without legs. One guy, his face was just torn to shit."

Reporter Megan Johnson's cell phone buzzed non-stop, but she couldn't return calls or even texts because of the spotty service. She and the group of wayward partygoers knew they were trapped in the midst of a terrorist attack and walked around in a fog, trying to get information. They shuffled around the mall for the next half hour or so as the grim scene outside became more apparent. The group eventually filtered out onto Stuart Street, where the families and friends of runners had gathered, holding up signs bearing their loved ones' names. These were signs that they had made to cheer on their family members and friends as they ran; now they were being used to track down the runners to ensure they weren't dead.

"Oh thank God! Thank God!" was a common refrain as families were reunited with runners. Tears flowed.

Megan made her way to Neiman Marcus, just across the street from where the second bomb exploded. There were people sitting on the floor everywhere. Runners wearing their Boston Athletic Association-emblazoned marathon jackets or wrapped in silver foil blankets covered the linoleum floor. The men's department became a makeshift recovery area. People offered jackets to each other, water, hugs.

"At Copley. Runners offering each other jackets to keep warm. Even in heartbreak there is good in people," she was finally able to tweet.

She heard a female runner call out a man's name. They ran to each other and embraced. Megan snapped a picture. It turned out the couple had just gotten married. The woman had been running near the finish line when the bombs went off. Megan tweeted out the picture with the words "Couple just reunited." The picture quickly went viral and wound up in the *Wall Street Journal* and *The Atlantic*, among other publications.

For any reporter, it was a tough story to cover. For Megan, who is not a hard news reporter, it was overwhelming. She felt on the verge of tears the entire time. She wanted to just go home and cry.

Police Commissioner Ed Davis needed to set up a command post. Initially, he had decided on the Boylston Street fire station, but there was a suspicious package there, so that was no good. They next went to the Copley Marriott hotel. Davis and two officers armed with rifles went into the hotel and asked to see the manager.

"We need your ballroom. We need to set up a command post," Davis told the manager.

"But, we have a wedding in there. It's all set up for a wedding!" the manager replied. In fact, as chaos ensued outside the hotel, staffers inside were busy stringing lights in the ballroom and organizing table settings, oblivious to the world around them. The city was now under siege, but the news still had not reached at least a few people — like this hotel manager — who were still going about their day, business as usual. Davis didn't know whether to laugh or cry.

Despite the uncertainty of the situation, the commissioner's softer side surfaced and he decided he didn't want to ruin someone's wedding. So they crossed the street to the Copley Westin hotel. Davis's group, which had now grown to several armed officers, went to the desk and told the manager they were taking over the ballroom. The army of cops eventually commandeered the entire third floor of the massive hotel.

Kurt Schwartz showed up at the Westin, as did National Guard General L. Scott Rice. He had two hundred troops in the city already for the marathon, and another thousand were on their way. With the help of state police and the National Guard, Davis and his colleagues managed to shut down twelve blocks in the busiest financial and retail district in New England.

Cell phone service had gone down, leaving not only terrified runners' families scrambling for information on their loved ones but also top law enforcement officials looking for ways to communicate. Davis and Schwartz had satellite phones, but service on those was spotty as well.

The only option was a single landline in the ballroom. Davis and FBI Special Agent in Charge Rick DesLauriers assigned a federal agent to guard the phone, making sure no one used it except top commanders. A call soon came in from United States Attorney General Eric Holder.

"Commissioner, how are you doing?" Holder asked.

"We're OK," Davis sighed.

"Whatever you need, we will take care of for you," Holder told him. "You have all the resources of the FBI at your disposal. If there's anything you need, call me. Good luck."

In addition to dealing with the scene itself, Davis had the city's overall security to think about. His mind raced. Could there be a larger cell about to activate? What was the fire at the JFK Library all about? Was it connected?

He also gave the order to lock down all the hospitals in case one of the terrorists was among the injured and his accomplices attempted to rescue him. Davis activated the department's stress unit to begin reaching out to traumatized officers. A team of cops from New York who had learned all too much about trauma on 9/11 was already on its way to Boston.

Javier Pagan was exhausted. His cell phone, like those of most everyone there that day, had no service. He walked to a pay phone and called his husband, Pedro.

"Pedro," Javier said, breaking down. He rambled, uttering the words *explosion* and *terrorist attack*.

"Huh?" Pedro said. "I can't understand what you're saying."

"I'm fine. I have to go," he said, and hung up.

He returned to the scene, and his captain came over and gave him a hug. Javier met up with his partner, George Diaz.

"There's a place for us over at the Lenox Hotel," the captain told them. "Get over there and get off your feet."

Javier walked into the Lenox, got a bottle of water, and went to use the bathroom. He splashed water on his face, glaring at himself in the mirror in an attempt to come to grips with what was going on. He couldn't.

He emerged from the bathroom and heard a woman yelling, "Evacuate the hotel!"

People started running. A beefy, athletic man with short, black hair was running toward him, holding a woman's hand and with two kids in tow.

"Officer, what's going on?" the man asked.

"I'm not sure," Javier responded. He recognized the man from television commercials for local life insurance company SBLI. It was Tedy Bruschi, a former New England Patriots star linebacker—now an insurance pitchman—who was at a fundraiser at the hotel when the bombs went off.

Javier is not a sports fan and didn't learn until later that the man from the commercial was one of Boston's most iconic sports figures.

"Oh my God, you're the guy from the SBLI commercials," Javier said.

Both men chuckled. Javier snapped back into cop mode and directed the retired NFL star and his family safely out of the hotel.

After helping evacuate people from the Lenox, Javier left, too. He walked up Exeter Street to Huntington Avenue and walked into the Copley Square Hotel, which was open to first responders.

Inside, there were dozens of cops. Some were on their radios. Some were just sitting quietly, taking breaks. Others were drinking bottled water or eating.

Javier was in a fog, but he realized he hadn't eaten all day. He was starving. He went to the kitchen and asked the chef to make him a burger.

Weary, hungry, and overwhelmed, Javier took a seat by the window alone. A TV overhead showed images from the terror attack on a constant loop. Javier sat somberly and ate his burger. His phone service was returning, and a steady flow of texts came in from other officers in the community service unit, asking if he was all right. He left the hotel and walked to the medical tent. EMS officers had golf carts, and one of them approached Javier and asked him to sit down.

"Are you OK?" the EMT asked.

Javier just sat there expressionless. He wasn't injured, but the EMT could see he was traumatized.

"Just sit here and relax," the EMT said.

As Javier looked around the tent, he realized the scope of what was going on. He thought about Pedro and his experience during the attacks on 9/11. He ruminated on all the ways that, over the years, he had thought he might die on the job. He had considered that maybe he would get shot or hit by a car. But it had never crossed his mind that he would be standing just a few feet away from a terrorist's bomb when it went off.

He felt lucky to be alive. He was.

He also thought about people in Tel Aviv, Cairo, and other cities where bombings are a more common occurrence. But this was not supposed to happen in Boston. Not at the marathon. Not ever.

He stayed in the medical tent for a while and then was assigned to stand watch on Boylston Street to prevent people from entering what was now the biggest crime scene in Boston's history.

Pedro wanted to check on Javier but wasn't sure if the city was locked down. He took a bus from the couple's West Roxbury home to the Back Bay MBTA station and called Javier.

"I can't really leave. I can't go over there," Javier told him. "Just go back home. I can't really get out of here. I'll see you later."

Pedro, remembering the mayhem of 9/11, understood and went back home.

Javier was relieved by a fellow cop around 11 p.m. He walked back to the South End station, got in his car, and drove home. He came to a stoplight that was red. He looked up at the light and started crying. When he arrived home, he walked into the house and hugged Pedro. Javier sobbed.

Back at the bomb scene, hotels in the twelve-block area had been evacuated. The Lenox Hotel was turned into a headquarters for the evidence technicians. It was a place where detectives like Danny Keeler could slip away from the madness of the moment, have a burger, and refuel.

Commissioner Davis sat in a briefing in the Lenox Hotel and gazed out the windows at Boylston Street—his beloved Boylston Street. Instead of smiling families, partying college students, and exhausted-but-triumphant runners, he saw stoic men and women in Tyvek suits, combing through the blackened bomb scenes. He saw agents from every conceivable federal and state agency: the FBI, the ATF, the US Marshals Service, Customs and Immigration, Homeland Security. And once again he saw the blood—lots of it.

Cops already had their eyes on a Saudi national who was at the scene and had raised suspicion after the bombings. He turned out to not be connected, but he was an early subject of intense questioning. Agents went to his house, and the media picked up on it, erroneously calling him a suspect. Today, Ed Davis says the person was an "important witness to talk to" but was never a suspect in the attacks.

The public needed answers. The public needed some comfort. A press conference was hastily called at the Westin. Reporters raced to the hotel, where they were met by heavy security. Bomb-sniffing dogs and machine gun-toting officers patrolled the building. Guests milled about aimlessly. They could not leave. Some sat by a fire reading. Others chatted nervously about the bombings. There was a line at the concierge desk as people scrambled for information.

Inside a second-floor ballroom, Commissioner Davis and other city officials were joined by authorities from local and state police, the Boston Fire Department, Boston Emergency Medical Services, the National Guard, the FBI—and Governor Patrick. The governor and his state police security detail had been at odds throughout the afternoon about the location from which the state's chief executive should monitor and manage the crisis. Once the bombs had exploded, Patrick demanded that he be taken directly to the state house, just a few short blocks from the crime scene. The state trooper responsible for his protection argued that the building was a potential target for the terrorists and that the governor would be much safer inside the MEMA bunker in Framingham. The trooper was probably right in his assessment, but Deval Patrick didn't care. His city and his state had been attacked, and the governor had to lead from the front, not the back.

Deval Patrick stepped forward and addressed the media and a live international audience. Mayor Thomas M. Menino was watching on TV from his hospital room at the Brigham.

"Good afternoon, everybody. Well, we've had a horrific attack here in Boston this afternoon," Patrick said somberly.

Camera shutters clicked softly as photographers captured the gravity of the moment, written on Patrick's face and the faces of those lined up behind him. Eerie silence filled the space between his words.

"Commissioner Davis is going to give some details about what we know so far, mindful that we don't have the whole picture yet. But we have gotten a good deal of information. Commissioner Davis will take all of us through the information that we have and then I'll come back and talk about some of the things and ways in which we're going to ask people to help us help you this afternoon."

Governor Patrick consciously set a tone right from the get-go that the focus of these officials' efforts was going to be to look *forward*. Yes, they were desperately seeking to piece together what had happened, and why. They were searching for those responsible and were determined to bring them to justice. But right out of the gate, the governor set a trajectory toward the future, recovery, and hope, and assured the public that we were all in it together. The slogan Boston Strong had yet to be coined, but the seeds of that sentiment were planted from the moment the first victim was treated at the horrifying scene.

"Thank you, Governor," Commissioner Davis said as he took the mic. "At 2:50 p.m. today there were simultaneous explosions that occurred along the route of the Boston Marathon near the finish line," Davis said. "These explosions occurred fifty to one hundred yards apart and each scene resulted in multiple casualties. At this point in time, all of the victims have been removed from the scene. We have sent officers to hospitals to be in touch with family members and possible witnesses."

In fact, it had taken just twenty-two minutes for first responders to clear the Boylston Street area after the bombings. Reporters scribbled furiously on their notepads as they received this first official response to the bombings.

"We immediately activated a system of response that the Commonwealth of Massachusetts and the federal government has in place for these types of incidents," Davis continued. "My first two calls were to the Special Agent in Charge of the FBI and to the Colonel of the State Police—both Rick DesLauriers and Tim Alben immediately sent resources."

Davis told the press that officials were still trying to determine what had caused the explosion at the JFK Library. He reminded everyone that it was still an active scene but that officials were treating the blasts on Boylston Street and in Dorchester as if they were related.

"We're recommending to the people that they stay home, that if they're in hotels in the area that they return to their rooms, and that they don't go any place and congregate in large crowds. We want to make sure we completely stabilize the situation."

The ballroom was silent, save for camera clicks, as the hulking police commissioner continued to deliver the latest information in his booming baritone voice. Governor Patrick stood stoically by his side.

"After this incident occurred, there were certainly a lot of people who were running from the scene," Davis continued. "Some of them deposited bags and parcels they were carrying. Each one of those bags and parcels is being treated as a suspicious device at this point in time. We have multiple EOD teams that are checking each one of these bags. But at this point, we have not found another device."

Present were reporters from every major news outlet in Boston, as well as many national outlets that had either been in town already to cover the marathon, or that had raced in after the bombings occurred. Reporters had many questions, but there was virtually no information given about what had actually happened. The media—and the public at large—was thirsty for answers, as well as some semblance of assurance that the situation was under control.

Governor Patrick returned to the microphone.

"You know, the marathon is a pretty special day around here," Patrick said softly. "I started this morning visiting Mayor Menino in the hospital, who was devastated that he couldn't be at the marathon today. He's on his way here now . . . from the hospital so obviously he is as concerned as the rest of us are about the safety of the people who come for this iconic experience here in the city."

He then described his phone call from President Barack Obama, a close and personal friend, who had assured him and the people of Massachusetts that they would have the full cooperation of the FBI and ATF, along with a fully deployed National Guard. He also urged anyone who had information to call law enforcement.

Patrick's plea for help from the public and Davis' vague descriptions of what exactly law enforcement knew about the attack left an uncomfortable silence in the large ballroom. The armed SWAT teams in the room and robot-like K-9 cops patrolling the hallway outside reminded reporters that they were in a war zone and underscored both the gravity and fragility of the developing situation.

Incredibly, the first question fired at Patrick came from a right-wing conspiracy theorist working for a fringe website who asked if it was possible the attack was a "false flag" operation. Beginning immediately in the aftermath of the bombings, conspiracy theorists, 9/11 "inside job" kooks, and crazed web trolls began posting images of the injured, claiming they were actors and that the whole marathon bombing had been plotted and staged by the government.

Historically, false flag attacks have been used by military organizations as a tactic in battle. The name originated from the practice of naval ships that would fly a banner belonging to a country other than their own in order to deceive an enemy. The term has come to be used by conspiracy theorists who claim the US government carries out covert operations — and in this case, a fake one — in order to drum up opposition to terrorist groups and legitimize military action against them.

Patrick was furious and snapped at the conspiracy theorist, "No."

Other reporters were stunned. It was an awkward, completely inappropriate moment that played out on live TV. It had the feel of one of those Howard Stern-listener sneak attacks on an unsuspecting CNN anchor reporting live on-air — except in this case, the questioner was a credentialed member of the media attending a press briefing on the first successful terror attack on American soil since 9/11.

The man was shouted down, and another veteran reporter steered the press conference back to reality, asking Davis if authorities were looking for a specific type of truck.

"No. There is no specific type of truck that we're looking for at this point in time," the commissioner said. "We are looking for any information that people have as to what they saw or might have heard at the site of the explosion or coming and going. We're investigating all leads right now."

"What about the death and injury toll?" another reporter asked.

"We don't have the number of casualties at this point in time. This is very early in the investigation, and I want to get out here to give you as much information as we have. But we cannot tell you exactly how many people have been injured."

Although Davis told reporters that the fire at the JFK Library was from a third explosion that authorities believed was "related" to the bombings, he later reversed course and ruled out the library blaze as being part of the attack. It was ultimately ruled an accidental fire caused by discarded smoking materials. There was an accelerant found at the scene, but authorities have said it may have been oil or some other flammable liquid from machinery in the room where the fire started. Some firefighters and other officials still wonder whether the fire may have been a diversionary tactic tied to the bombings.

There were also multiple reports of more bombs that did not detonate. Most famously, there were reports that explosives were found at the Mandarin Oriental hotel and under the VIP grandstands. These reports were never confirmed. At the press conference, Davis said of additional devices: "They may be blowing things up over the course of the next few hours. But at this point in time, we have not found another device on Boylston Street."

"Was there any warning of an attack?" a reporter asked.

"None," Davis said. "We talk about the threat picture all the time as we lead up to this particular event but we have no information that this was going to happen."

"Is this a terrorist attack?" another journalist asked.

"We're not being definitive on this right now but you can reach your own conclusions based upon what happened," the commissioner said.

Mayor Menino watched the first press conference from his room at the Brigham. He was as shocked as the rest of the city and country. But this was *his* city. This was not supposed to happen on his watch.

He knew he was the city's public face and unquestioned leader. He had no choice but to get out of the hospital and get over to the Westin hotel. Menino is notorious for his stubbornness, so when he made up his mind that he was checking himself out of the hospital to go address the city—and the world—the doctors, nurses, and all his aides knew there was no stopping him. So they helped him.

He got himself dressed and into his wheelchair and was brought over to the hotel. Steve MacDonald, the Boston Fire Department's veteran spokesman, gave the news to reporters that the mayor was indeed on his way. Reporters scrambled, calling their desks to put them on alert that Menino had checked himself out of the hospital and would be addressing the media soon.

The mayor arrived at the Westin and met privately in a function room with Patrick, Davis, DesLauriers, and others. In the ballroom, MacDonald gathered the media.

"Everyone got sound?" MacDonald said from the podium. "All set? OK. Mr. Mayor?"

Menino was wheeled out by a Boston police officer.

"Good afternoon," he started. "Very typically, this is a great day in the city of Boston. But we had a tragedy. Several explosions happened on Boylston Street in the past few hours. Boston police, state police, all the public safety officials are working together on this issue. The governor and I have spoken to the president of the United States just a half hour ago and he's offered all the assistance he can to us during this investigation. Myself as mayor, I offer my condolences and prayers to the families that were involved in these explosions."

He gave out the city's hotline phone number and urged folks to call with any tips or issues related to the bombings.

"This is a tragedy. We're going to work together on this," he finished.

Commissioner Davis returned to the podium and gave some further details about the JFK Library incident.

"The device at the JFK Library was actually an incendiary device or a fire," he said. "We haven't linked that directly to this incident. Right now, the information is two explosions occurred on Boylston Street. The information we got about 15 minutes prior to the last press conference may have been premature."

He was asked again if there were any warnings or indications that an attack on Boston was imminent.

"There was no specific intelligence. We certainly increase our posture around an event like this. There was no specific intelligence that anything was going to happen," he said.

It was one of the most emotional press conferences Mayor Menino had ever been a part of. Certainly, it marked the darkest moment in the city's history in his twenty years as its chief executive. The fact that it was taking place as his career was winding down and as he was physically ailing only added to the melancholy feeling the seventy-year-old politician felt inside.

His heart broke for Boston. He loved this city and he was not going to take this sitting down.

13

KEELER'S GHOSTS

In death, she was smiling. Krystle Campbell looked serene as she lay on a stretcher in the back room of the medical tent on Boylston Street. Danny Keeler didn't know who she was as the young woman had no identification, driver's license, or ATM card on her body. She did have black gunpowder marks covering the freckles on her face. An attendant turned Campbell onto her stomach briefly while Keeler inspected her injuries further. Her skin was charred, and her back had been blown apart by scalding shrapnel. Keeler thought about the anguish and anxiety felt by families across New England—across the country—who had yet to hear from their loved ones at the marathon. He thought about his own kids. Keeler looked down at the lifeless body on the stretcher and silently grieved for her parents, whoever they were.

Keeler rounded up a group of detectives and brought them over to the California Pizza Kitchen restaurant, located inside the Prudential Center mall, to decompress for a moment after what they'd seen and done during the past hour. Keeler would never admit it, but at that point, he needed a break, too. He could not shake the image of Denise Richard leaning down over her son Martin. Keeler's eyes welled up again at the thought. *Stay focused, dude*, he whispered to himself.

His mind then shifted again to his own family. His cell phone had been lighting up. Keeler's kids and his girlfriend, Carol, had been watching the live coverage on television and he had yet to speak to them. Keeler fished for his cell phone and called home.

"How bad is it?" Carol asked.

"It's a mess," Keeler responded. "We're gonna be down here for awhile."

"How're you doing?"

He paused before answering. Sadness quickly turned to rage.

"We're gonna get these motherfuckers!"

Danny Keeler had investigated over two hundred murders in the city of Boston, and now he had at least three more to solve: those of two women who just a few hours earlier had been brimming with life, and that of a little boy who would never have the chance to grow up. For years, Keeler had been the shoulder to cry on and the man to call on those torturous nights when grieving family members felt as if they couldn't go on any longer. The crimes that haunted him the most were those against children — children like the boy who now lay under a white sheet in front of Forum.

His career up to this point had been one of both triumph and frustrating disappointment. When Keeler joined the department in 1979, he stood out from his peers almost immediately. In August 1980, Keeler — still just a rookie — ripped off his uniform and jumped sixty feet off the Boston University Bridge into the Charles River to save a man who was attempting suicide. Through Keeler's quick actions, the man lived, and Danny was awarded the department's Medal of Honor. He joined the Boston Police homicide unit in 1992. At the time, the unit was overwhelmed by a record-setting number of murders — most of them unsolved. Keeler got to work right away. In November 1992, he walked into Carney Hall at Boston College and arrested a night school student named Michael Finkley for the deadly shooting, two years earlier, of Frederick "Peanut" Brinson on a busy Dorchester street in broad daylight. Finkley was convicted and sentenced to life in prison. Keeler later captured the killer of eighty-six-year-old Nordella Newson. The elderly woman had been stabbed and strangled by her drug-addicted nephew in an attempt to steal five hundred dollars. Keeler was working and closing the books on murder cases at breakneck speed. His success earned him the nickname Mr. Homicide on the streets and inside the courtrooms of Boston.

The Brinson and Newson murders were slam dunk cases, but others proved more difficult. First was the murder of nine-year-old Jermaine Goffigan on Halloween in 1994. Goffigan was shot on his front porch while counting candy. The murder rocked the city, and Keeler and his partner, acting on a tip, made a swift arrest. The suspect, a teenager named Donnell Johnson, was later convicted and would serve five years in prison. The conviction was overturned, however, when it was learned that the alibi Johnson had given Keeler and his partner, William Mahoney, was never turned over to prosecutors. Two other men later pleaded guilty to Goffigan's murder. Johnson sued both Keeler and Mahoney, claiming they withheld evidence that could have exonerated him. Despite calling the actions of the homicide detectives "deeply troubling," the judge threw out Johnson's lawsuit. Mahoney was suspended for thirty days, but no discipline was taken against Keeler.

In 2004, Keeler got an audiotaped confession from a twenty-two-year-old man who said that he had helped bury alive his fourteen-year-old pregnant girlfriend on the grounds of the abandoned Boston State Hospital. Kyle Bryant told Keeler that he hid in the bushes while his friend Lord Hampton stabbed, choked, and bashed the girl's head in with a rock. The victim, Chauntae Jones, was eight months pregnant with Bryant's child at the time. Hampton admitted to investigators that Bryant wanted Jones killed out of fear that her family would accuse him of statutory rape. "As I'm throwing dirt on her, he's [Bryant] jumping up and down on her and yelling, 'Hurry up and die, bitch,'" Hampton told police. "She gasped all the way through until she was completely buried."[31]

Yet the jury refused to convict Bryant because it felt that prosecutors had not presented enough evidence. There was no blood, no fingerprints to connect Bryant to the grisly murder.

When the verdict was announced, both Keeler and the family of Chauntae Jones were stunned and outraged. The victim's mother had to be retrained by five court officers while her cousin vowed to kill Kyle Bryant one day. Danny Keeler understood their explosive reaction.

"You tell the disenfranchised people of this world like the Jones family the system works," Keeler told the *Boston Herald*. "We told them, 'Don't react to the situation with violence. Wait, we've got him, he's confessed.' And now this? They believed in us and we let them down. There wasn't one person on that jury who couldn't say, 'I'm holding out. I know he did it?' It was a total lack of civic responsibility."[32]

Justice would finally catch up to Bryant, but not before he killed again. He was convicted six years later of fatally shooting a man outside a Brockton, Massachusetts bar.

Keeler faced scrutiny himself when he arrested a man accused of decapitating his own brother. The detective made the bold arrest while being videotaped by an ABC News crew for the documentary *Boston 24/7*. William Leyden had discovered his brother John's headless body rolled up in a blanket and hidden under a bed inside his East Boston apartment. Keeler pointed the guilty finger at Leyden and provided ABC News with unprecedented access to the man's arrest. Leyden was booked and released on one hundred thousand dollars bail, but he lost his job at a print shop as the cloud of guilt loomed over his head. Three years after the arrest, a serial killer named Eugene McCollom admitted to killing John Leyden, whom he had befriended at an Alcoholics Anonymous meeting, and burying his head at a park in Fort Lauderdale, Florida. Leyden's sister, Mary Ellen Dakin, had strong words for Detective Keeler, whom she blamed for inflicting further damage on her grieving family. She blasted the Boston Police and the "misguided influence" of Danny Keeler, and William Leyden called the detective an "incompetent and self serving cop."[33]

In 2006, Keeler would suffer more embarrassment after he was caught on surveillance video taking a pair of sunglasses from a store on Newbury Street while he was investigating a theft there. He was suspended for thirty days but was saved by a clerk-magistrate who found there was not enough evidence to charge him with a crime.

Mr. Homicide was now Mr. Controversy. One of the reasons Keeler remained on the job was the fact that he was one of the most instinctive detectives the department had ever seen. He also knew how to work a crime scene as good as, if not better than, anyone.

Boylston Street was now the biggest crime scene Keeler had ever encountered. He walked behind the bar at the California Pizza Kitchen and grabbed a bottle of Jameson's. He poured himself a shot, downed it, and thought about what to do next. The FBI was now on the scene with members of its cyber crimes unit, which Keeler found odd. *Where are the FBI's bomb techs?* he asked himself. He could feel the FBI beginning to close ranks and take control of the crime scene, so Keeler grabbed one of his detectives and an ATF agent and told them to head back to Boylston Street to develop what evidence they could.

Governor Patrick would later tell the *Boston Globe* that the hand off between Boston police and the FBI was "seamless." "There wasn't any fussing about it," he claimed.[34]

In truth, it was a tug-of-war from the outset. First, the FBI agent in charge had to be convinced it was an act of terrorism.

Suffolk County District Attorney Dan Conley, who was also running for mayor, witnessed the bombings while he was campaigning at the finish line. "Agent Rick DesLauriers seemed panicked when we first spoke," Conley recalls. "He kept asking me in an agitated way, 'Is this terrorism? Do you think this is terrorism?'"

Conley told DesLauiers that "of course" they were dealing with terrorism—either foreign or domestic.

The FBI also refused to allow Keeler's men to begin their work.

"Let's develop it [the crime scene] now," the ATF agent told his FBI counterpart.

"We're going to wait."

"No, no. Let's get the fucking lights down here now and let's start working on this now."

The FBI agent refused to budge.

Word got back to Keeler. He returned to Boylston Street and could not believe the bodies of Lingzi Lu and Martin Richard had not been moved yet.

"Our guys were absolutely beside themselves that Martin Richard was still left on that street," Keeler says with a trace of anger still present in his voice. "It was positively no reasonable explanation other than the inexperience of the FBI to leave that kid there."

Martin did not look like the photograph his family would later release to the media. His face and body were covered in soot. Some officers fresh to the scene thought he was African American at first. Keeler and his men were furious. They stood nose-to-nose with the FBI agents as the Feds tried to order them away from the scene. The Boston cops wouldn't budge, especially Boston Police Captain Frank Armstrong, a father of five, who stood his ground and stood vigil over the boy's body, while another officer stayed with Lingzi Lu.

"Whoever this boy is," Armstrong said to Keeler, "I want to be able to tell his father that 'Your son was never left alone.'"

Captain Armstrong stayed with the bodies of Martin Richard and Lingzi Lu until they were finally removed at 2 a.m.

"We stood there not so much as cops, or veterans, but as fathers," Armstrong later told the *Boston Herald*. "Every one of us there that day thought but for the Grace of God that could be my child coming in to watch the marathon on a beautiful day."[35]

Like other police officers from all over the Commonwealth, Sean Collier was doing what he could to support his fellow cops while they worked frantically to restore order and find out who was responsible for the deadly attack on Boston.

The twenty-six-year-old officer was manning the phones at dispatch for the MIT Police Department. MIT's territory had expanded on this night to include all of Cambridge, as the city cops were assisting the BPD in its investigation on Boylston Street. Collier had always wanted to be a cop; he always wanted to help people. His mother thought he'd make for a great police officer and an even better priest. Collier was the kid who stood up to the bullies in his neighborhood and school when others wouldn't.

"He talked about becoming a police officer his whole life, even when he was little and still hugging his Care Bears," His mother, Kelley Rogers, remembers. "He always just jumped right in."

He had jumped right in on this day. Although he wasn't on the front lines of the investigation or joining the hunt for suspects, Collier felt that he was still doing important work. Someone had to respond to the other emergency calls coming into the station on April 15.

Collier had been dreading a day like this since 9/11. He was a sophomore in high school during that time, and his older sister, Nicole, was having difficulty coping with the tragedy.

"Sean was my savior," Nicole Collier Lynch says. "I slept in his room for a few months after it happened. I slept on a chair. My room was in the basement, and I was too scared to sleep alone. I don't deal well with that stuff."

Sean Collier could deal with it. He'd already overcome a great deal at that point. Another sister, Krystal, had died from a lung infection when she was just three days old. Sean was born a year later in 1986, and he immediately filled the void in his mother's aching heart. His parents were still married at the time, but their union wouldn't last much longer. Sean was just four years old when his parents divorced. His father, Allen Collier, moved to New Hampshire and saw his children every other weekend, but there was always a sense of instability as Sean's dad bounced from marriage to marriage. However, the elder Collier did infuse in Sean and his younger brother, Andy, a love for racing. Dad would take the boys to Queen City Speedway in Manchester, New Hampshire, to race foot-long slot cars, which are a little bigger than a traditional soap box derby car. The Collier brothers enjoyed it so much that they eventually got part-time jobs at the track. They used the money they saved to buy go-karts, which they raced around an eighth mile asphalt track in Ware, New Hampshire. Sean was always a big kid but had avoided contact sports like football in high school because he preferred zipping around the track. He had the racing bug, but his brother's was even bigger. Andy Collier now works for NASCAR.

Sean was a concert nut, too, the rock band Linkin Park being his favorite when he was younger. His musical taste changed after high school and college, when Sean's appreciation drifted toward country acts like Jason Aldean. But he never wavered in his commitment to becoming a cop or his commitment to helping those in need. While in college at Salem State University, just north of Boston, Collier became an active donor to the Jimmy Fund, a charity organization more than half a century old that raises money for pediatric cancer patients at the Dana-Farber Cancer Institute in Boston. The Jimmy Fund had been made popular by Red Sox legend Ted Williams, and the team's connection to it remains strong today. Each year WEEI radio, a local sports talk station, holds a radio-thon to raise money for the Jimmy Fund, and on that program Sean heard the first-hand stories from young cancer patients about their struggles and their triumphs. He was working part-time with his sister at Harvard Vanguard, where their mother worked as a nurse and health administrator. Collier earned little money, yet he made regular donations to the Jimmy Fund from his checking account and would continue to do so regularly.

After graduating from Salem State with a degree in criminal justice in 2009, Sean found work as a clerk with the Somerville, Massachusetts, police department. Collier was the department's IT guy—a civilian. Still, he saw it as a foot in the door and a step in the right direction. Sean's combination of eagerness and intelligence drew praise from his bosses at Somerville PD, who sponsored him for acceptance into the MBTA Transit Police Academy. Collier would still have to pay his own way, and his initiation into the academy would be a point of humor and embarrassment for years to come.

At the academy, cadets were ordered to sew their names into their caps and to have all their grooming gear kept in a shaving case. Sean rushed out to CVS and purchased what he thought was the right accessory and reported for duty.

"Collier!" the instructor barked. "You mean to tell me that you stole your sister's makeup case?"

"No sir, no," he replied, blushing.

He had mistaken a makeup kit for a shaving case. For this, he was ordered to skip around the gym like a girl a dozen or so times.

Like most cadets, Collier was strapped for cash while going through the academy. Normally a giving person, Sean now needed to rely on the kindness of others, and he sought help from his large, blended family. By now, his mother, Kelley, had remarried. Her new husband, an attorney named Joe Rogers, had brought his two children, Rob and Jenn, to live with them in their large Wilmington home. That made for a household of six kids, and they all grew very close.

"When he was in the academy, he used to call me and my husband Brendon and say, 'Hey can I borrow twenty bucks to put gas in my car? Don't tell Mom though, please don't tell Mom that I keep asking you for money,'" sister Nicole says. "It was every week, and Brendon would say, 'I will throw a couple hundred in.'" Nicole would kid Sean and remind him that the loans would be coming out of his nieces' college funds.

"He paid us back within days every time."

Upon his graduation from the Transit Police Academy, Sean was asked by his mother if there was any way for him to avoid getting his head shaved with the rest of the cadets. Her reason: Sean's sister was getting married, and mom did not want his head shaved for the wedding pictures. The dutiful son asked his instructors for special dispensation, but was denied.

Sean Collier graduated from the academy in 2010 with the highest academic score in his class. While there he also befriended another cadet, Richard "Dic" Donohue. The two spoke often about the challenges of the academy and felt truly excited about their opportunities to help people. Dic Donohue stayed with the transit police, while Collier was offered a job at the Massachusetts Institute of Technology. Taking the MIT police job was not an easy decision. Collier had been working details in the town of Lincoln, about twenty miles west of Boston, and had applied for a full-time position with its police department. When Lincoln's police chief was slow to present an offer, Collier accepted a job with MIT's patrol division, which is responsible for the safety of the school's students and staff members over a 168-acre area in the city of Cambridge. Lincoln's offer came immediately after, and Collier debated whether to take it since it was a municipality, as opposed to an institution. Sean decided that keeping his word meant more to him than anything else, so he called the police chief in Lincoln and gave him the news. The chief knew that he was losing a good officer and asked Collier if he liked that fact that he was now considered part of a "campus club."

"No," Collier admitted. "But this is the job that I've accepted."

Sean took to the MIT job with relish, and his mom was happy, too.

"I thought by working on a college campus, he'd be safe," his mother says.

During his first week on the job, Collier told his family that someone had pulled a knife on him during a traffic stop. MIT may house many of the world's great minds, but it's also located in the middle of an urban area where drugs and violence are commonplace. It was a sobering realization for Collier's mom.

"Oh, crap, this is not what I thought it was," she thought at the time.

Collier found an apartment on Curtis Street in Somerville, which he shared with five roommates. He was your typical bachelor, which meant that he ate most of his meals out of a take-out container and kept his room in a disheveled state. When his sheets had been on his bed for too long, laundry was out of the question. Sean simply ran over the sheets with a vacuum until they were clean again—at least in his mind. He grew particularly proud of his job and his campus. He enjoyed showing his family around MIT and where he usually parked his police car, which was in the middle of the courtyard.

"I like parking here because I like talking to people," he beamed. The one part of the job he detested was casting off some of the local homeless people for vagrancy. Collier understood that it was his job to get them off campus, but he also didn't want them to freeze to death during the unforgiving New England winters. During one particularly cold winter day, Collier was asked to remove a homeless man from sleeping on a campus grate, but he refused. The man was soaking wet, and Sean knew that he wouldn't survive much longer outside. Instead, Collier sneaked the homeless man into the basement of the MIT library, got him some dry clothes, and allowed him to stay there until the snow squalls passed by. The two men became friends after that.

In 2013, during the winter storm dubbed Nemo, Collier responded to a call from an MIT graduate student and his wife about their newborn daughter, Sophia. The baby had just arrived home from the hospital and she was not breathing. Collier was the first responder to the scene. He cleared space in the hallway and the baby's room so that paramedics could perform their duties swiftly. The baby was treated for dehydration and recovered after a two-day hospital stay. When the parents returned home, they received an email from Collier that read, "My name is Sean Collier. I was the first responding officer to your apartment where your child (I believe her name was Sophia, although I'm not positive with all the chaos) was having difficulty breathing. I wanted to follow up and find out how Sophia is doing?"[36]

The email came as a surprise to the couple. Sophia's parents were amazed by the officer's engagement with the community.

Still, he felt he could do more. The shootings at Sandy Hook Elementary School had a profound effect on Sean, who posted a note on Facebook saying that he wished he had been a first responder in the hope that he could have done something to stop gunman Adam Lanza.

Military service was also an option Collier explored. He asked his sister Jennifer if she believed their mom would "freak out" if he joined the National Guard.

"Yeah, I probably will too," replied his protective older sister. "Why would you do that?"

"I like my job, but I feel that I'm just not doing enough at MIT," Collier responded. "It could be a good supplement for my work."

Sean visited with a National Guard recruiter just a couple of months before the Boston Marathon. Around this time, he received the news he had been waiting for. There was an opening at the Somerville Police Department, and the chief wanted him for the job. This opportunity was too good to refuse. Collier told MIT that he would be moving on, and all wished him well. He would start his new job in June.

On Monday, April 15, Sean Collier worked his normal 3–11 shift, then continued on through the night as law enforcement everywhere remained on alert and on the hunt for those responsible for the bombings at the finish line.

[14]

A FAMILY'S ANGUISH

Bill Richard was dying inside. His wife, Denise, was in surgery at Beth Israel Deaconess Medical Center having her injured eye stabilized; his daughter, Jane, was being operated on at Boston Children's Hospital a short distance away on Longwood Avenue; and his son Martin was still out there on the cold street. Jane had suffered burns over much of her body. Her hair was singed to the scalp, and — like her father — she had endured a perforated eardrum.

Bill knew his son was dead, but the official word came from Boston Police Sergeant Billy Doogan, a grizzled veteran in charge of the BPD's Cold Case Squad. He had dealt with hundreds of victims in the past and was no stranger to the delicate balance one must use when dealing with those whose grief is immeasurable. He approached Bill Richard in the hospital hallway. Richard was still in shock, his clothes charred and stained with the sad detritus of the marathon attacks. And his hearing was almost non-existent — he had lost all hearing in one ear and had just thirty percent in the other.

"Mr. Richard. I'm sorry," Doogan started.

"What?" Richard shouted.

The cop raised his voice.

"Mr. Richard, I'm very sorry," the detective continued.

"What?" Richard repeated.

It was an agonizing exchange as the cop tried desperately to inform Bill Richard that his eight-year-old boy was dead. The father finally heard enough of the officer's words and saw enough in his eyes to understand fully that his boy was gone.

He screamed in agony. It was a pain Doogan had never personally felt, but knew all too well. The two men embraced as Richard nearly collapsed in grief.

Bill's friend Larry Marchese was monitoring Facebook to check on his friends who had been in the city that day. By early evening, Larry believed he had accounted for everyone he thought had attended the marathon—everyone except for Bill Richard.

"Aw, shit," Larry mumbled to himself as he dialed Bill's cell phone. The call went directly to voice mail. He texted a couple times but again got no response.

Finally the phone rang. It was Bill Richard, and his voice was cracking.

"We lost Martin," he told Marchese.

Larry was confused and tried to put his friend at ease. "He'll show up. Don't worry, we'll find him."

Bill asked his friend to speak up, and Larry repeated his hopeful words.

"No," Bill told him. "He's dead."

Marchese was standing by the window in his office and fell back in his chair, his eyes welling up with tears. He could see the boy's gap-toothed smile in his mind's eye. He could hear Martin's thick Boston accent, one that neither Henry nor Jane had. Larry sat still in his chair.

Such a funny and sweet little boy. How can he be dead?

Larry and his wife, Nina, got a babysitter for their kids and raced into Boston, where many of the roads were shut down. He called a state trooper buddy who told him to drive to the state police barracks in South Boston and leave his car. The trooper then drove Larry and Nina to Beth Israel Hospital. The couple rode an elevator to the fifth floor, where they met Bill Richard in the hallway. Larry embraced his friend, and both began crying. He placed his hand on Bill's head and felt the man's burned hair coming off like flakes in his hand.

"Bill's pants were ripped," Larry remembers. "He was a zombie."

"Martin is out in the street," Bill cried. "My baby boy is out in the street!"

The two men hugged even tighter.

A specialist had been flown in to stabilize and repair Denise's right eye.

A six-millimeter ball bearing from Dzhokhar Tsarnaev's pressure cooker bomb had penetrated her eyeball and stuck to one of her optic muscles. In order to save her eye, the surgeon would eventually have to remove the sclera—the tissue that makes the eye white—the pupil, and the retina, and then rebuild it layer by layer.

"It was like peeling an onion and then putting it back together again," Marchese said.

The FBI interviewed Denise Richard at 11 p.m. on the day of the bombings, after she had undergone five hours of surgery. Nina Marchese was there at her bedside.

"I pray to God that you've forgotten everything," Nina thought as she looked at her friend, whose head was covered in thick layers of bandages.

Instead, Denise's recall of the bombing was remarkable. She was able to describe the scene with pinpoint accuracy.

She also knew that her beloved son Martin was dead.

Over at Massachusetts General Hospital, there was confusion. Patty and Billy Campbell arrived at the hospital at around 2 a.m. with the hope of being reunited with their daughter, Krystle. Fifty-two-year old Karen Rand, Krystle's friend and former colleague, had been brought to Mass General by ambulance hours earlier. The two friends had been standing close to each other when the first bomb exploded behind them. Rand suffered major damage to her left leg. While she was undergoing surgery, a handbag that had accompanied her to the hospital was searched in an attempt to determine her identity. A staff member found a driver's license in the bag with the name Krystle Campbell. The staffer matched the bag to the patient, whom they now believed was Campbell. When her parents entered the hospital, doctors came over and explained that the artery in Krystle's left leg had been severed. They could not save the leg, but they managed to repair the artery and save her life.

The news was devastating, but at least their daughter was still alive.

The Campbells were then escorted to an intensive care room to check on their daughter. Billy Campbell looked at the woman lying in bed who was missing her left leg, and his heart nearly stopped.

"That's not my daughter, that's Karen!" he shouted. "Where is my daughter?"

The nurses were as shocked as the parents were.

An hour later, a Boston Police detective arrived at Mass General and showed Billy Campbell a photograph of his daughter taken at the medical tent. The father looked at the picture and collapsed.

When Michelle L'Heureux awoke from surgery, she had no idea how long she had been unconscious. The first thing she did when she opened her eyes was look down to see if she had her left foot.

She saw it and said aloud, "Thank God."

It turns out she had been in surgery for nine hours. She went in around 4 p.m. on April 15 and came out about 1 a.m. on April 16.

A doctor entered her room and told her the wound to her arm had just missed her main artery. Had that artery been severed, she almost assuredly would have lost her arm—and quite possibly died.

"You're very lucky," the doctor said.

She didn't sleep most of that first night. Brian and her best friend, Sare Largay, were there. Michelle started reading posts on Facebook and was sickened by the news of what was happening. At length, she drifted off.

When she awoke, she smelled flowers. Her friend Caroline was in the bed next to her, and their room was filled with deliveries of flowers, chocolates, gift baskets, and stuffed animals. Some were from friends, some were from Michelle's co-workers, others were from Caroline's friends. Michelle was overwhelmed. There were so many that she told one of the nurses to send some to other patients in the hospital who didn't have any.

And then a stream of visitors arrived. Among the first to visit was her friend Nicole. She told Michelle she saw the first explosion, then heard the second one behind her and didn't know where to run.

"I was so scared I didn't know whether to run or hide under a car or behind a bush. I was worried about you guys," she said.

She and Caroline talked about what had happened. Their other friend Christian nearly lost his leg, but doctors were able to save it. Caroline learned during her treatment that she was two weeks pregnant and that the baby was unharmed. In December 2013—roughly eight months after the attacks—Caroline gave birth to a healthy baby girl, whom the couple named Marlowe Eve.

Around noon on Tuesday, Michelle's dad arrived at the hospital. He walked in, gazed deeply at Michelle in her hospital bed, and leaned over to gave her a big hug. Not normally an emotional guy, the gruff firefighter was overcome, and tears welled up in his eyes.

"You're going to be OK, doll. You're going to get through this," he told her. "I'm very proud of you. You got through this."

Paul L'Heureux, besides being a retired firefighter, served in the military and is active in the American Legion. It was very hard for him to see his daughter injured by terrorism on American soil. He stayed in Boston for three days, bedding down at a nearby hospital, and visited daily.

While bombing survivor Jeff Bauman, who lost both legs, was under heavy anesthesia, one of the men credited with saving his life was under heavy scrutiny about his actions before the bombing. Carlos Arredondo had reunited with his friend John Mixon at the apartment of John's daughter. Mixon had just gotten off the phone with the FBI.

"They want to talk to you," he told Carlos. "They mentioned what happened in Florida."

Mixon was referring to his friend's highly publicized suicide attempt. When Arredondo returned to his home in Roslindale, Massachusetts, early that evening, he was met by a Boston Police detective and an FBI agent who asked him for his shoes, pants, and T-shirt. Carlos immediately obliged. The federal agent also seized his camera, which had several photos he had snapped at the marathon.

"Can you retrace your footsteps during the race?" the agent asked. "Where precisely were you when the bombs went off? What did you see? What did you do?"

Arredondo answered the questions as best he could. The grilling lasted for about forty minutes.

When Jeff Bauman arrived at Boston Medical Center, he told a police officer there, "I know who did it."

Bauman remembered locking eyes with a suspicious-looking man outside Marathon Sports just before the bomb went off. The man wore a thick, hooded coat, and he looked serious. Bauman found his demeanor odd given the party atmosphere around them. He turned his attention away briefly, and when Bauman looked back—the man was gone.

Bauman was rushed into surgery before he could explain what he saw. Hours later, after he woke up, he asked for a pen and a piece of paper. On it, Bauman wrote, "Bag. Saw the guy. He looked right at me."

Earlier that same Monday night—just hours after his bombs had blown apart so many lives—one of the Tsarnaev brothers wrote a message of his own.

"Ain't no love in the heart of the city," Dhzokhar Tsarnaev tweeted. "Stay safe people."

He followed that Twitter message with another at 12:34 a.m. on Tuesday.

"There are people that know the truth but remain silent & there are people that speak the truth but we don't hear them cuz they're the minority."

Boylston Street just moments before the first bomb exploded in front
of Marathon Sports. Courtesy: Colton Kilgore

A pair of bloodied jeans and socks removed from a bombing victim by EMTs on Boylston Street. Courtesy: Colton Kilgore

Exclusive image taken from a video camera inside the first bomb blast.
Courtesy: Colton Kilgore

The Tsarnaev brothers captured on surveillance cameras walking down
Boylston Street shortly before the bombings. Courtesy: FBI

Boston Police Detective Danny Keeler, aka Mr. Homicide. Photo by Dave Wedge

Boston Police Officer Javier Pagan was just one of the heroes who saved others on Boylston Street. Courtesy: Javier Pagan

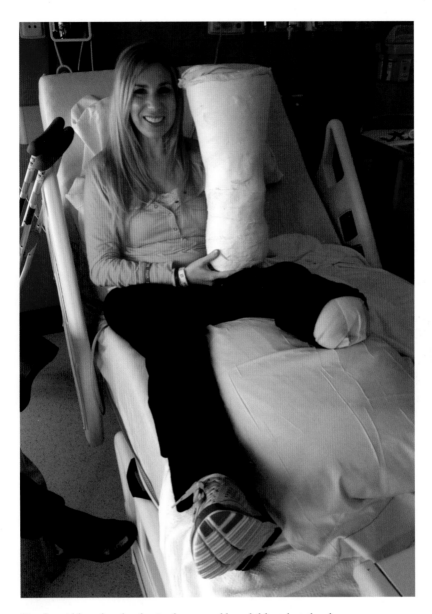

Heather Abbott lost her leg in the second bomb blast, but thanks
to her courage and resiliency, she is back doing the things she loves.
Courtesy: Heather Abbott

The Richard family, seen here on a
trip to Washington, DC, attended the
Boston Marathon just about every year.
Courtesy: Larry Marchese

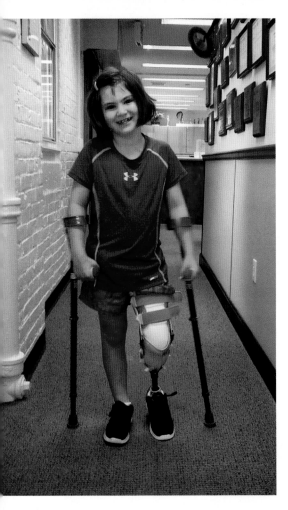

The first words Jane Richard spoke when she awoke from a coma were: "Martin, where are you?" Courtesy: Larry Marchese

Tracy Munro and her daughter, Stella. The Cambridge mom helped comfort Jane Richard after the bomb blast. Courtesy: Tracy Munro

MIT Police Officer Sean Collier on a trip to Nova Scotia in March 2013, one month before he was murdered. Courtesy: Sally Miller

Sean Collier's comrades stand at attention over his casket during a memorial service for the fallen officer at MIT. Courtesy: Governor Deval Patrick's Office / Spencer Crispino

The World Series trophy placed on the finish line during the celebration parade for the Boston Red Sox. Photo by Dave Wedge

Marathon survivors Sabrina Dello Russo and Michelle L'Heureux discover a touch of home in Cluny, France. Photo by Casey Sherman

Marathon hero Jeff Bauman spending a late night on board the Marathon Heroes Cruise through the south of France. Photo by Casey Sherman

Marathon hero Carlos Arredondo shares a moment with survivor Mery Daniel at an event in Boston. Photo by Casey Sherman

Arredondo comforts Jun Lu, father of victim Lingzi Lu, aboard the Marathon Heroes Cruise. Photo by Casey Sherman

Seventy-one-year-old survivor Bill White, shown here on the cruise to France, lost a leg in the bombing at Marathon Sports. Photo by Casey Sherman

Governor Patrick and his wife, Diane, walk with Denise and Jane Richard down Boylston Street on the first anniversary of the marathon bombings. Mayor Martin J. Walsh and girlfriend Lorrie Higgins are on the far right. Courtesy: Governor Deval Patrick's Office / Eric Haynes

Denise Richard holds daughter Jane during the memorial service marking the first anniversary of the marathon bombings. Courtesy: Governor Deval Patrick's Office / Eric Haynes

[15]

CITIZEN SOLDIERS

Late Monday night, Kurt Schwartz suggested to Commissioner Davis, Mayor Menino, and the governor that three hundred soldiers from the Massachusetts National Guard be used to help secure the perimeter of what was now a twenty-block crime scene around Boylston Street. The troops were on duty for the marathon, and Schwartz held them over after the bombing. Schwartz wasn't sure whether he would get approval for the idea, as the thought of armed soldiers patrolling the streets of Boston might create even more panic.

"Yeah, I can use them," Davis said without thinking twice.

Mayor Menino did not say anything.

Schwartz then turned to Governor Patrick. "Are you OK with that?"

"Absolutely," the governor replied.

Schwartz immediately got a hold of the National Guard troops' commander, Major General L. Scott Rice, and told him about the plan. Both men decided that three hundred soldiers were not enough, so with the governor's approval they activated one thousand soldiers to join city, state, and transit police to guard every hotel, every train station, and every spot in the city where people gathered in large groups—including Boston's most popular tourist attraction, the marketplace at Faneuil Hall.

It was the largest deployment of soldiers in the city of Boston since 1919, when then Governor Calvin Coolidge ordered five thousand guard members into action to quell the violent Boston Police Strike, which left nine people dead and sections of the city in rubble.

As dawn broke on Tuesday, April 16, law enforcement still had no idea exactly what they were dealing with. Information was trickling in from members of the FBI's evidence response team who had recovered bomb fragments, the accounts of victims and witnesses who were giving statements of things they saw, and from the thousands of photographs and videos taken with smartphones before and after the bombers struck.

Though he'd had very little sleep the night before, Governor Patrick knew that he had to remain visible and helpful, yet not to get in the way of the cops and others out there trying to do their jobs.

"I visited the BAA office just outside Copley Square," he recalls. "People there were just devastated. They were really shaken, crying. I tried to comfort them by telling them they had performed beautifully."

He also visited Mass General and shook hands with the doctors and nurses who had managed to save every life that had come through their doors over the previous twenty-four hours. In fact, no responding hospital lost a single person injured in the bombings.

The governor then returned to the command center at the Westin hotel, where he gave the first media briefing of the day, surrounded by members of the Massachusetts congressional delegation who had gathered in a show of support. Governor Patrick first wanted to address rumors that a third bomb had been discovered under the grandstand on Boylston Street.

"It's important to clarify that two and only two explosive devices were found yesterday," he said. "Other parcels, *all* other parcels in the area of the blast have been examined but there were no unexploded bombs."

The governor then announced that FBI Special Agent in Charge Rick DesLauriers would head the probe.

"This will be a combined federal, state, and local effort. It will be an ongoing investigation. It is a criminal investigation," DesLauriers said in the news conference. "The FBI is bringing substantial—very, very substantial—federal resources to bear along with our federal partners. The ATF is well-represented here."

He described it as a "potential terrorist investigation"—marking the first time officials had publicly done so—and asked the public for a "heightened state of vigilance" because the bombers were still at-large.

"We will bring those responsible to justice as quickly as possible," he said.

Boston Police Commissioner Ed Davis echoed those remarks.

"This cowardly act will not be taken in stride. We will turn over every rock to find those responsible."

Davis then acknowledged ominously: "There is no suspect."

He did let the media know that there were people of interest that investigators were now speaking to.

The city was in full security mode. Armored Humvees cluttered Boston Common, where the colonial militia had mustered before the American Revolution. Hotels, hospitals, colleges, and government buildings were patrolled by federal, state, and local cops, all armed with semi-automatic rifles. Copley Plaza was cordoned off with yellow tape and police barricades.

TV satellite trucks were parked around the Common and at the mouth of desolate Boylston Street. CNN's Wolf Blitzer and Fox News Channel's Bill Hemmer gave live updates from tents set up at the corner of Boylston and Arlington streets.

The fact that no international group took responsibility for the attack only added to the confusion and mystery surrounding the bombings.

"It means we know less than we thought we would at this point," US Senator Elizabeth Warren said at the news conference. "It means the investigation needs to remain very open."

US Representative Stephen Lynch also spoke at the media briefing. The congressman was especially close to the situation because the Richard family had worked on his campaigns over the years, and also because Denise Richard worked at Marian Manor, a senior living facility in Lynch's South Boston neighborhood. The blue-collar congressman, a former iron worker, lives in Southie, just a mile or so from the Richard home in the Ashmont section of Dorchester. He's a leader in the Massachusetts Democratic Party and had grown to become friends with Bill Richard and the family. At the Westin, Lynch talked about visiting the distraught family in the hospital.

"They're close friends [of mine]," Lynch said. "Bill has ball bearings from the blast embedded in his skin. The older boy, Henry, has post-traumatic symptoms. It shows just how random this violence is, that one son was taken and one was not."

Lynch, a member of Congress's Armed Services Committee, knew plenty about the IEDs American troops faced in Iraq and Afghanistan. He had traveled to the war-torn regions several times with congressional delegations and was a crucial driving force behind efforts to improve the quality of armored vehicles used by American soldiers. Lynch had seen IEDs up close in Iraq and even had to take cover in bunkers during attacks while visiting Iraq in 2008.

Lynch knew that the ball bearings used in the bombs and "the timing" of the coordinated blasts had all the hallmarks of a jihadist attack.

"This isn't some kid in his garage," he said. "Having two explosions, eleven seconds apart—that points to someone who has training and expertise.... It's an antipersonnel device. They were trying to cause carnage here."

Special Agent in Charge DesLauriers said that items were still being collected from the scene, including BBs, nails, and pieces of black nylon believed to be from the bombers' backpacks. Pieces of the pressure cooker bombs were recovered from rooftops. People reported smelling gunpowder.

All of the items, along with thousands of pictures and videos—including eleven from outside Forum—were sent to the FBI's crime lab in Quantico, Virginia. More than two thousand tips had flooded in to the FBI and Boston and state police.

"We are doing this methodically and carefully, yet with a sense of urgency," DesLauriers said. "The investigation is in its infancy, but rest assured, we are working hard. The range of suspects and motives is wide open. Someone knows who did this. Cooperation from the community will play a crucial role in this investigation."

The initial shock having worn off, reporters and pundits turned their questions to second-guessing: Did the city perform bomb sweeps that morning? Could the attacks have been thwarted?

It was far too early in the probe to know the answers, but Lynch and

Davis tried to calm the public's fears. Lynch said authorities took "all the appropriate steps" and believed the devices were brought into the area after police did a security sweep.

"There was nothing to lead us to believe that what we were doing, what the mayor was doing, what the governor was doing, was less than appropriate," he said. "The staffing was there, the sweeps were there.... They did their due diligence. But . . . under these circumstances, it was very difficult to stop."

Added Davis: "There were more officers assigned this year than ever before. We were particularly concerned with the finish line this year."

The reason for the increased security wasn't a specific threat; rather, it was because the 2012 marathon had seen one of the biggest crowds ever at the finish line.

"There was no specific threat for this event," Davis reiterated.

Governor Patrick called for people to donate blood, noting that many victims required multiple transfusions.

"There is a need for blood on a sustained basis," he said.

He also offered prayers for the wounded and the families of the dead. He thanked first responders for their extraordinary efforts in preventing the death toll from getting higher and announced initial plans for an interfaith prayer service to help the city and the state to heal.

"That was a priority for me," Patrick recalls. "I wanted to make sure that we allowed all folks an outlet to express their grief and to come together."

The governor urged survivors to take advantage of a support center which had been set up at The Castle at the Boston Park Plaza where workers from the American Red Cross, Salvation Army, and the Boston Public Health Commission reunited lost friends and loved ones who had been separated after the bombings, helped locate bags that had been abandoned at the finish line, and provided immediate psychiatric care for those who had witnessed the kind of horrific bloodshed and destruction they'd only ever seen in the movies, but never before in real life.

In a token gesture, the Boston Athletic Association brought over a section of the adhesive finish line to allow runners who had been stopped during the marathon before they got to Boylston Street a chance to cross the tape and receive their medals. Runners had trained for months, even years, for a chance to compete in the Boston Marathon, and the sense of shock and frustration was overwhelming for some.

"I was stopped at mile twenty-five [just outside Kenmore Square]. It was heartbreaking," Jeannie Hannigan of Keene, New Hampshire, said. "I just wanted to keep going because I was having a really good race until then. This year I was going for it; I knew I had it. It was shocking. I wish everyone would have been able to finish, but I'm glad I have it [the medal]."[37] This year's medal would have special significance, like those from other athletic contests marred by historic events, such as the infamous 1936 Summer Olympics in Adolph Hitler's Berlin, or the 1972 Summer Olympics in Munich, where eleven members of the Israeli team were murdered at the hands of Palestinian terrorists.

While law enforcement continued to focus its attention on the twenty-plus blocks around Boylston Street, the heart of Boston shifted that evening to a small park in Dorchester where Martin Richard once played with his friends. By now, his photograph had traveled the world and back. The image of the young boy at school holding a blue poster board with the words *No More Hurting People—Peace* surrounded by two red hearts drawn with magic marker, had become a symbol of both hope and tragic loss. Larry Marchese was also getting inundated with phone calls and texts from Richard family friends and relatives who wanted him to establish some kind of fund for the family.

"You all need to relax," Marchese told them. "We need to do this right."

At that point, Marchese did not know whether he could legally accept donations or what the tax implications would be.

"What are we gonna do?" friends of the Richard family asked Marchese and his wife, Nina.

"I don't know," Larry replied. "We're gonna hug Bill."

He also spent the day on Tuesday with an MIT student who was a neighbor of the Richards' at the lake in New Hampshire. Together, they built the Richard Family Fund website. Larry then sat down with Bill and worked on this statement they would release to well-wishers and the media:

My dear son Martin has died from injuries sustained in the attack on Boston. My wife and daughter are both recovering from serious injuries. We thank our family and friends, those we know and those we have never met, for their thoughts and prayers. I ask that you continue to pray for my family as we remember Martin. We also ask for your patience and for privacy as we work to simultaneously grieve and recover. Thank you.[38]

Larry and Nina Marchese did their best to shield Bill, Denise, and Henry Richard from the outside world while they remained at Brigham and Women's Hospital. There was a virtual news blackout. In the family room, where Henry spent most of his time, the television was locked on the Discovery Channel. Henry's uncle Brad Richard spent time keeping the eleven-year-old entertained and occupied.

"Brad was a rock star," Marchese recalls. "He and Henry were hanging out in the corner of the room acting like two little boys."

Denise's father, Bob, arrived from Florida and the moment he saw his daughter—he let go, tears spilling down his cheeks. He had been especially close to his grandson Martin, even sleeping in a bunk bed in the boy's room when he visited.

Staffers at the Brigham moved an additional hospital bed and a cot into Denise Richard's room so that the family could sleep together, while over at Children's Hospital little Jane remained in a medically induced coma. But Jane was never alone, and she was semi-conscious now, beginning to move and reach for tubes and push nurses' hands away. Her aunts rallied around her, as did Nina Marchese. They held prayer vigils at her bedside.

"When I saw Jane for the first time, she didn't look like herself," Nina recalls. "Her tiny body was covered by machines working to keep her alive."

Nina did her best to stay calm and focused while she was in Jane's hospital room. Crying would not do the little girl any good. Nina held her tears for later, when she broke down and asked herself—and God—*How will this little girl recover? How will she live and move forward with her life?*

As darkness fell over the Richard family's Dorchester neighborhood, thousands of candles were lit by friends, neighbors, and total strangers alike who gathered at Garvey Park to pray for Jane, Martin, Denise, Henry, and Bill.

"Nobody knows what to do, but this is the only thing we can think of to do," said neighbor Maria Deltufo. "To come together and be with each other and just show how strong a community we really are because Dorchester really is a strong support system. There's nothing any of us wouldn't do for that family right now."[39]

The vigil closed with an emotional and impromptu chorus of "God Bless America," with thousands of attendees singing through tears.

As Bill Richard mourned in seclusion while watching over his injured wife and daughter, the mother of Krystle Campbell shared a glimpse of her grief with the world from the front porch of her Medford, Massachusetts, home. Patty Campbell, who just hours before had suffered the doubly cruel fate of mistakenly believing that Krystle had survived the attack, stood before a pack of reporters and photographers and shared memories of her twenty-nine-year-old daughter.

"Krystle Marie, she was a wonderful person," Patty Campbell said, fidgeting with her reading glasses, her voice failing. "Everybody that knew her loved her. She loved her dogs. She had a heart of gold. She was always smiling. You couldn't have asked for a better daughter. I can't believe this has happened. She was such a hard worker at everything she did. This doesn't make any sense."[40]

Nothing made sense. The city was paralyzed and bewildered by the events of the past two days—two days unlike any other in Boston's turbulent history. Confusion was also felt on the campus of Boston University, where students scoured Sina Weibo, a Chinese social media site, for any word of their missing friend, Lingzi Lu. BU's Chinese student organization was also put on notice.

Lingzi's aunt Helen Zhao was working in the Boston area when she first saw television reports of the bombings. As shocked as she was to see the explosions and destruction on Boylston Street, it never entered her mind that the tragedy would hit so close to home. Still, she called her niece to see if she was OK but got no answer. A college friend of Lingzi's contacted the aunt and told her not to worry, that Lingzi was probably tending to one of her friends at a hospital. At 11 a.m. the next morning, Helen Zhao received a phone call from the Boston Police.

"They said they wanted to come and talk to me," Helen Zhao said in an interview with WCVB television. "They walked in and sat and they said, 'Sorry, we have really bad news. The third victim was Lingzi.'"[41]

When word finally came that the graduate student was among the three people who perished in the bombings, both friends and total strangers took to social media to express their condolences. Just days after her death, a memorial page was created on Facebook entitled "R.I.P. Lu Lingzi." On it, mourners wrote brief notes such as, "My heart breaks for you. R.I.P. lovely girl" and "The world has lost a beautiful, intelligent woman. So, so sad!"

BU's Marsh Chapel, where Martin Luther King Jr. had formulated his pacifist beliefs while pursuing his doctoral studies in the early 1950s, was now surrounded by a garden of flowers along with handwritten notes from Lu's heartbroken classmates. Her parents responded to the notes and the overwhelming love for their daughter in a statement issued on their behalf days later by Boston University. The statement read in part:

> We are grieving and at a loss for words to describe the pain and sadness we are experiencing following the sudden passing of our daughter, Lingzi. She was the joy of our lives. She was a bright and wonderful child. We were thrilled to watch her grow into a beautiful and intelligent woman. . . . It has always been her dream to come to America to study. While she was here, she fell in love with Boston and its people. . . . While her dream has not been realized, we want to encourage others who have Lingzi's ambition and dreams, and want to make the world a better place, to continue moving forward. . . . We hope that everyone who has now heard the story about Lingzi will keep a memory of her in their hearts."[42]

"She felt love with Boston," Helen Zhao said. "The food; the culture. She one time told me that every corner you turn is a picture . . . it's like why her? What has she done?"[43]

Approximately forty minutes after the bombings, Tamerlan Tsarnaev received a call on his cell phone from Khairullozhon Matanov, a native of Kyrgyzstan who had been living in the US since 2010. Matanov lived in an apartment in Quincy, Massachusetts, and drove a cab. He had known both

Tsarnaev brothers but was particularly close to Tamerlan. The two men had discussed hiking a mountain in New Hampshire to train like the mujahideen. Matanov invited the brothers out to dinner on the night of the bombings. When he returned home from the restaurant, a friend pulled Matanov aside and told him that he wished the bombers weren't Muslim.

"The bombers could've had a just reason if it was done in the name of Islam," Matanov said coldly. "I'd support the bombings if the reason was just or if the attack had been done by the Taliban and the victims had gone to paradise."[44]

On Tuesday, nearly twenty-four hours after the murders of Lingzi Lu, Martin Richard, and Krystle Campbell, and the injuries to 268 others, Dzhokhar Tsarnaev resurfaced in Cambridge, where he demanded the return of a white 2007 Mercedes Benz station wagon that he had dropped off two weeks before for repair. Dzhokar wore nine-hundred-dollar Louis Vuitton shoes and Burberry pants. His hair was cut shorter than usual.

"Where is the car?" he asked the mechanic, Gilberto Junior.

"The car is in the parking lot," Junior replied. "But I haven't worked on the car yet. I've only removed the rear bumper and the tail lights."

"I don't care, I don't care," Tsarnaev said nervously. "I need the car right now, right now."

The mechanic noticed that his customer, who was normally laid back, was fretting about something. Dzhokhar bit his fingernails repeatedly as he pressed Junior for the vehicle.

"Gimme the key. I don't care. I'm gonna take the car the way it is."[45]

Tsarnaev told the mechanic that the car belonged to his girlfriend and that she wanted it back. The mechanic had known Dzhokhar for two years but had never seen him in such a state. Tsarnaev walked in a circle and stared at the ground. Gilberto Junior thought the young man was on drugs.

Dzhokhar drove back to UMass-Dartmouth on Tuesday afternoon and hung out at his dormitory, Pine Dale Hall. By now he had his nerves under control. Andrew Glasby, a classmate who sat next to him in a psychology class, later described Dzhokhar as nonchalant. "He acted like it was just another day." Glasby said Tsarnaev even offered him a ride to his home in Waltham that Friday.[46]

Later that night, Dzhokhar worked out at the campus fitness center.

There he bumped into another classmate, Zach Bettencourt, who brought up the bombings.

"Man, can you believe that happened?" Bettencourt said. "I thought that only happened in Iraq or Afghanistan with those bombs."

"Yeah, man, tragedies can happen anywhere in the world."[47]

Dzhokhar went back to his Twitter account late Tuesday and early Wednesday. In the months before the marathon, his tweets usually centered on his favorite television shows, including *Sons of Anarchy*, *Game of Thrones* and *Breaking Bad*.

"Breaking Bad taught me how to dispose of a corpse," Tsarnaev tweeted in January 2013.

On the day after the bombings, his messages turned to denouncing twitter rumors that a man on the cusp of proposing to his girlfriend found her dead on Boylston Street.

"Fake Story," Dzhokhar tweeted out at 5:09 p.m.

Hours later, at 1:43 a.m. on Wednesday, Tsarnaev tweeted again. This time, he attempted to recapture the laid back attitude he'd been known for before Marathon Monday.

"I'm a stress free kind of guy," he announced.

On Wednesday, April 17, two days after the bombings, Commissioner Ed Davis was summoned to a briefing with several video experts, detectives, and federal agents. They had a break in the case. Agents had analyzed endless streams of video until they came upon one particular clip that stood out from all others. The clip showed a man acting suspiciously—suspiciously *calm* in the wake of overwhelming terror. He was then dubbed White Hat.

Davis watched the video, which would be released to the public the following day, over and over. He also saw in the footage a taller man walking in front of White Hat.

"They were walking at the same cadence," Davis recalls. There was no sense of panic or concern in either man. They almost appeared to be marching. *These look like our guys*, the commissioner thought to himself.

Detectives examined the videos more closely and identified the second man as potentially involved. He was wearing a dark baseball cap and sunglasses and was dubbed Black Hat.

Investigators now had their suspects. They just needed to figure out who they were. They watched more videos, and they also spotted the suspects in surveillance photos and in pictures taken by spectators. Governor Patrick was also shown the images and briefed on the situation. The problem was that neither man looked like a prototypical jihadist terrorist; rather, they looked like two everyday college kids in a city filled with more than two hundred thousand students. They were so nondescript that one popular men's website, Barstool Sports, proclaimed that the city had been bombed by two random "bros."

Ed Davis demanded that the photos be released on Wednesday. The sooner those images were out there, the sooner this nightmare could be brought to a close. Surprisingly, Davis was met with fierce resistance from the FBI and federal prosecutors. For Davis, it was a public safety issue. These guys were still on the loose. He wanted to get their pictures out there with the hope that someone would recognize them, so that they could be caught before anyone else got hurt. But prosecutors were not focused on the immediate danger. Instead, they feared that releasing the pictures could taint public opinion and jeopardize a future trial. President Obama was coming to town on Thursday for an interfaith service, and there was a Boston Bruins game scheduled at the Garden that night. Public pressure for information was building. Did officials have any idea who committed these acts of terror?

There were also rumblings that the FBI knew exactly who the two men were. Tamerlan Tsarnaev had been on a federal terror watch list and was known to Russian authorities as a potential threat.

Was the FBI withholding information about the two suspects? Ed Davis needed to find out. In one meeting, Davis called Rick DesLauriers of the FBI and demanded information on the suspects.

"I want their names," Davis demanded. "This is my fucking city!"

The fact that they were on a watch list and that the Russians had warned the US about them would mean that their pictures should have been on file with the Boston FBI office and with the Immigration and Naturalization Service. But no one involved in that previous case came forward to identify the brothers in the days following the marathon attack.

To make matters worse, there was a flood of misinformation and disinformation flowing throughout both the blogosphere and traditional media. Speculation was rampant about who may have been responsible for the bombings. Was it the Taliban? Was it al-Qaeda? Was it a homegrown cell? Unlike many terror attacks, no international group claimed credit for the bombings.

Would-be cyber sleuths were muddying the waters by analyzing and dissecting pictures from Boylston Street, trying to pinpoint who the attackers may have been. Not surprisingly, there were some dark-skinned and bearded men whose mere presence at the marathon finish line made them suspects in the eyes of some online vigilantes. The website Reddit had an entire section overrun with wannabe detectives trying to identify the bombers.

The *New York Post* splashed a story on its front page with the headline: "Bag Men: Feds seek these two pictured at Boston Marathon."[48]

In its front-page photo, the *Post* circled two men in red and indicated they were suspects. The story quoted a law enforcement memo that sought information about the two men. Neither of them, however, had anything to do with the bombing. Both were mere spectators enjoying the day. One of them was a high school track star from Massachusetts, who later filed a lawsuit against the paper.

Governor Patrick, Commissioner Davis and other officials threw cold water on the *Post* story in press conferences and criticized other media outlets for running with stories based on sources that turned out to be false. Lawyers for the tabloid would later argue that because its reporters had been working off an FBI email seeking more information about the men, and because the paper had never labeled the men as "suspects," the story was accurate. *Post* lawyers also insisted that the "Bag Men" headline was merely an attention-getter and was not defamatory.

Local media also found itself wanting in the hours and days after the attacks. Every newspaper, every TV station in the city and beyond had dedicated all of their resources to covering what would be the biggest Boston story of their lifetimes. In the frenzy to break news, the *Boston Globe* erroneously reported that police had a bombing suspect in custody and that he was en route to federal court. Other outlets began reporting similar bulletins, and suddenly there was a mad dash to the John Joseph Moakley United States Courthouse, located in the Seaport section of South Boston. Reporters huddled for more than two hours waiting for some type of hearing to get underway. Courthouse staffers, caught up in the excitement and uncertainty of the situation, began discussing how they would handle the large crowd of reporters and spectators and whether they needed to provide a live television feed of the proceedings for those who couldn't cram into the courtroom. While this was going on, the US Attorney's office reached out to court officials to say there would be no hearing. Before this news trickled down to the media, however, the courthouse was evacuated because of a bomb threat. Throughout it all, Bostonians stayed glued to the live TV coverage, then texted friends and took to social media to pass along the latest information — information that was all wrong.

The bombing survivors had little use for flashy headlines or news organizations looking to get a jump on one another. They were merely trying to stay alive, or to cope with their lives that were now forever changed.

Mery Daniel woke up in her hospital bed at Mass General on Wednesday. Her doctor entered her room and described to her all the things a team of surgeons had done to keep her heart beating.

"Your heart stopped twice after you arrived," the doctor informed her. "We had to massage your heart to save your life."

As a medical student, Mery tried to absorb and understand what the doctor was saying. She understood that a pancreatic laceration had left her with internal bleeding. She was confused, however, when she looked down at her legs. Her right leg was wrapped in bandages because doctors had cut away muscles and tendons that had been ripped apart by shrapnel. And her left leg — was gone. While she had been lying on Boylston Street and while she was being carried into Mass General, Mery had realized that — if she lived — she might lose a leg. But she had thought that the damage to her right leg was much more significant than the injuries sustained by her left. The doctor explained that the arteries and nerves in her left leg had been cut deeply and that the only way to save her life was to amputate. Mery was physically broken, but she did not cry.

"I'm glad to be alive," she says. "Losing the leg didn't seem that significant to me."

Her husband and other family members visited her that day. Mery's daughter, Ciarra, was kept at home for fear that the image of her mother lying in a hospital bed would frighten the little girl. Yet, Mery knew she was fortunate for two big reasons. Once again, she thought about her decision not to take Ciarra to the marathon. It was a decision that quite possibly saved her little girl's life. Mery also knew that she would be returning to her daughter—that Ciarra would not have to grow up without her mother. Mery would be there for her. She would be able to dress Ciarra for her first school dance. She would be there when Ciarra got her driver's license. She would be able to hug her daughter on her graduation and wedding days. Mery closed her eyes and thought about this, about returning home to her child. This thought would feed her determination in the days and weeks to come.

Michelle L'Heureux went back in for a second surgery on Wednesday. She went into the operating room around 7:30 a.m. and was there for more than eight long hours. During the first surgery, doctors stabilized and cleaned her wounds and implanted small vacuum-like devices in her arm and leg to stave off infections. The second surgery was performed to clean up the wounds even more and to partially close the huge gash on her arm.

Like Jane Richard, Michelle was never left alone. Because she was the daughter of a Maine firefighter, a station house in Boston—Engine 7, on Columbus Avenue—had adopted her as its own. Each day, a firefighter was assigned to Michelle's bedside—to bring her gifts and to get her anything she needed. The firefighters were also there for Michelle's dad, allowing him to park his truck at the station and giving him a ride to the hospital each day to visit his daughter.

Heather Abbott was also going in for a second surgery so doctors could determine if her foot could be saved. She was faced with several difficult decisions and an agonizing recovery ahead. Heather had just learned from her doctor that, because her foot was in such poor condition, the chances of her returning to normal were virtually zero.

"If you keep the foot, you might never be able to walk on it again," her doctor told her gently.

Even with the effort of the world's best surgeons, her foot would be fixed permanently in a flexed position and would remain severely mangled. Also, if she kept the foot, her left leg would most likely be shorter than her right, giving her a permanent limp.

By contrast, she was told, a prosthetic leg would improve her chances of resuming a normal life. Advances in prosthetic technology would give Heather a better shot at getting back to walking, paddleboarding, even running—if she opted for a prosthetic leg rather than retaining her mangled limb. The doctors brought in runners and athletes who had suffered horrible lower leg injuries and had had to make similar decisions to amputate. Some told her they wasted years of their life by refusing to amputate. Others told her horror stories of repeated surgeries that were all for naught.

All four of her surgeons recommended amputation.

Heather looked at the situation very logically and matter-of-factly.

This is what it is and I can't change it, she told herself.

"I don't really feel like I have a decision to make," she told her doctors. "To me, the decision seems very clear."

Heather Abbott decided to go with the doctors' recommendations and have her injured lower leg removed. A surgery was scheduled for that Monday—exactly one week after the bombings. She didn't watch any news reports on the attacks and didn't go to any of the hospital's support groups set up for victims and survivors. Being a single, independent woman, she decided to handle the situation the way she handles everything in her life: on her own.

"She's my hero," her father told the Associated Press. "She's stronger than I am. I'm constantly having meltdowns, and she knows what has to be done, and she's right there with it."

MIT Police Officer Sean Collier was back on normal duty on Wednesday night. He was on foot patrol on campus, and despite the tension gripping the city—he was bored. Nothing was happening on campus, and students were staying inside or close to home. Sean's mother called his cell phone and they spoke briefly. She never mentioned the bombing, as she figured the culprits were long gone by now. They chatted briefly about their day, and Sean told her that he had to get back to work.

"Be careful and I love you."

"Back at you," Sean replied.

At 5:04 p.m. on Wednesday, Khairullozhon Matanov, the Quincy cabbie who had befriended the Tsarnaev brothers, tried to reach Dzhokhar on his cell phone. There was no answer. Next, he called Tamerlan but did not connect. He made several more calls to the brothers before finally getting Tamerlan on the line. The two agreed to meet at Tsarnaev's apartment in Cambridge later that night.

16

THE FLAME IS KINDLED

Air Force One touched down at Logan Airport early Thursday morning. Governor Patrick and his wife, Diane, met President Obama and the First Lady on the tarmac. The two old friends shook hands and embraced.

"You know, I've done too many of these," President Obama said somberly.

Patrick and his wife rode with the first couple from the airport to the Cathedral of the Holy Cross, where they were both scheduled to speak at the interfaith healing service.

"We were just in Newtown, and now this," Michelle Obama observed as she stared out the window of the presidential motorcade.

The governor had been pushing for a healing service. Someone had suggested Trinity Church in Copley Square, but that remained essentially a crime scene and was too close of a reminder of what had happened. Instead, Patrick and others chose the Cathedral of the Holy Cross on nearby Washington Street. Begun in 1866 and dedicated in 1975, the Cathedral was built in classic Gothic Revival style and towers 120 feet high. It has always been a place for healing. During his first visit to the United States in 1979, Pope John Paul II used the cathedral for a prayer service with two thousand priests. More than a decade earlier, in early 1964—just months after the assassination of President John F. Kennedy—Richard Cardinal Cushing celebrated a requiem in the late leader's honor that was broadcast nationwide. Today's service would also be seen across the United States—and across the globe.

The governor, like Commissioner Davis and others, was exhausted. He had barely slept since Monday, and his adrenalin was finally getting low. He had taken a few catnaps on the couch in his office, but they were always interrupted by news about the investigation or about the victims. He thought about what New York City mayor Rudy Giuliani had endured in the days following 9/11. Giuliani had pushed through his fatigue in order to provide leadership for his people, and Patrick would do the same. He met with first responders, with survivors, and with families of the victims, including the Richard family.

A well-known Democratic activist, Bill Richard, along with his wife, had worked on Patrick's 2005 campaign. "We have a photo on our mantle of Martin, at two years old, holding a Deval Patrick sign," Denise Richard told Patrick during his visit to the hospital. Tears welled up in the governor's eyes. They welled up again when he paid a short visit to Jane Richard's hospital room and saw the little girl covered by bandages and tubes.

"Out of all the politicians who visited, Deval Patrick made the biggest impact on Bill and Denise," Larry Marchese recalls. "He was so human, and he just connected with them as others could not."

The governor had to split his attention and efforts between providing emotional support to millions of Massachusetts residents, and tracking down those responsible. *The killers are still out there*, he reminded himself.

How do you strike a balance between comfort and getting to the other side? he asked himself time and again.

Patrick received phone calls from his predecessors, former governors Mitt Romney and Bill Weld, both Republicans. Romney and Weld offered their counsel and assistance. The former governors had weathered their share of crises as the state's chief executive, but neither could fully grasp what Deval Patrick was facing now.

Security was airtight along the perimeter surrounding the Cathedral of the Holy Cross. Members of the US Secret Service joined other federal agents, state troopers, and Boston police in a sweep of the area. Marathon survivors and families of the victims were invited to attend, as were first responders and public officials. The service was also open to the public on a first-come, first-served basis. All had to pass through steely-eyed security screeners who were on the lookout for bags, sharp objects, or liquids that could pose a threat.

President Obama entered the cathedral hand in hand with the first lady.

They were followed by Governor Patrick and his wife, Diane, under a rousing chorus of "Amazing Grace." After everyone was seated, Reverend Liz Walker, an iconic former Boston TV news anchor turned minister, stood tall at the podium and pondered two questions.

"How can a good God allow bad things to happen? Where was God when evil slithered in and planted the bombs that exploded our innocence?"

Walker told those gathered inside the cathedral and those watching from across the country on live television that God is "here in this sanctuary and beyond." She called Boston a "city that has always faced the darkness head on."

Walker was right. Boston is a city that has successfully repelled invaders for centuries. The fighting spirit is ingrained in its people. Testimonials of this fighting spirit stand like sentinels across the city, from the towering monument at Dorchester Heights where 1,200 of our forefathers watched the mighty Royal Navy sail away in 1776 after an unsuccessful siege on Boston, to the inspiring memorial on Boston Common to the 54th Massachusetts *Glory* Regiment that stood tall during the Battle of Boykin's Mill in the Civil War. Studying the crowd, Reverend Walker could see that the fighting spirit of those brave men had been passed down to the citizens of Boston today.

That spirit was about to be exemplified by the actions of the city's longest-serving mayor. Tom Menino had been escorted into the cathedral in his wheelchair. On this day, like all others, he had refused to take any pain medication.

"Please stay in your wheelchair," his handlers had urged him.

But the mayor had made up his mind long before that. He had visited with many of the survivors and families of victims in the preceding days. Menino was moved and inspired by their collective resilience. The victims were his neighbors, his friends.

"Papa, I know that little boy," Menino's granddaughter had told him about Martin Richard.

"These people had so much courage," Menino recalls. "When it came time to deliver my remarks, how could I not stand?"

The mayor was wheeled to the podium. The congregation remained silent. Menino then lifted himself up and stood, to the amazement of the crowd.

"We are one Boston. No adversity, no challenge, nothing can tear down this city and the resilience and the heart of this city and its people," Menino said, his voice breaking. "We love the fathers and the brothers who took shirts off their backs to stop the bleeding, the mothers and the sisters who cared for the injured."

The mayor praised police and firefighters, doctors and nurses, business owners and ordinary Bostonians who — to his mind — had all performed miracles, working tirelessly for those in need. "This was the strength of our city at work . . . nothing can defeat the heart of the city, nothing can take us down."

Governor Patrick, an accomplished orator whose eloquence rivals President Obama, was equally inspiring.

"How very strange that the cowardice unleashed on us should come on Marathon day, on Patriots' Day, a day that marks both the unofficial end of our long winter hibernation and the first battle of the American Revolution," he said. "Massachusetts invented America. . . . An attack on a civic ritual like the Marathon, especially on Patriots' Day, is an attack on those values. And just as we cannot permit darkness and hate to triumph over our spiritual faith, so we must not permit darkness and hate to triumph over our civic faith. That cannot happen. And it will not.

"We will recover and repair. We will grieve our losses and heal. We will rise, and we will endure," he said.

Patrick introduced his longtime friend Obama. The two men shook hands and embraced in the pulpit. Both wore solemn — almost defiant — looks upon their faces.

"Boston is the perfect state of grace," the president said, citing a poem written long ago by E. B. White, ". . . and so we come together today to reclaim that state of grace, to reaffirm that the spirit of this city is undaunted and that the spirit of this country shall remain undimmed."

Boston Police officer and first responder Javier Pagan sat directly behind First Lady Michelle Obama during the service. The cathedral is just across the street from the District 4 police station on Harrison Avenue where he works every day. He, too, had barely slept since Monday. On Tuesday, he was back up and out of the house early and was assigned to a traffic post at the corner of Massachusetts Avenue and Albany Street at 6 a.m. Later that day, he and other cops were ordered to meet with a department stress unit that included New York City police officers who had worked on 9/11.

Javier knew he was traumatized by what he had seen and also that he wasn't one of those cops or firefighters to keep it all bottled up inside. He went in and talked privately with a therapist.

She told him, "There's people that are going to accept that this happened and it's tragic and it gets filed away in the back of their head and they function. There are some people who can still function but are going to constantly be reminded. And there are some people who can't function and they're going to commit suicide or leave the job."

Javier wasn't sure which category he fit into, but was pretty sure it wasn't the third one. At least that's what he hoped.

The picture from *Sports Illustrated* showing Pagan in action went viral. Soon, he was getting all sorts of calls from media across the globe. CNN anchor Anderson Cooper tracked down one of Javier's sisters.

"It was such a shock to me. I just go to work and do my job. I don't do this to get accolades," he said. "I get paid to do a job and I do it. If I get credit for it, that's fine. If I don't, I don't. That's fine."

There was also some subtle resentment behind the scenes from cops who maybe did more at the scene than Javier or perhaps had a larger role in the investigation. Javier became news because he was in the *Sports Illustrated* picture, and also because he was gay.

Javier brushed aside the backbiting. "Policing is very cliquey, " he says. "But I'm not in high school. I had friends when I got this job."

Javier Pagan drew strength from the interfaith service, from the words by Mayor Menino, Governor Patrick, President Obama, and others—and he was also struck by how good the First Lady's hair looked. He raves to his friends about it to this day. As he left the church, regular folks walked up to him, shook his hand, patted him on the back, and thanked him.

Following the service, President Obama met with race volunteers at nearby Cathedral High School and praised them for their selflessness. He then visited with bombing victims and caregivers at Mass General Hospital, while Michelle Obama met with patients at Children's Hospital and

Brigham and Women's. During his visit to Mass General, the president met with Mery Daniel. Mery remembers shaking hands with the commander in chief—but not much else, as the pain medication was wearing heavy on her that day.

The president and the governor also visited Krystle Campbell's friend Karen Rand in the hospital. Months before the bombings, Deval Patrick had lunch at the Summer Shack and had met Karen then. The governor didn't recall the meeting but was reminded of it during the visit.

When Patrick and Obama entered her room, Rand was groggy from medication and surgery, but her boyfriend, Kevin McWatters, recounted to Patrick the tale of their Summer Shack meeting. They took pictures, and Rand told Patrick and Obama that she would be in Chicago in June.

Two months later, Patrick returned to Chicago—his hometown—for a ceremony re-naming a street in his honor in his old South Side neighborhood. Patrick stood that day at the building where he grew up, surrounded by press taking pictures as the street sign was unveiled. As he walked from the site, a couple approached him.

It was Karen Rand and Kevin McWatters. The two were in town on vacation, and Karen had thrown out the first pitch at a White Sox game with President Obama. The couple had read in the local paper that Patrick would be in Chicago that same weekend, so they made the time to go to the event to say hello to the governor again.

"It was a very touching occasion," Patrick said. "It was incredibly moving to me. . . . The whole thing has been so intimate. I can't think of another, a better word to describe how connected people either were or became."

After the White Sox game, Rand told ESPN Chicago that she was most excited to meet Coco Crisp, a member of the 2007 Red Sox World Series team. She also hailed Obama for following through on a promise he had made to her in her hospital room to meet up with her when she was in Chicago.

"I just happened to be one of the people that [the president] came to see [in the hospital]," Rand said. "He was great. He came in our room like he was an old neighbor and an old friend and really talked to everybody in the room and was really compassionate about the terrible thing that happened. We mentioned we were coming to Chicago, and he said, 'When you are out there, we want to make sure you have a really nice trip.' So that's how it happened. They followed through, and here we are."

After meeting with Mery, Karen, and others, President Obama and Governor Patrick had lunch with Mayor Menino in the basement cafeteria, where they dined on sandwiches.

Heather Abbott got a surprise visit from the First Lady at the Brigham. As Heather lay in her bed, surrounded by friends, Michelle Obama popped her head into her room.

"You are so brave," she told Heather.

"Thank you," Heather replied.

Michelle Obama then handed her a presidential challenge coin, which are traditionally given to wounded soldiers. After the deadly massacre at Fort Hood in 2009, President Obama had placed challenge coins on the memorials of the soldiers killed during the shooting rampage.

There were no TV cameras. The Obamas specifically requested that the visits be personal and not staged PR appearances. Many of the survivors did snap their own pictures of the visits and posted them on their Facebook walls.

At this same time, the investigation was about to get a jolt. The FBI had finally agreed to release the photos of Black Hat and White Hat. In late afternoon, the Bureau announced on its website that it would hold a news conference at 5 p.m.

"Our collective law enforcement team has pursued thousands of leads and tips," DesLauriers announced at the briefing. The agent said that on Wednesday, they had developed a single person of interest. During further investigation, a second suspect was also identified. The Feds then posted two charts side by side with four photos each of the suspects.

"They appear to be associated. Suspect One is wearing a dark hat. Suspect Two is wearing a white hat," DesLauriers pointed out. "Suspect Two set down a backpack at the site of the second explosion just in front of the Forum restaurant."

He urged patrons who had been at Forum to contact the FBI if they had not done so already.

He also urged the media and the public to share and further publicize the photographs and video of the suspects found on the FBI website. DesLauriers stressed that the eight images being presented were the only ones that the public should deem credible. The FBI did not want a repeat of the *New York Post* fiasco.

Sean Collier was one of millions of people to post the FBI images on his Facebook page immediately following the FBI briefing. He was back on his 3–11 shift and expected another slow evening. He had become friends with a young woman who also worked at MIT. She worked at a campus bar called The Thirsty Ear, dubbed "the Institution of the Institute," over on Albany Street. Collier texted her at around 10:30 p.m.

"Are you working tonight? I think I might come by after my shift."

17

TRAITORS

Dzhokhar Tsarnaev returned to UMass-Dartmouth just a few minutes after 4 p.m. on Thursday. The cloak of anonymity would shield him for another hour before the FBI released clear photos of him and his brother to the world. The FBI still did not have his name. He was only known as Suspect Two or White Hat, but anyone who knew him well would be able to identify him from the pictures.

After the televised FBI news briefing, the campus was buzzing with students who chatted among themselves about how their friend and classmate looked like one of the bomb suspects. Even then, the talk was mostly in jest as no one could imagine that a sleepy-eyed stoner like Dzhokhar could be responsible for the first successful terrorist attack on American soil since 9/11. They wanted to talk to Dzhokhar, but at that point—he was gone.

A girl who followed his Twitter account tweeted him a photo of White Hat with the message: "lol, Is this you? I didn't know you went to the marathon!!!"

Tsarnaev never responded to the tweet. Instead, he drove his green Honda Civic back to Cambridge where his brother, Tamerlan, was waiting. The noose was now tightening around their necks as people everywhere, from schoolchildren to grandparents, pushed their faces out on Twitter, Instagram, and Facebook. The pictures of the bomb suspects were shared and re-shared.

"Somebody out there knows these individuals as friends, neighbors, co-workers, or family members of the suspects," DesLauriers had told the nation in a 5 p.m. press conference. "Though it may be difficult, the nation is counting on those with information to come forward."

He called them "extremely dangerous."

"No one should approach them," he said. "No one should attempt to apprehend them except law enforcement."

Sean Collier was sitting in his police cruiser parked at Main and Vassar streets, near Kendall Square in Cambridge. It was a popular cut-through for drivers looking to avoid a red light. Collier was on the watch for anyone taking an illegal turn through campus, but he was also on high alert, like every cop in the region, because of the at-large terrorists.

His boss, MIT Police Chief John DiFava, pulled up next to Collier around 9:30 p.m. DiFava was the state police colonel from 1999 to 2001 and was put in charge of security at Logan International Airport in the immediate aftermath of the September 11, 2001, attacks.

He was known as a cop's cop: he chased Irish mob boss James "Whitey" Bulger, headed the state police underwater recovery team for years, and was acknowledged as one of the best field tacticians of his era. He liked eager, honest young cops like Sean Collier.

"What're you up to?" DiFava asked.

"Just trying to make sure everyone behaves," Collier smiled.

After a brief chat, DiFava drove away.

The eyes of the world were now on Dzhokhar and Tamerlan Tsarnaev. The brothers had to get out of Cambridge, out of Massachusetts. America's most wanted men decided to drive to Times Square in New York City for one final bloody crescendo. Tamerlan knew that he'd never see his wife or infant daughter again and resigned his younger brother to the idea that both were on the cusp of martyrdom—paradise awaiting.

Their arsenal was low. They had five more pressure cooker bombs; a Ruger P95 9mm semiautomatic handgun, which is described as a rugged and reliable pistol; a BB gun; a hunting knife; and a machete. If they were bringing war to New York City, the Tsarnaevs would need more weapons.

The brothers drove through Cambridge and spotted Collier's squad car. The hooded men crept up from behind as the officer kept his attention on the intersection in front of him. One brother went to the driver's side of the vehicle while the other approached the passenger side. At that moment, Tamerlan opened the door and fired the Ruger at the unsuspecting officer—hitting him five times, including two bullets to the head.

Sean Collier was killed instantly. Dhzokhar then reached into the vehicle and tried desperately to free Collier's service weapon but failed because he did not know how to remove it from its holster. MIT had recently issued its officers new holsters equipped with three-way locks. Collier had told his family about it. The brothers struggled to steal the officer's gun but soon abandoned their efforts.

Calls flooded 911 dispatchers reporting the gunshots. There were early reports, which turned out to be wrong, that Collier's shooting may have been tied to the robbery of a nearby convenience store. It took roughly thirteen minutes for EMTs to reach Collier.

"That is confirmed, a gunshot wound. CPR in progress," one EMT radioed. Collier was rushed to Massachusetts General Hospital but was dead on arrival.

News of the shooting spread quickly. Cops across the Boston area heard the horrifying radio transmissions that one of their own had been executed.

"They just shot an MIT cop," a friend told Danny Keeler by phone.

"You're shitting me," Keeler responded.

While some questioned whether the attack was random, Danny Keeler sensed right away that somehow White Hat and Black Hat were involved. He grabbed his jacket and his gun and headed out the door for Cambridge.

Commissioner Davis got the call at his home shortly after 10:30 p.m.

"It's gotta be related to our guys," Davis said.

The commissioner was told that it appeared to be a simple armed robbery.

He didn't believe it. Davis began connecting the dots in his head as he, too, rushed out the door. He had his police badge but had forgotten to take his gun, which he'd placed in a safe at his home earlier that evening.

Brendan Lynch, Sean Collier's brother-in-law, arrived home in Dracut late that night after having a few beers with friends from work. His wife, Nicole—Sean's sister—was already in bed. Brendan sat in his living room working on his iPad with the television on in the background. The eleven o'clock news on WCVB Channel 5 opened with breaking news from Cambridge. There had been a shooting at MIT. He ran into the bedroom and awoke Nicole.

"It's Sean, it's Sean!" Nicole screamed, shooting upright in her bed.

"That's ridiculous, they didn't say anything about a police officer being involved," Brendan told his wife, trying to calm her nerves.

Still, Nicole could sense that something tragic had happened to her brother.

She called her sister, Jen, and together they debated whether to call their mother.

"We didn't want to worry her unnecessarily," Nicole says. "We tried to decide who should call Sean because we didn't want him to get mad at us like last time."

Jen began tracking the story on Twitter. She tried getting in touch with a friend who was an EMT to see if he had heard anything come over the scanner. Twitter updates came streaming in. "First, we learned it was a shooting," Nicole remembers. "Then it was a cop, and then it was an MIT cop."

Sean Collier's mother, Kelley Rogers, had just retired for the evening after doing a few hours of work at home. Her phone rang close to 11 p.m. It was DiFava.

"I'm sending some police officers to get you and bring you to Mass General," he told her.

The mother started screaming.

DiFava did not tell her that Sean had been shot. Instead, he informed her that her son had been seriously injured.

Kelley then called her daughter Jen with the news.

"You need to get John [Jen's husband], you need to get in your car and get to Mass General," she said in tears. "Sean has been hurt and I think it's going to be the last time you see him."

Both Jen and Nicole rushed from their homes to be with their brother. Nicole had to get a neighbor to watch her two children, who were sick at home with high fevers. As her husband drove, Nicole monitored the news on her smartphone. An update came across stating that the unidentified MIT police officer had been killed. Nicole called Jen with the news.

"Then I called the person who was watching my kids just to say, 'He was killed but I am still going in there,'" Nicole recalls. She continued to follow the news updates even when Brendan pleaded with her to put her phone away.

"Don't look at it," he told her. She didn't listen to him. She was glued to it.

They arrived at Mass General and were stopped by police on the street near the entrance.

"The MIT police officer is our brother," Brendan told the cop.

"Okay, just pull up as far as you can and just go in," the officer replied. "Don't worry about your vehicle."

There were more than a dozen armed police officers gathered outside the hospital. The family noticed the familiar markings of the MIT Police Department among that crowd.

When Jen arrived, she and her husband, John, were met by a police officer at the entrance. He began moving and motioned for the couple to follow.

"The officer was practically running through the hallways. My husband and I were struggling to keep up with him," Jen recalls. "I remember thinking, *This isn't good*. Then he just dropped me in this spot with all these people in the hallways, and I didn't know where to go."

A staffer pointed to a small room. "Your mother is in there," she said.

Jen walked in to find a distraught Kelley Rogers. "Jenny, he died."

Jen's husband tried to get a hold of Sean's younger brother, Andy, in North Carolina. At this time, the family was approached by Collier's partner, who had found the body slumped over in his squad car. The MIT cop broke down and wept.

Nicole finally connected with Andy on his cell phone.

"I picked up my phone and I said, 'What's going on?'" Andy said. He knew there was no way Nicole would be up that late, so he realized that something bad had happened—but not to Sean. "I immediately thought of my nieces and nephew."

"Andy, you need to come home," Nicole said.

"Wait, what's going on?"

"Sean's been shot. He's dead."

"No," Andy cried.

After learning about his brother's murder, Andy went to Sean's Facebook page and posted the following: "Sean I love you. You are a great brother and I never told you enough."

The family had to identify Sean Collier's body through photos. They were forced to see the bullet hole in the young man's forehead.

Investigators still had not mentioned anything to the family about Sean Collier's killers. As the sisters were saying their goodbyes to their loving brother, they heard rumblings in the hallway about police activity in Watertown.

Jen looked at Nicole. "How weird would it be if it was the marathon bombers?"

Roughly twenty-five minutes after firing the shots that killed Sean Collier, the Tsarnaev brothers were looking to steal something else—this time a car. They pulled Dhokhar's Green Honda Civic behind a late model Mercedes Benz ML 350 that was parked along a curb on Brighton Avenue. The driver, a twenty-six-year-old Chinese man, had stopped to answer a text when he heard a knock on his passenger side window. He lowered the window, and Tamerlan Tsarnaev stuck his long arm in, unlocked the door, and climbed inside.

"Don't be stupid," Tamerlan said, waving the Ruger that killed Officer Collier. "You know about the marathon bombings?"

The driver nodded yes.

"I did that," Tamerlan said matter-of-factly. "And I just killed a policeman in Cambridge."

He demanded money. The driver carried only forty-five dollars in cash, which Tamerlan begrudgingly took. He then ordered the driver to turn right onto Fordham Avenue, while Dhzokhar followed close behind in his Civic. The Mercedes traveled through Brighton, Watertown, and then back to Cambridge, where an army of police officers was now combing the streets for Sean Collier's killers.

In an exclusive interview with the *Boston Globe*, the driver—who was referred to only by the nickname Danny—spoke about the tense ninety minutes he was forced to chauffeur the most-wanted killer since Osama bin Laden around metro Boston.

"Death is so close to me," he told the *Globe*. "I don't want to die. I have a lot of dreams that haven't come true yet."[49]

Tamerlan ordered the driver to keep his eyes on the road. "Don't look at me!" he shouted. "Do you remember my face?"

The driver said no. His hands were clutching the wheel tightly in an effort to stop them from shaking. Tamerlan studied the driver, who was Asian—but was he Chinese American or something else? When the driver spoke, Tsarnaev had difficulty understanding him.

"OK, that's why your English is not very good. OK, you're Chinese. I'm a Muslim."

The driver smiled. He now saw a glimmer of hope to his desperate situation.

"Chinese are very friendly to Muslims," the driver announced. "We are so friendly to Muslims."

Tamerlan leafed through the driver's wallet and found his ATM card. He asked for the ATM code and got it. When they arrived in East Watertown, the driver was ordered to pull over onto Fairfield Street, a quiet side street. When he did, Dzhokhar parked behind him and got out. The brothers spoke briefly on the street and began transferring their arsenal from the Honda Civic to the Mercedes. Tamerlan ordered the driver to move over to the passenger side and got behind the wheel. Dzhokhar climbed into the back seat behind the Chinese man.

They stopped at a nearby Bank of America, where Dzhokhar retrieved some money with the driver's ATM card. The brothers spoke openly in their native language about going to New York City. The driver could only pick up the word *Manhattan* in the conversation. The Tsarnaevs then asked him if his car could be driven to New York City. As he drove, Tamerlan fidgeted with the radio, going from station to station but avoiding any news. They returned to Fairfield Street where, once again, the brothers retrieved some items from the Honda Civic. Tamerlan slipped an Islamic prayer CD into the Mercedes's stereo and then got back on the road. The driver got a text from his roommate and then a phone call.

"If you say a single word in Chinese, I'll kill you right now," Tamerlan warned.

"I'm sleeping in my friend's home tonight," the driver told his roommate. "I have to go."

Tamerlan nodded and smiled. "Good boy. Good job."

At this point, they needed gas. They spotted a Shell gas station at River Street and Memorial Drive in Cambridge. Dhzokhar tried to fill the tank using the driver's credit card. The credit card reader was down.

"Cash only," he told his older brother, who then gave him a fifty dollar bill. Dhzokhar walked inside the Shell mini-mart. The Mercedes driver had a decision to make: stay in the car and be killed like the MIT police officer and all those innocent souls at the Boston Marathon, or try to make a run for it. There was only one option and it was clear. With lightning speed, the driver unbuckled his seatbelt, opened the passenger door, and sprinted. The driver kept running and did not look back. He heard no shots fired, he felt no pain. He was free.

[18]

WAR IN WATERTOWN

Watertown Police Officer Joe Reynolds was on routine patrol around 12:40 a.m. when he got the call that a stolen Mercedes was headed his way—Cambridge police had called Watertown, notifying them that there had been a carjacking around midnight.

Police were tracking the vehicle through GPS, and it was on its way to Watertown.

It wasn't a highly unusual call for the Watertown night shift cops. The bedroom community borders Boston and is a safe town, but occasionally bad guys from Boston make their escapes through Watertown's leafy side streets, thrusting the local cops into action.

Reynolds spotted the stolen SUV, riding along closely to a green Honda Civic. He didn't know the accused marathon bombers were behind the wheels of both vehicles. He also didn't know the drivers were connected to Sean Collier's shooting. Joe Reynolds thought it was just another simple carjacking and that he might have to chase a couple of punks through some yards.

As he drove along Dexter Avenue, radio broadcasts called out the house numbers as the stolen SUV drove along the street.

"I see that car. Do you want me to stop it?" Reynolds radioed.

"Hold on, Joe. Let's get you some backup before you do it," Sergeant John MacLellan replied.

Reynolds was driving toward the SUV, coming from the opposite direction on Dexter Avenue. As he passed the vehicle, he focused solely on the stolen SUV and paid no attention to the Civic.

After the cop passed the vehicle, he made a U-turn and got behind the SUV. MacLellan was a few blocks away at a 7-Eleven convenience store on Auburn Street. He sped toward Dexter Avenue.

"Give me a minute to get closer, Joe," MacLellan radioed. He closed the gap.

"Okay, Joe. Now light 'em up," MacLellan said.

Reynolds flicked on his blues and tried to stop the SUV as it turned onto Laurel Street. The vehicle drove about three-quarters of the way down Laurel Street and stopped. Reynolds stayed in his car for a few moments, waiting for backup.

Suddenly, out of the darkness, Tamerlan Tsarnaev emerged from the SUV and started walking toward Reynolds's cruiser. He was shooting a gun.

Reynolds threw the cruiser in reverse and floored it, flying backwards toward Dexter Avenue and MacLellan.

MacLellan came around the corner on the left side of the road. Suddenly, thunder erupted in the night.

"Shots fired!" Reynolds shouted into the radio.

Reynolds was ducking as he drove furiously in reverse away from the crazed shooter. MacLellan came flying around the corner, just missing Reynolds's cruiser, and drove down the middle of the street toward Tamerlan Tsarnaev. A round came right through the center of MacLellan's windshield, and glass exploded into the interior of the car. He felt the sting of glass cutting his face. The bullet whizzed right past his head, singing the tiny hairs and skin on his ear. The bullet buried itself into the driver's seat headrest right behind him. MacLellan, a twenty-four-year veteran cop and father of one daughter, had no time to react. He continued down the street and stopped on the left side of the road and jumped out. Tamerlan kept firing as MacLellan took cover behind his cruiser. Bullets pinged off the vehicle while MacLellan tried to reach inside to grab the patrol rifle between the two seats. He was under heavy fire and was a sitting duck. The officer's training had never prepared him for this. This wasn't police work—this was combat.

He then made an unconventional, snap decision—he slammed the car into drive and let it roll down the street, hoping it would distract the shooter. MacLellan ran alongside the vehicle, maintaining his cover. It was trash day, so residents had their barrels out. The cruiser banged into barrels, knocking them over, as it rambled down the street.

MacLellan saw his chance and ducked out of the line of fire, sprinting into a driveway and taking refuge behind a tree. Reynolds ran over to the sergeant and joined him behind the tree, which felt like a giant sequoia to the two terrified cops—but in reality it was a thin oak barely big enough to provide cover for one person, never mind two.

As the vehicle continued to roll down the street, one of the Tsarnaev brothers lobbed a pipe bomb into the middle of the road. It exploded with a thunderous *boom* that blew out the windows of the stolen SUV.

"Sarge, we're too close!" Reynolds yelled.

The two cops ran around the side of a house as another bomb came roaring up the street. This one landed even closer to them.

"Oh shit, this is gonna hurt," MacLellan said, bracing himself for the worst. But the device was a dud.

They ran behind the house. Reynolds hopped a fence.

"Sarge! Come on! Jump!" he shouted.

MacLellan decided to stay in the yard and went back to the tree. He stood behind the tree, looking at the pipe bomb that didn't detonate. He thought about running over and grabbing it and tossing it back at the attackers, but he quickly changed his mind.

Maybe it's a triggered device and they'll detonate it as soon as I get close, he thought.

Just then, a third bomb tumbled down the street with a terrifying *tink, tink, tink!*

This one did go off, and it was even louder than the first. MacLellan felt the compressions. His eyeballs rattled, and he felt his brain bouncing off the insides of his skull. He put his hands up to his eyes to make them stop moving.

Just then, Officer Miguel Colon showed up on the scene with a spotlight and shone it down the street. It was immediately shot out. Colon quickly took cover with Reynolds.

"Sarge! Get back here! Take cover!" Colon yelled to MacLellan.

Radios roared with reports of shots fired and explosions in the street.

"They're throwing bombs at us!" MacLellan screamed into his walkie-talkie. "We've got them pinned down! We need help!"

Inside an apartment at 62 Laurel Street, twenty-three-year-old Andrew Kitzenberg heard the shootout and started taking pictures with his iPhone. He live-tweeted the mayhem unfolding right outside his window, starting with this post at 12:55 a.m.: "Shoot out outside my room in Watertown. 62 Laurel St."

Sergeant Jeff Pugliese, a thirty-four-year veteran of the department who had survived a heart attack a few years earlier, had wrapped up his shift at midnight and should have been fast asleep at home. But a report he had written earlier in his shift got deleted accidentally, so he stayed late to re-write it. He was on his way home in his family minivan when he heard the report of the carjacking on his scanner.

Pugliese figured it was a routine stolen vehicle but decided to swing by and help out, thinking the culprits would not recognize the van. On his way to the scene, he heard the mayhem erupt. A lifelong Watertown resident, he knew the neighborhood well, so he took a quick turn onto School Street to get a better position on the shooters. He was running through backyards toward Laurel Street when another pressure cooker bomb went off. This one was in the middle of the street and was louder than the others, which were pipe bombs. A plume of fire erupted from the bomb and lit up the street, briefly turning darkness into daylight. Pugliese had seen video of such a thing from news reports on the wars in Iraq and Afghanistan, but he never imagined that he would see something like this in his hometown.

The shrapnel packed into the bomb shot straight up into the air and rained down from the sky on top of the crouching cops. The bomb landed on its side, and the pavement blunted some of the shrapnel explosion. The device was just feet away from MacLellan.

Pugliese was still running when a resident came out his back door and darted across his own backyard. Pugliese didn't know if the guy was one of the terrorists, but he saw he didn't have a gun. The man hopped a fence and sprinted away. Pugliese called it in over the radio and continued running toward his cornered comrades.

He got closer and came to a spot where he had a clear view of the two brothers behind the SUV. Pugliese started firing. The Tsarnaevs were covered, so he tried to skip bullets off the pavement under the car to strike them. Officials believe Pugliese hit at least one of the brothers.

Tamerlan emerged from his cover and charged toward Pugliese like a mad bull. He had a gun in his hand, and Pugliese had little cover—he was standing at the side of a house with nothing but two cars parked in a driveway between him and the brothers.

They were about fifteen feet away from each other, and both fired repeatedly. Bullets screamed past Pugliese's head, embedding themselves into the house. Pugliese returned fire, striking Tamerlan as many as seven or eight times. But—incredibly—Tsarnaev didn't go down. Bullets were going right through the Chechen boxer, but he kept coming. Tamerlan was closing on Pugliese when he suddenly stopped. He had either run out of bullets or his gun jammed. He looked at Pugliese and threw the useless gun at the cop.

The wounded terrorist turned and ran down the driveway and up the middle of the street toward MacLellan. Pugliese gave chase. MacLellan didn't see a gun but feared Tamerlan had another bomb. MacLellan was out of bullets but aimed his gun at the terrorist anyway.

"Stop or I'll blow your fucking head off!" he screamed.

With all the chaos unfolding, he tried another trick: he pretended his gun was shooting, faking the recoil. Word spread quickly via police radios of the shootout and bomb-tossing going on in the normally quiet suburban neighborhood. Cops from Boston, Arlington, the MBTA, and the state police sped to the surreal scene and took up positions on the surrounding streets.

As MacLellan stood in the street fake-firing his gun, Pugliese bolted out of the shadows and tackled Tamerlan to the ground. The Chechen's hands were under his chest, but he wouldn't give up without a fight. MacLellan hopped on the pile and the pair struggled desperately to handcuff the suspected bomber.

Reynolds came running to help just as Dzhokhar Tsarnaev hopped into the stolen Mercedes SUV. The vehicle sped toward the mass of bodies brawling on the pavement. Reynolds and MacLellan leaped out of the way but Pugliese continued to struggle with Tamerlan until the last second.

Pugliese rolled off just as the SUV sped toward him and struck Tamerlan, pinning him underneath the carriage and dragging him several yards. Reynolds and MacLellan thought Pugliese was under the vehicle, too.

The SUV went flying up the street and smashed into a cruiser, dislodging Tamerlan's battered body. Pugliese looked at the other two cops, and all three breathed an exasperated sigh of relief, their hearts still pounding.

Pugliese looked down at Tamerlan, who was still alive. The officer left nothing to chance. He pounced on Tamerlan again, and despite heavy wounds, the brother continued to fight back.

The cops then heard a radio transmission of "officer down."

It was Sean Collier's police academy friend, thirty-three-year-old Richard "Dic" Donohue, a cop now with the Massachusetts Bay Transit Authority.

One of dozens of officers who had arrived on the scene as backup, Donohue was struck in the leg by one of the three hundred bullets sprayed around the neighborhood during the shootout. It's widely accepted that Donohue was the victim of friendly fire. The bullet severed Donohue's femoral artery, and he appeared to be bleeding out. Two Harvard University cops and a Boston police officer were doing CPR. One of them tied tourniquets around Donohue's leg to stem the gushing blood.

Watertown firefighters Pat Menton and Jimmy Caruso rushed to the Dexter Street scene with an ambulance. Donohue looked bad. He was ghastly white and was drifting in and out of consciousness.

The cops and firefighters loaded him into the ambulance. Menton worked on Donohue's breathing while Caruso applied pressure, trying desperately to stem the blood loss.

"We need a driver!" Menton yelled.

Menton's brother, a Watertown cop named Tim, had been in the firefight. Now he leaped into the driver's seat and sped toward Mount Auburn Hospital. A state trooper rode in the back with the two firefighters, and all three worked to save the young cop's life.

Back on Laurel Street, Tamerlan lay cuffed and dying on the pavement. EMTs arrived and loaded him into an ambulance. Tamerlan spit at one of the EMTs. He looked another one in the eyes. The EMT described it as the most chilling look he had ever seen.

Meanwhile, Dzhokhar had sped from the scene. He dumped the SUV on Spruce Street, which is actually a continuation of Laurel Street. Cops surrounded the SUV but kept at a safe distance, not knowing if he was inside or if the vehicle was booby-trapped with bombs.

Watertown Police Chief Ed Deveau had spent Thursday night winding down at the Charles River Country Club after another long day. Several of his officers were deployed throughout Boston, backing up Boston police, helping patrol the city, and beefing up security for President Obama's visit that day.

Throughout the day Deveau, a lifelong Watertown resident and former high school basketball star, had been monitoring the manhunt through news reports and was aware that the FBI had released pictures of the two bombing suspects. He attended a board meeting at the country club and had dinner and a drink with a couple of friends before going home and hitting the sack around midnight. He was unaware when he went to bed that Sean Collier had been killed in nearby Cambridge.

He wasn't asleep for more than a few minutes when his cell phone buzzed on the nightstand next to his bed. It was Watertown Police Lieutenant Jamie O'Connor, who was the shift commander that night. Deveau knew immediately it was bad news. It was never good news when the officer in charge called you that late at night.

"Oh shit," the chief muttered.

"Chief, they're shooting at us and throwing bombs at us and I think it's related to the MIT officer being killed!" a panicked O'Connor shouted into the phone. The chief could hear loud radio traffic in the background, and then he heard an explosion.

"What the *fuck*?" Deveau shouted. "I'm on my way!"

He got dressed quickly, ran out of the house, and sped toward the terrifying scene that was still unfolding at the corner of Dexter and Laurel streets. He realized on the way that, like Ed Davis, he had left his sidearm behind, but he did have a gun in the trunk of his cruiser.

Deveau gripped the steering wheel tightly as he listened to the chaotic radio broadcasts from his men. When he arrived, uniformed cops from several departments were running around with guns drawn. Smoke filled the air. Deveau was in plain clothes and just wanted to find his guys to make sure none were hurt.

He started to pick up bits of information. The Boston Marathon bombers had struck again. This time though, one was dead—the older one—while the younger one was on the run. The furious battle had involved three pipe bombs, two pressure cooker bombs, and hundreds of rounds fired. One cop was shot and was en route to the hospital. Three cruisers were totaled in the battle, and several homes were riddled with bullet holes. War had been waged right in the middle of a residential neighborhood, but—somehow—no civilians had gotten injured.

One of the first officers Deveau spoke to was MacLellan. The cop was exhausted—and a little bit nervous.

"So Chief, I violated policy," MacLellan told him as they stood at the intersection of Dexter and Laurel.

"What are you talking about?" the chief said.

"I couldn't get away from the SUV and the bullets kept bouncing off the cruiser, so I rolled the car down the street and it smashed into something and there is a lot of damage," MacLellan said. Instead of focusing on the fact that he had survived, MacLellan was worried about destroying a department vehicle.

The chief looked him square in the eyes.

"John, are you kidding me? You're fucking alive. I just want to hug you," Deveau said.

The two men embraced.

When Commissioner Davis and Danny Keeler arrived at Laurel Street moments later, the acrid stench of gunpowder hung in the air. Davis surveyed the scene. He spotted hand grenades on the ground, surrounded by a litter of spent shell casings. The Watertown cops were walking around like zombies, dazed and confused, most with hearing loss from explosions that had blasted their eardrums. Watertown Police Officer Dennis "D. J." Simmonds, who also exchanged gunfire with the suspects that night, would continue to struggle with mental and physical injuries for the next year. Simmonds died days before the first anniversary of the marathon bombings from what officials described as a "medical emergency on the job." He was only twenty-eight years old.

"I'm sorry we let him [Dzhokhar Tsarnaev] get away," another one of the cops told Davis the night of the shootout. The commissioner told the officer not to worry. *These men have gone through hell*, Davis thought to himself. *They've just experienced mortal combat, something most cops will never see in the course of their careers.*

As Davis walked over to Chief Deveau, his friend of twenty years, he could hear the crunch of debris under his shoes. Normally, preserving the crime scene would be his top priority, but not on this night. *We gotta get this guy,* Davis thought. *I don't give a shit about evidence right now, we just gotta get this guy.*

The commissioner also needed a gun. Rushing out of his house, he had forgotten to retrieve his service weapon from his safe. An officer handed Davis a weapon, and he spent the next few minutes discussing the situation with Deveau.

Davis then turned his attention to Keeler.

"Watertown knows the terrain, but we have the resources."

They both focused their eyes on the stolen Mercedes SUV, still sitting on Spruce Street where the younger Tsarnaev had abandoned it.

"The car was shot to hell from both sides," Keeler recalls. "It got the shit shot out of it. How he ever made it out of the car is beyond me."

The Watertown cops told them that Suspect Two jumped out of the vehicle and fled to the left through a backyard.

"Take that car and draw a twenty-block perimeter around it," Davis ordered.

Keeler got his men organized. "If you have a vest, you're in. If you don't have a vest, you're out. Two guys into each yard, and remember to announce yourself going in. Don't move to the next yard until this yard is clear. Check the houses, check the occupants and get them up and be comfortable that they're not being held by someone inside their home." Keeler thought back to the FBI's decision against releasing photos of the suspects the day before. *Maybe, just maybe, this bloodstained night could have been prevented,* he said to himself. But he couldn't dwell on anybody's past mistakes right now. At this moment, he needed to help capture, cage, or kill Suspect Two.

The manhunt got off to a rocky start, however. Believing that the FBI's tracking dog had identified the scent of the suspect, armed officers followed the canine through several backyards—until the dog's handler realized that it had been chasing after a squirrel.

THE LOCKDOWN

Dic Donohue was clinging to life when he was rushed into Mount Auburn Hospital. Doctors would later say that he had barely a drop of blood left in him when he arrived. He had gone into cardiac arrest during the ambulance ride. As Tim Menton drove, his brother, Pat, and Watertown firefighter Jimmy Caruso did their best to apply pressure to Donohue's gushing wound. Blood covered their hands and arms, and both men feared that Donohue would be DOA. When they reached Mount Auburn, doctors worked for forty-five long minutes to revive him. Once they got his heart beating again, they whisked him into surgery.

A short time later Donohue's wife, Kimberly, arrived at the hospital, where doctors and a priest were waiting to greet her. She had not heard from her husband since midnight, when he had texted the following: "Phone dying, gonna be late." Kimberly read the text and went back to sleep. She was awakened at around 1:30 a.m. by their seven-month-old baby, Richie, who was wailing in his crib. As she attended the infant, the doorbell rang. It was the police.

"You are my worst nightmare," she told him. "If Dic is dead, you'd better tell me right now. Don't walk in this house. Don't come past the door. Tell me if Dic is dead."[50]

When she got to the hospital, Kimberly was shocked to learn that doctors had just gotten Dic's pulse back. They gave Kimberly her husband's wedding ring, his police badge, and his cell phone. His life would hang in the balance for the next eight hours as surgeons worked to repair the three-quarter-inch wound near the top of his right thigh.

As she sat in the hospital waiting room, Kimberly thought of their son, Richie. Would he grow up without a father? Would he know his dad only through a collection of medals and citations and some pictures on the wall? Dic Donohue had embraced life during his thirty-three years. He'd been a track star at Winchester, Massachusetts, High School and had graduated from the Virginia Military Institute in 2002 before becoming an officer in the US Navy. He'd served in the military, but he never saw combat until he returned home. VMI's motto is "In Peace, a Glorious Asset, In War, a Tower of Strength." The city of Boston was now at war, and Kimberly Donohue prayed that her husband's name would not be added to the growing list of those killed by the Boston Marathon bombers.

After Dic's surgery, Kimberly was allowed into the recovery room, where she saw tubes coming out of his chest, mouth, and nose. She turned to his doctors.

"We have a seven-month-old baby," she said, her voice shaking. "He has to come through. It's not a question. You cannot come back in this room and tell me anything else. That's the only answer I want."

Sean Collier's sister was seeking answers of her own. How was she going to break the news to her young daughters that their beloved uncle was dead?

"When we got home and they had come into my room, I told them that Uncle Sean had died at work, and still to this day that is pretty much all that they know," Nicole says. "Each comes out with different stories as to how maybe Sean has died. My middle one actually told me the other day that she had figured it all out — she knows exactly how Sean died. He climbed a ladder at our house up onto our roof and fell off, and that is her story."

Sean's brother, Andy, was also struggling to come to grips with what had happened. His family had booked him a flight from North Carolina to Boston, but the plane was not scheduled to take off until 7 a.m. Andy sat alone with his thoughts and took a Xanax to calm his nerves. Sleep was impossible, so he turned on the television to watch continuing coverage of the drama unfolding back home.

"The first thing I saw was a picture of this one guy [Tamerlan] lying face down on the ground," he recalls. "And I just broke down again."

Governor Patrick had been woken up at midnight by a call from MEMA director Kurt Schwartz, who had been monitoring the action in Watertown on both his state police and Boston police radios. He had heard the shootout start. He heard officers screaming about bombs. He immediately called the governor. Patrick did not answer his cell phone, but Schwartz was able to reach him on a landline.

"Governor, I'm trying to piece this together. It sounds to me as though the terrorists are in a shootout with police right now. It sounds to me as though there's at least one cop dead and that a second cop has been shot. It doesn't sound good. I'm on my way to Watertown right now."

"I need updates from you every hour," the governor told him. "You keep me informed."

Schwartz sped from his home in Concord with blue lights flashing.

With one suspect still on the loose, the state's Executive Protection Unit was put on alert, and security was tightened around the governor's home in Milton. The one piece of positive information was the fact that police had told Schwartz that Black Hat was down.

Tamerlan Tsarnaev was rushed to Beth Israel Hospital, where Denise Richard and other victims were still recovering from their wounds. He was barely breathing, but he was shackled with handcuffs and surrounded by an army of police officers. According to his autopsy report, Tamerlan suffered "gunshot wounds of the torso and extremities" as well as "blunt trauma to [his] head and torso."[51]

Many of his injuries had been inflicted by his younger brother when Dzhokhar hit him with the stolen SUV. Surgeons made an attempt to save his life by inserting a breathing tube into his mouth. Those efforts were futile. Suspect One fell into cardiac arrest and was pronounced dead at 1:35 a.m. He spoke his final words as he was being loaded into an ambulance from the Watertown scene. He peered deep into a cop's eyes and sneered, "Rot in hell."

Back in Watertown, Commissioner Davis, the state police, and the FBI had set up a command post at the Arsenal Mall, less than a mile from Laurel and Dexter streets. Davis was dead tired, but his mind was still racing. Where was Suspect Two? Was he headed for New York City as the carjacking victim had suggested to police? Had a terrorist cell been activated?

The commissioner consulted with Governor Patrick, Kurt Schwartz, and State Police Colonel Tim Alben.

"How far could he [Dzhokhar] have gone?" Patrick asked.

They studied a map of the area and all the possible escape routes. They could not fully engage in a house-to-house search in the dark, so they had to hold the perimeter until first light. Then they would be able to set up a grid search pattern and bring in enough police to walk the twenty-block grid.

Alben, Davis, Deveau, and other officials held a press conference at 1 a.m., confirming Collier's death at the hands of the alleged marathon bombers. They also provided details of the Cambridge carjacking and Watertown shootout.

A stone-faced Alben stood before a crush of local and national media and issued the lockdown order for Watertown.

"The most important message we are doing right now . . . is we are asking people to shelter in place for the time being and not to leave their homes," Alben said, photographers' shutters clicking in the night air. "If they see something suspicious . . . they should call 911 immediately. To motorists: they should not stop for anyone or pick up anyone on the side of the roadway."

Then, he issued this warning about Suspect Two: "He should be considered armed and dangerous. . . . Please, use extreme caution and stay inside your homes."

He also said there were teams of explosives experts at the site inspecting devices found in the streets.

"Some detonated and some did not," he said.

"We're trying to protect the safety of people living there," Davis added. "There's a twenty-block perimeter."

But by that time, the bombing suspect could have been anywhere. Members of the bomb squad reported that they believed they had recovered a triggering device from a suicide vest. At that point, police had to assume that Suspect Two could still have been carrying a backpack filled with explosives and perhaps a gun.

MBTA Police Chief Paul MacMillan spoke up. The time was now 4:30 a.m.

"Guys, at about five o'clock, trains and buses are gonna start going live," MacMillan said. "What are we gonna do about Watertown?"

There was no way law enforcement would let buses roll through Watertown. They could not let Suspect Two flee by bus.

"Well, what about the Harvard Square [MBTA] station?" someone asked. "Can he get to Cambridge and the T and blow that up?"

"How confident are you that you've got this guy contained in the twenty blocks?" Schwartz asked the police commanders.

"At best, fifty-fifty," he was told.

The answer wasn't what Schwartz wanted to hear.

"What are we gonna tell the public?" Schwartz asked. "Folks are just getting up and heading out the door for work."

MacMillan told the group it would be impossible to partially shut down the transit system at that point.

"I can't close one station and one line in thirty minutes," MacMillan said. "I would need a couple of hours to do that."

What MacMillan could do was shut the entire system down. "It's all or nothing," he said.

Schwartz could not make the call to shut down the transit system on his own. He coordinated a conference call with Governor Patrick, Commissioner Davis, Mayor Menino, and others.

"Here's our recommendation," Schwartz said. "We shut down the entire T system right away. We also want to ask people in Watertown and communities that border Watertown to shelter in place. He [Suspect Two] may be wounded, but we don't know how far he's gonna go."

Law enforcement officials agreed on the plan, but the politicians were unsure. Mayor Menino was originally against the idea. He was worried what kind of message it would send to the public. Schwartz reiterated the notion that there was only a fifty percent chance that cops had the suspect cornered within that twenty-block grid in Watertown. He also stressed that the fugitive could be carrying more bombs. Adding to the nightmarish worst-case scenario was information coming in that a terrorist cell had indeed been activated and that another bomber had traveled by cab to South Station while an accomplice was en route from New York. That piece of information later proved to be false, but the uncertainty of the situation was not only terrifying—it was also something no one in the room had ever dealt with before.

Menino would not allow any more blood to be spilled on his streets. He agreed to the plan, as did the governor. Menino also asked that the shelter-in-place order be expanded to include all of Boston. When people woke up that day to go to work, they were informed by TV, radio, text, email, and reverse 911 calls to their homes that the city of Boston was effectively shut down and that no one should drive in to work. An entire American city was completely locked down for the first time in our nation's history.

The sound of car horns blaring; the sight of waves of people pouring out of MBTA stations talking incessantly on their cell phones during the walk to work. It's a normal routine for a city like Boston, but on this day—there was none of it. The streets were deserted. The city was silent, save for the roar of a police cruiser or armored vehicle responding to one perceived threat or another. Every major corner and every major attraction in Boston was guarded by armed soldiers and cops, all of them on the lookout for Dz-hokhar Tsarnaev—America's most-wanted man. Locations symbolic of Boston and the birth of our nation garnered special attention from law en-forcement, which covered much of the city in a protective blanket. Faneuil Hall, where Samuel Adams called for the removal of British troops after the Boston Massacre, was now defended by a new generation of American patriots drawn from communities across the Commonwealth and dressed in Kevlar and armed with M16s. The state house and South Station were also fortified. There was quiet in the historic North End, South Boston, and Roxbury districts, where residents young and old remained housebound and glued to their television sets and computer screens. Indeed, the whole world was watching their beloved city and offering voices of support. New Hampshire native and Hollywood star Adam Sandler summed up what many were feeling that morning when he tweeted: "Boston is probably the only major city that if you fuck with them, they will shut down the whole city, stop everything and find you."

The collective mood of the city's neighborhoods had shifted from fear and uncertainty to one of overwhelming resolve. *You are trapped; we will not let you get away.*

In neighboring Watertown, where the search for Dzhokhar Tsarnaev was centered, Police Chief Ed Deveau marveled at the number of law enforcement teams and media crews that had descended on his quiet community. The only other time on Deveau's watch that the town had found itself at the center of international news was in 2010, when a Watertown man named Aftab Ali Khan was arrested following the failed Times Square bombing in New York City. Khan, who had only lived in the town for a short time, was accused of sending $4,900 to Faisal Shahzad, a jihadist convicted of the botched bombing plot. Khan was deported to Pakistan in May 2011.

This time, the terrorism had come to Deveau's front door—literally. He lives just a short ride away from Dexter and Laurel streets. Deveau knew Boston's top cop from Davis's days in Lowell. Both Lowell and Watertown are part of the North Eastern Metropolitan Law Enforcement Council (NEMLEC), a consortium of fifty-eight police departments that combine resources for emergencies. NEMLEC's SWAT team was activated, and several officers from the unit were already patrolling the neighborhoods surrounding the zone where the shootout had gone down just minutes earlier.

Neither chief anticipated an exhaustive search as they presumed that Dzhokhar was injured, bleeding, and on foot. With several tracking dogs on the street, they figured it wouldn't be long before the terrorist was found. Police were vigilant, and so were civilians. Residents in the neighborhood received automated calls at their homes and on their cell phones telling them to lock their doors and not to open them except for uniformed police officers. Watertown's 911 lines lit up with reports of suspicious men walking around the neighborhood. All cars in the twenty-block perimeter were stopped. Pedestrians were ordered to put their hands up, show ID, and get off the streets. During these hours of heightened tension, the fog of war was apparent as false alarms continued to pour in. At one point, a report came in about a man who dove into the Charles River, just a few blocks south of Dexter and Laurel. There was no man in the river. There was another report of police in Kenmore Square stopping a cab that may have been carrying the bomber. It turned out to be false. Similarly, someone reported that a cab took a fare from the Arsenal Mall in Watertown to South Station, just as trains were leaving the hub for New York City. Again—false. A train was stopped in Connecticut and searched, but nothing suspicious was turned up.

There was a report from a woman that her daughter was being held at gunpoint in a Watertown home. Authorities thought they had their guy. SWAT teams and hostage negotiators were alerted. It turned out that the woman was calling about a psychiatric patient, and the incident had no connection to the at-large terrorist.

Concern spread to the south coast of Massachusetts and onto the campus of UMass-Dartmouth, where officials were shocked to learn about their student's lead role in the bloody drama unfolding up in Boston. At 11:15 a.m., a caravan of state police vehicles sped down Old Westport Road and onto the college campus. Armed troopers patrolled the grounds and searched Dzhokhar's dorm room at Pine Dale Hall, while two Black Hawk helicopters from Camp Edwards on Cape Cod circled overhead and landed with additional troops. Just after 2 p.m., UMass-Dartmouth Chancellor Dr. Divina Grossman, who was just finishing her first year on the job, issued a statement which read in part:

> On Tuesday, we drew strength from a campus vigil that attracted hundreds
> of people in remembrance of the victims, and today we learned that a sus-
> pect is one of our students. We closed and evacuated the campus to assure
> the safety of our students, faculty and staff.[52]

A few miles away in New Bedford, officials shut down Bristol Community College. Thirty miles to the north on the campus of Bridgewater State University, security personnel evacuated two halls following the discovery of a suspicious package. The most innocent among us were also being pulled from harm's way as child care centers in Dartmouth—including the Schwartz Center for Children, which teaches special-needs kids—were shut down.

Inside dorm room number 7341 at Pine Dale Hall—Dhzokhar's room—FBI agents retrieved several BBs, a large firework, and the black jacket and white hat that were believed to have been worn by Dhzokhar at the Boston Marathon. Tsarnaev's laptop computer and a backpack stuffed with fireworks were missing. Those items had been taken out of Dzhokhar's dorm room the day before by his college pals Dias Kadyrbayev and

Azamat Tazhayakov, both exchange students from Kazakhstan. Tsarnaev normally hung out at their apartment at 69A Carriage Drive in New Bedford, and Kadyrbayev had been a frequent guest at Dzhokhar's home on Norfolk Street in Cambridge and had met several times with family members, including Tamerlan. Dhzokhar had made a disturbing revelation to his friends Tazhayakov and Kadyrbayev over lunch just one month before the bombings. "It's good to die as a Shaheed (martyr), as you would die with a smile on your face and go to Heaven," he told them.[53] Tsarnaev also informed his friends that he knew how to make a bomb and went on to describe the ingredients needed to build an explosive device.

Ninety minutes after the marathon bombings, Tsarnaev texted his friend Azamat Tazhayakov. "Don't go thinking it's me," he wrote.[54] The next day, the two young men were captured on surveillance cameras entering and leaving the gym at UMass-Dartmouth. Dzhokhar appeared nonchalant and smiling on the video.[55]

On Wednesday, April 17, 2013, just forty-eight hours after the bombings, Kadyrbayev met briefly with his friend Dzhokhar during his last visit to campus. While chatting in the student lounge inside Pine Dale Hall, the Kazakh exchange student noticed that Tsarnaev had cut his curly black hair a bit shorter. They continued to make small talk while Kadyrbayev smoked a cigarette. Dzhokhar then returned to his dorm room alone. A day later, when the FBI released its photographic evidence connecting Suspect One and Suspect Two to the bombings, Kadyrbayev turned on the news and thought his buddy Dzhokhar looked an awful lot like the killer in the white hat. He texted Tsarnaev about it and got a reply moments later.

"lol," Tsarnaev answered. "You better not text me. Come to my room and take whatever you want."[56]

The Kazakh thought Dzhokhar was joking. Then he wasn't so sure. Kadyrbayev huddled with their mutual friends Azamat Tazhayakov and Rob Phillipos, and all three went to room 7341 at Pine Dale Hall and were allowed in by Dzhokhar's roommate, Andrew Dwinells. Tsarnaev and Dwinells were not friends—they had been randomly chosen to room together in Pine Dale Hall. They ran in different social circles and did not share much with each other. In the days after the bombings, Dwinell did notice that Dzhokhar slept longer than usual. The roommate did not know the names of Tsarnaev's friends who asked to enter the room.[57] Once inside, the trio noticed a backpack containing fireworks. There were seven red tubes; each one was six to eight inches long. The explosives had been opened and emptied of gunpowder. The moment he saw the empty fireworks, Kadyrbayev knew that his friend was one of the Boston Marathon bombers. He also spotted a tube of Vaseline that he believed Dzhokhar had used to make the bombs. Instead of calling 911, however, the Kazakh grabbed the backpack—the potentially damning evidence—and left the room. He took the laptop also so that Dhzokhar's roommate wouldn't think he was stealing or acting suspiciously by taking just the backpack. The three men then drove to the apartment on Carriage Drive in New Bedford, where they monitored TV reports throughout the night.

"Kadyrbayev and Tazhayakov started to freak out because it became clear from a CNN report that [Dzhokhar] was one of the Boston Marathon bombers," Rob Phillipos later told FBI agents.[58]

The Kazakhs began speaking rapid-fire in Russian, which Phillipos couldn't understand.

"Should I get rid of the stuff?" Kadybayev later asked Phillipos.

"Do what you have to do."

The trio then made a pact to destroy the evidence linking their friend to one of the bloodiest crimes in American history. At 10 p.m., Kadyrbayev stuffed the backpack and the fireworks into a large trash bag. He also gathered trash from the apartment and dumped it on top of the evidence before tossing the bag in a dumpster outside.

On Friday, April 19, law enforcement agencies swarmed the apartment complex on Carriage Drive and arrested all three men. Exactly one week later, authorities recovered Dzhokhar's backpack from a New Bedford landfill. The backpack was partially enclosed in a black garbage bag with red drawstring handles. Inside the backpack, agents found the fireworks, the jar of Vaseline, and a UMass-Dartmouth homework assignment sheet from a class Dzhokhar was enrolled in.

Khairullozhon Matanov was also busy trying to get rid of evidence. He had been following the story throughout the night on his laptop computer and knew his friends had now been identified as the suspected marathon bombers. Matanov called Dzhokhar on Friday morning but got no answer. He then begged a friend to take some cell phones he had in case the FBI raided his Quincy apartment.[59] The friend refused. He then asked the friend to help him scrub his computer and delete large amounts of data from his Google Chrome Internet cache. Once again, the friend said no.

"You're not a good brother," Matanov told him.[60]

Matanov performed the task himself. Another friend urged Matanov to go to the police before the police came for him. Matanov consented, so they drove to the Braintree Police Department, where Matanov was questioned by detectives. Matanov would bury himself during the interrogation. He told police that he had not seen the surveillance photos of the Tsarnaev brothers and only knew them from the mosque and through playing soccer. Both statements were lies. Matanov would later face a series of charges, including making false statements and destroying documents. Twenty-one-year-old Stephen Silva, another Tsarnaev friend, was later indicted on charges of heroin trafficking and possession of a Ruger model P95 9mm pistol—the same model Tamerlan had used to execute Sean Collier—that prosecutors say Silva had on him in February 2013, just two months before the bombings. The weapon's serial number had been obliterated.[61]

Law enforcement was tightening the noose around Dhzokhar's friends and associates—but there was still no sign of the young bombing suspect himself.

Back in Watertown, the epicenter of the manhunt, grid searches of the neighborhoods were in full swing. At 89 Nichols Street, a woman summoned a reporter and asked for a police officer. A state trooper talked to the woman, who believed that she had seen blood outside and that someone might have gone into the basement of her brick apartment building. Officers with K-9s went to the building and talked to the woman. Within minutes, a heavily armed SWAT team clad in black body armor and riding in an armored truck rolled up to the building. The National Guard pushed back media and spectators, shouting, "Get back!" Guns were drawn.

The officers approached the house and went inside. The building was cleared, but trickles of blood were found in the back yard. The area was cordoned off with yellow police tape. A few hours later, another commotion erupted at the top of Willow Park, a small side street in the neighborhood. There was a report of someone finding a rocket or a rocket launcher in the basement. There was another report of someone seeing a man in a hoodie on the street. The National Guard again pushed everyone back and sealed off the area. Machine guns were drawn, and cops ran down Quimby Street to Willow Park, where they took cover behind cruisers and armored vehicles. An officer on a loudspeaker shouted, "Come out!"

The house was cleared. Similar scenes continued throughout the early afternoon as cops responded to various reports and investigated suspicious activity. Media reports trickled out, quoting cops overheard on police scanner traffic claiming that Dzhokhar had posted a message online: "I will kill all of you. You killed my brother."

Police spoke to reporters at the scene, pleading with them to stop tweeting their exact locations. They feared Dzhokhar and anyone he might be conspiring with could be monitoring media feeds to see where the cops were and, more importantly, where they were not.

Fear, uncertainty, and panic gripped the sleepy suburban neighborhood. Cops were on edge. One of their brothers had already been killed, and another was fighting for his life. Time was of the essence to catch this madman. Wounded or not, Dzhokhar Tsarnaev was still a dangerous jihadist bent on killing as many innocent people as he could.

By the afternoon, talk shifted to how long the lockdown should stay in place. There were as many as a thousand cops now on patrol. Watertown was a fortress. Armored vehicles from all over New England rumbled through the streets as residents remained inside their homes, many without enough food to get through the day. One cop involved in the manhunt, Brookline Police Officer John Bradley, learned this firsthand when a young couple with an infant son shared their problem. Kevin and McKenzie Wells told Bradley they hadn't enough milk to feed their seventeen-month-old son, Holden. Bradley then marched to the corner store and retrieved two gallons of milk and delivered them to the couple. The thankful parents offered to pay for the milk, but Bradley said no way. Kevin Wells snapped a photo of the courteous cop with his cell phone and posted it onto his Facebook page. The Boston Police Department then tweeted the image out during the lockdown, and it would be shared more than sixty thousand times over the next few days.

Tracy Munro, the mother who had provided comfort and support to Jane Richard in the moments after the bombings, was sitting inside her apartment in Cambridge. She was scared and she was alone. Her daughter, Stella, was visiting with her dad a few miles away, and there was no way to get to her. Munro had been living a nightmare since the marathon, and now she was wondering if she'd ever wake up. After tending to Jane Richard outside Forum, Munro had made her way to the Cask 'n Flagon restaurant next to Fenway Park, where she was reunited with her cousins and with her Uncle Robby, a runner who had been stopped at Kenmore Square before reaching the finish line. The next day, she watched the news reports and learned the full names of Jane and Martin Richard.

"I couldn't believe the two children I had encountered were related," she recalls. Tracy Munro broke down and wept. She had been having a difficult time since the tragedy, and now it continued to evolve around her: MIT Police Officer Sean Collier was murdered less than a mile from her Cambridge apartment. She awoke on Friday morning to the sound of police cars screaming by her bedroom window. Munro phoned her boyfriend, Brian.

"I hear police sirens," she told him. "I'm afraid to look outside."

"Don't look," the boyfriend advised. "Turn on some music and tune out awhile."

Munro heeded the advice and listened to Mazzy Star on her iPod. The singer's soft voice comforted her as it had when she delivered Stella a decade before. Munro was heartbroken to be separated from her daughter. She called Stella at her dad's place and was relieved to find that she was alright. Stella was enjoying time with her father, but she was feeling overwhelmed by the situation.

"You understand that police are here to take care of us, right?" Munro asked.

"Yes," Stella replied. "But can we still go to the park?"

"No, baby," the mom replied. "The point of this is to stay inside."

People were confused and scared—and little progress was being made. By 5:30 p.m., the entire twenty-block perimeter in Watertown had been thoroughly searched. Dzhokhar Tsarnaev had vanished.

Governor Patrick conferred with State Police Colonel Tim Alben, Commissioner Davis, Police Chief Ed Deveau, Rick DesLauriers of the FBI, Mayor Menino, and others. They debated whether it was time to lift the lockdown and try to resume some sense of normalcy—hoping that the young bomb suspect would be caught riding in a cab, fleeing on a train, or hiding in the woods; hoping that he would be found *somewhere* before he harmed anyone else. Patrick spoke to President Obama, and they decided to lift the lockdown.

The governor and Alben, both weary from a sleepless, terrifying night, stepped to the swarm of microphones to update all those who had huddled inside their homes since dawn.

"You're all tired, we certainly are as well. But we remain committed to this," Colonel Alban said. "We do not have an apprehension of our suspect this afternoon, but we will have one. We're committed to that."

Alben went on to describe the complexity and fluidity of the volatile day. He said that a forensic team had finally removed all exploded and unexploded bombs from Laurel Street and that a decision had been made to draw back tactical teams from the area. The shelter-in-place order was officially lifted, but the state police would provide the Watertown community with additional patrols over the next three days. The MBTA was being reopened immediately, but life was far from getting back to normal. Alben and Governor Patrick stressed the need for Watertown residents and all Bostonians to remain vigilant and on alert for any suspicious activity.

"Remember, there's still a very, very dangerous individual at large," Patrick said.

The plan was to avoid a situation where large groups would gather. Therefore, scheduled home games for both the Red Sox and Bruins were cancelled for the night. The tent had been erected at City Hall Plaza for the Big Apple Circus, but the evening performance would be postponed as well. Those venues would simply offer too large and too soft a target. Law enforcement knew that all animals, including Dzhokhar Tsarnaev, were most dangerous when cornered and wounded.

Like all Watertown residents, Dave Henneberry and his wife, Beth, had been monitoring the chaos unfolding on TV as they sat in their modest two-story home at 67 Franklin Street. Henneberry was going a bit stir crazy. He looked out the window at one point and saw that the white plastic shrink-wrap on his Seabird powerboat, the *Slip Away II*, had been lifted up and that some padding he'd put inside to protect the twenty-four-foot vessel was on the ground. The newly retired phone company installer needed to protect his boat—and he also wanted a cigarette. So when Governor Patrick gave the OK to resume normal activity, Henneberry went outside, had a smoke, and checked on the *Slip Away II*.

Neighbor Dan Cantor, who had lived in the neighborhood for twenty years, spoke with Hennebery outside just after the lockout was lifted. The two men had been among the residents cooped up all day, and they chit-chatted in the street. Henneberry said he was upset because the shrink-wrap was partly off his boat. He thought police had taken the cover off to look inside and hadn't put it back properly. He was going to go see what the hell was going on.

Henneberry climbed up a stepladder next to the boat and lifted the shrink-wrap to have a look inside. What he saw was blood splattered on the deck and a body curled up near the steering console. America's most wanted man was hiding out inside Henneberry's pleasure craft.

Oh my God, he's in there, Henneberry said to himself. He had listened to the gun battle on Laurel Street the night before and watched the explosive images later on television. He could not imagine such violence in his own backyard.

He hopped off the ladder and scampered into the house, yelling to his wife: "He's in the boat! He's in our boat!"

Beth dialed 911 and handed the phone to her husband.

"There's somebody in my boat! There's blood in the boat!" he shouted into the phone.

"Did you say there's a body in your boat?" the dispatcher replied.

"There's someone in my boat and a lot of blood."

The police dispatcher asked Henneberry if the man was still in the boat. He brought the phone outside and looked closer.

"He's still in the boat."

"Stay in the house," the dispatcher ordered.

Seconds later, Commissioner Davis's cell phone rang. The ringer was set to the sound of a revving motorcycle, and the noise jolted him. "I was ragtime," Davis recalls. "I'd been up for thirty-six hours straight, so it took me a couple of seconds to compute what was happening." When he first learned about the boat, Davis thought it was on the water somewhere, not in somebody's backyard. He, Colonel Alban and FBI Special Agent in Charge DesLauriers spoke briefly and then sent an army of officers to Henneberry's home. Detective Danny Keeler, who was back at District 4 in Boston, grabbed several of his officers and raced to the scene. If this was indeed Dzhokhar Tsarnaev, Keeler wanted the opportunity to look the alleged killer straight in the eye — if he was to be taken alive.

Moments later, three of the officers closest to the scene reached Henneberry's front door and knocked.

"Come on. I'll show you the boat. I think he's dead," Henneberry told the officers.

"No, no, no. Go in your house, and we'll figure this out," one told him.

After lifting the shelter-in-place order, Governor Patrick and his state police driver headed to the governor's home in Milton for a little dinner and some rest. He and his wife, Diane, had decided on a few orders of food from their favorite Thai restaurant in Quincy.

"Call in the order, and I'll pick it up on the way home," he told her.

The governor soon arrived at the restaurant, where he found a big brown bag stuffed with cartons of spicy noodles waiting for him. At that moment, he received a call from State Police Colonel Tim Alben.

"We think we have the suspect."

The governor's eyes grew wide. "We're heading back to Watertown," he told his driver. "They think they got him."

There was just one problem—the bag of Thai food. Governor Patrick had a job to do, but he was also a husband and father who had to feed his wife and daughter. He called Diane.

"Honey, you have to meet me just off exit 10 at St. Agatha Parish," he told her. The governor's driver took him to Squantum Street in Milton and then to the church on Adams Street, where Patrick jumped out of the vehicle, handed his wife the Thai food, gave her a quick kiss, and sped back to the highway.

Relieved that the lockdown was over, Tracy Munro and her boyfriend went down the street to Lord Hobo, a pub in Inman Square for dinner and a few beers. Munro had read the online chatter from people who were pissed off at the government for suspending their civil liberties for the day.

"What the hell are people upset about?" Munro asked her boyfriend. "I'm extremely proud of the police. I was willing to do whatever they asked me to do."

Tracy Munro had seen the bloodshed carried out by the bombers at close range. She was still very shaky over what she had witnessed, and the lockdown had only added to her stress. When she went to relax at the restaurant, she left Stella with her dad, as there was no need to disrupt the child's night. But her girl was safe, and that was what mattered most.

Munro was also trying to cope with her newfound notoriety as her story had been reported in the press, and friends were now flooding her Facebook page with messages of support. They were calling her a hero.

Hero? Munro thought. *I can barely keep it together. All I know is that I'm alive and I'm scared.*

She thought that Dhzokhar Tsarnaev might be hiding in plain sight, now that it was easier for him to move around.

Where could he be? she asked herself.

Munro sat down at the bar and ordered off the menu. Everyone was still glued to the HD television sets overhead. The station they were watching suddenly flashed the breaking news graphic CORNERED. Her heart began racing again as it had on Boylston Street days before.

In Dave Henneberry's back yard on Franklin Street in Watertown, cops assumed the boat where the bombing suspect was hiding was booby-trapped with bombs—and that Dzhokhar Tsarnaev had a gun. There was a gaff in the middle of the boat, and the black handle that was poking out looked to authorities like a rifle barrel.

In fact, Tsarnaev did not have a gun. Instead, he had a pen and a piece of paper, which he used to scrawl this note:

> I'm jealous of my brother who ha[s] [re]ceived the reward of jannutul Firdaus (inshallah) before me. I do not mourn because his soul is very much alive. God has a plan for each person. Mine was to hide in this boat and shed some light on our actions. I ask Allah to make me a shahied to allow me to return to him and be among all the righteous people in the highest levels of heaven. He who Allah guides no one can misguide. A[llah Ak] bar! The US Government is killing our innocent civilians but most of you already know that. As a [illegible] I can't stand to see such evil go unpunished, we Muslims are one body, you hurt one you hurt us all. Well at least that's how muhhammad (pbuh) wanted it to be [for]ever, the ummah is beginning to rise [illegible] has awoken the mujahideen, know you are fighting men who look into the barrel of your gun and see heaven, now how can you compete with that. We are promised victory and we will surely get it. Now I don't like killing innocent people it is forbidden in Islam but due to said [illegible] it is allowed. All credit goes [illegible]. Stop killing our innocent people and we will stop.[62]

Dhzokhar Tsarnaev scribbled this manifesto with the presumption that they would be his last words. He believed the day would end with his death as it had begun with the death of his brother. Before leaving his Cambridge apartment for good the day before, Dzhokhar emailed his mother, telling her that he would see her in this life or the next one.[63]

Officers from multiple departments surrounded the boat, each with guns drawn. Noticing sudden movements inside the vessel, one cop fired and then bullets started flying everywhere. Cracks of gunfire echoed through the neighborhood and for several seconds, there was chaos.

"As soon as one cop shot everybody shot," Deveau recalls. "A significant amount of rounds went off."

Next-door neighbor Dan Cantor, a Berklee College of Music professor who moonlights as a drummer for indie rock band Jim's Big Ego, heard the gunshots. His family had spent much of the lockdown in his soundproof basement music studio, so the kids wouldn't hear explosions and gunshots ringing out in the neighborhood. As cops moved in on Dzhokhar, gunfire rang out again. Cantor estimates he heard between thirty and fifty shots. He rounded up his family and they all hid under a bed together—away from the windows—as the gunshots erupted just outside. Some of the cops were using Cantor's Toyota Prius as a shield.

Boston Police Deputy Superintendent (and future commissioner) William Evans screamed out "Hold your fire!" several times until the gunshots ceased.

Danny Keeler was on the scene also and was relieved to know that no Boston police officer had drawn their weapon during the tense seconds when the boat was fired upon.

"Nice job on the fire discipline," he shouted to William Evans. Keeler examined the bullet-riddled vessel. *What the fuck would we have done if it wasn't that kid in there*, he muttered to himself.

The FBI's Hostage Rescue Team took control of the scene. They had been brought up from Virginia, and several of the operatives spoke with slow Southern drawls.

When Governor Patrick returned to Watertown, he met with the FBI's tactical supervisor in a trailer at the command post. The Fed wore a headset and had control of several remote cameras at the scene.

"He had this big bulge of chewing tobacco in his lower lip," Patrick recalls. "He was describing the action while spitting into a Gatorade bottle." The supervisor resembled a minor league baseball coach calling in signals from the dugout.

In Watertown, another FBI agent was perched on the second floor of Henneberry's home, overseeing the situation below. A state police chopper whirred overhead and took thermal images of the boat, revealing the outline of the terrorist in hiding. Television stations tapped into the state police camera's live feed, and soon all of America could see a figure moving slowly under the tarp inside the vessel.

Flashbang grenades — small, non-lethal explosives that stun their targets — were lobbed toward the boat in a bid to disorient Dzhokhar Tsarnaev. When that failed to work, the FBI had another idea. One agent on scene, a big Southern man with a long beard, nudged Danny Keeler as he pointed over to the BearCat, an armored, tank-like vehicle that had been brought in by state police. He too was chewing tobacco and spitting in a cup.

"You know, I'd like to take that truck you have," he told Keeler and William Evans, "and ram that fucking boat a couple of times and shake that motherfucker up a little and see what he wants to do. Is that OK with you?"

Evans gave him the nod and the BearCat moved into position. The vehicle's motor cranked and its tires tore through the sod in Henneberry's yard as it powered toward the boat.

The small tank crashed into the vessel — *bam!*

"Motherfucker ain't moving," the FBI agent said. "What'dya say hit him a couple more times."

They tried the tactic again, but the boat trailer was too strong to let the vessel be lifted fully off the ground.

A negotiator from the FBI's Hostage Rescue Team then grabbed a bullhorn and delivered a message from Dzhokhar's wrestling coach at Cambridge Rindge & Latin that urged his former student to surrender. The question was: would he go down fighting as his brother had, or was Dzhokhar ready to give himself up?

Members of the SWAT team were then selected to advance on the boat to capture the suspected terrorist — or kill him if they had to.

At this point, Tsarnaev was positioned along the starboard side of the boat. His arm emerged from beneath the shrink-wrap. He stood up, and a sniper's scope beamed a red dot on the bloodied, battered teenager's forehead. Dhzokhar Tsarnaev was dead if he made a wrong move. He was unsteady on his feet and bleeding profusely from the neck and head. He lifted his shirt to alert police that he was not wearing a suicide vest.

"Show me your hands!" one member of the SWAT unit shouted. "Show me your hands!"

A phalanx of cops grabbed him, tore him out of the boat, and thrust him to the ground where he was gang-tackled by several officers. Dzhokhar Tsarnaev screamed out in pain. His arms and legs were patted down for explosives. His hands were pried open and searched for detonators—all while he continued to cry out.

Two transit police officers, comrades of Dic Donohue, were given the honor of handcuffing the suspected bomber.

Dzhokhar Tsarnaev was placed on a stretcher and led through a group of cops that included Danny Keeler. Each officer stared angrily at the terror suspect who had damaged—but had not broken—their beloved city. A few cops spit in Tsarnaev's face as he went by.

As Danny Keeler looked at Tsarnaev, he saw the faces of Krystle Campbell, Lingzi Lu, and Martin Richard in his mind's eye. Their faces, both in life and in death, would be with him forever. He thought about their families and the families of *all* the murder victims he had fought for during his long career.

"We got you, motherfucker," Keeler whispered as Dzhokhar was led past him in shackles on a stretcher.

"I owe you, everybody, a drink after this one," Keeler told his boss, Ed Davis.

"The rounds are on me," the commissioner responded.

Watching the dramatic arrest from a pub in Cambridge, Tracy Munro saw the breaking news banner CAPTURED fly across the television screen. She placed her head down on the bar and wept uncontrollably.

[20]

CAPTURED

Moments after the bombing suspect was taken into custody, Mayor Tom Menino got on the police radio. He was exhausted and overcome with emotion.

"Your mayor is very proud of you," he told his men.

"We did it for you, boss," an officer replied immediately.

At 5:58 p.m., the Boston Police Twitter feed broke the news to the world: "CAPTURED!!! The hunt is over. The search is done. The terror is over. And justice has won. Suspect in custody."

Residents in both Boston and Watertown took to the streets in celebration. On Mt. Auburn Street in Watertown, a large crowd gathered to honor the police officers. Cops made their way back to their vehicles amid the sounds of cheering and clapping. Many jubilant residents broke from the crowd to offer hugs and a pat on the back to their protectors. Police officers responded with a wail of sirens and lights flashing in celebration. One armored vehicle came through with several cops riding on the back in their SWAT gear. The officer riding shotgun got on the loudspeaker and chanted, "U.S.A.! U.S.A.!" to thunderous applause. The chant extended to the throng partying in the streets. In Boston, meanwhile, a spontaneous celebration broke out on Boston Common. It was reminiscent of a Red Sox, Bruins, or Patriots world championship win. But on this night Bostonians weren't celebrating some shiny trophy, instead they were celebrating something much more meaningful—their freedom and their safety.

The party raged into the wee hours. Mayor Menino was back at the Parkman House at 33 Beacon Street, close to the Common. He had been staying at the historic, city-owned residence while recovering from surgery. He could hear the loud cheering on the next block, and he smiled.

Soon, he got a call from Commissioner Davis.

"Mayor, they're drinking and partying on the Common. What do you want us to do?" the commissioner asked.

The mayor wished he could be out there celebrating with his people. "Who cares?" Menino replied.

If the city was going to heal itself, let that healing begin tonight, he thought.

Earlier that evening, the mayor had participated in a news conference along with Governor Patrick, Commissioner Davis, Colonel Alben, and others in Watertown.

"We are so grateful to be here right now. We're so grateful to bring justice and closure to this case," Alben said. "We are eternally grateful for the outcome here tonight. We have a suspect in custody. We're exhausted, folks. But we have a victory here tonight."

Commissioner Davis echoed Alben's sentiments.

"Four days ago my city was ruthlessly attacked" a stern Davis said. "[This result] makes me proud to be a Boston police officer."

Governor Patrick brought the night back to the victims and their families.

"On behalf of Krystle and Martin and Lingzi," Patrick said, "on behalf of the MIT officer who was lost last night, and the transit police officer who was injured; and on behalf of the hundreds of people that were hurt by the explosions at the marathon, I want to say how grateful I am . . . to all of the law enforcement who worked so long and so hard together, to bring us to tonight's conclusion. It was a very, very complicated case. A very challenging case. It's a night that I think we're all going to rest easy."

The final tweet from the Boston police that night read, "In our time of rejoicing, let us not forget the families of Martin Richard, Lingzi Lu, Krystle Campbell and Officer Sean Collier."

Michelle L'Heureux had undergone eight hours of surgery on Friday morning. It was her third surgery in less than a week. She was aware of Sean

Collier's execution and the Watertown shootout the night before, and she knew there was an intense manhunt underway for Dzhokhar Tsarnaev, brother of the man who had tried to kill her on Boylston Street.

Doctors performed skin grafts to close up her arm and leg and removed the vacuum apparatus from her arm. As she was being wheeled back from surgery that morning, she held up both her arms to show her nurses that she had no more hoses attached to them. It was a small but important victory for her. Back in her room, she asked one of the nurses, "Did they catch him yet?"

The answer was no. Because of the lockdown ordered by Governor Patrick, she didn't have any visitors that day. The hospital was eerily quiet. For the first time since the bombings, there were no flower deliveries, no well-wishers dropping by. When she awoke from surgery, Michelle picked up her iPad and immediately began surfing the web for information on the manhunt. The television set in her hospital room was tuned to CNN. As the day wore on and the intense pain returned, she was given medication to make her sleep. At around 7 p.m. on Friday night, Michelle was awakened by the sound of nurses, doctors, and others cheering out in the hallway.

Someone yelled into Michelle's room, "They caught him!"

She turned on the TV and confirmed that Dzhokhar Tsarnaev was indeed in custody.

"Thank God," she said to the TV. "Thank God!"

Boston Police Officer Javier Pagan watched the surreal, chaotic events of Friday's manhunt from home. He got text messages all day from his fellow officers who were on the scene.

When Dzhokhar Tsarnaev was finally in handcuffs, a friend texted Javier, simply, "We got him."

Javier's reaction was one of relief, but he was also sad about Sean Collier's senseless murder. He felt the anxiety of his brother and sister officers, all of whom knew these terrorists were not only capable of killing a cop—they wanted to do so.

"The stress level was so high," he recalls. "But you have to give it to the city, you give it to the state, you give it to all the agencies involved—from Monday to Friday, we got them."

Danny Keeler stopped off at a package store before returning to District 4. He purchased two thirty packs of beer for his men, all of whom had been pulling eighteen-hour days for the past week and were physically and emotionally drained. Some were crying in the station house. Keeler himself wept privately for those who were lost and the hundreds more who would never be the same again. Keeler took the party over to J. J. Foley's, a legendary cop bar in Boston's South End. The cops drank, hugged, and de-stressed from the most intense hours they had ever faced on the job. Keeler raised a glass of Jameson's, looked around the bar, and toasted his men. His eyes welled with tears, and his heart filled with pride.

"It's like some of the guys are racehorses and you have got to reward a racehorse or something afterwards," Keeler explains. "They'd been going at it real good. They need to unwind and the drinks are on me. It was very satisfying to know that those guys were there when you needed them."

Dzhokhar Tsarnaev was brought by ambulance to Beth Israel Hospital, where twenty-six survivors, including Denise Richard, were still being treated for their injuries. Beth Israel was the closest Level One trauma center to Watertown. It was also the same hospital where Tamerlan Tsarnaev had been pronounced dead hours before. The younger Tsarnaev brother was flanked by armed guards as his stretcher was wheeled into a resuscitation room where ER nurses and doctors worked from thirty to forty minutes to stabilize him for surgery. A breathing tube was placed in Dzhokhar's mouth, which made it impossible for him to communicate. Staring down at the suspected terrorist, staffers felt conflicted, but they knew they also had a job to do.

"They look at the perpetrator as someone absolutely horrible and ask themselves, 'What have we done? We just saved him,'" said Dr. Richard Wolfe, head of emergency medicine at Beth Israel.[64]

There was also outrage among victims and their families recovering at the same hospital.

"The bastard is downstairs," Bill Richard said as his own wife lay in a hospital bed and his daughter remained in a medically induced coma at Children's Hospital. The reality of the situation was distressing, as was the planning for their son Martin's funeral. Bill Richard and his friend Larry Marchese had both gotten word that members of the infamous Westboro Baptist Church were planning to protest at the eight-year-old's funeral. The church, located in Topeka, Kansas, is made up of about forty radical zealots who leverage media attention surrounding funerals for American soldiers to espouse their hatred for gays. Firefighters and members of local biker gangs had offered to form a protective barrier around services for the little boy, but the Richard family wanted to avoid such a spectacle at all costs.

They were forced, despite their enormous grief, to stage a decoy funeral for Martin. Only a small number of family members were told where and when the real service would take place. Flowers were sent to a different funeral home as a diversion. The owners of John J. O'Connor & Son Funeral Home in Dorchester, where the actual service was held, also participated in the ruse by pretending they were closed and by giving most employees the day off. A select group of pallbearers and ushers were brought in for the funeral. On Monday, April 21, exactly one week after Martin's murder, family members were given information about where to be at 7:30 a.m. the following morning. On Tuesday, April 22, a bus with tinted windows picked up the family from the hospital chapel and drove them toward the service with a police escort. When two TV satellite trucks followed the small convoy, state police blocked an intersection to stop the media.

Inside the funeral home, Martin lay in an open casket, wearing his Boston Bruins jersey. The Bruins were his favorite Boston team, and forward Patrice Bergeron was his favorite player. A marathon medal and his football were placed in the casket with him.

Larry Marchese was angry. He prayed before the boy's body and got angry with God.

"You didn't learn from your own son?" Larry demanded, looking up at the crucifix above the coffin.

Denise Richard attended the funeral for her little boy, but Martin's sister could not.

"Jane was still being cared for by a group of angels at Children's Hospital," Marchese recalls. By *angels*, he meant the nurses who spent every hour with the child, changing the dressing on her bandages and comforting the little girl with soothing voices.

"Now, Jane, we're going to lift you up so we can clean you," a nurse would tell her while she was unconscious. The nurses talked to the little girl constantly to let Jane know that she wasn't alone. They even painted the toenails on her remaining foot while she was sleeping.

Denise Richard, on the other hand, wondered if she was being told the truth about her own injuries. Nina Marchese had taken Denise to a small coffee shop in the lobby of the hospital where the day's newspapers were filled with stories of the bombings and the aftermath. Denise noticed her son's photo on the cover of one paper and asked to read it. Thus far, friends and family, including Larry and Nina Marchese, had done everything they could to shield Bill and Denise from the intense media coverage.

"Can I get a copy of the paper?" Denise asked Nina.

"Sure," Nina replied, although she was unsure it was the right decision.

Denise read the cover story about her family and commented on the photo of little Martin. Her reading was slowed by the heavy bandage over her right eye. She paused halfway through the article and looked up at Nina.

"This article says that I have brain damage," Denise said. "Nina, do I have brain damage?"

"No," Nina Marchese replied. "No you don't. That report is false."

And it was. A projectile from the pressure cooker bomb had damaged her optic nerve but had stopped short of her brain. Denise Richard was relieved. Despite the enormous pain her family had endured, she also knew that she would have to be a strong mom for her eldest son, Henry, and her daughter. When little Jane Richard was finally brought out of her coma, she looked around the room and stared up at the ceiling.

"Martin, where are you?" she asked.

The Richard family would have a flood of support flowing from people all over the world who had been touched by their plight and by the photo of Martin holding his hand-drawn sign that read: *No More Hurting People — Peace*. Boston's professional sports teams, which are ingrained in the character of the city like few other places, also stepped up to help.

On April 17, just two days after the bombings, the Bruins invited Martin's older brother, Henry, to a game against the Buffalo Sabres at the Garden. It was a great opportunity to help the grieving boy and get him away from Beth Israel hospital, if only for a short while. Larry Marchese and his son, who was Henry's age, accompanied the boy to the game. It was the city's first major sporting event since the tragedy, and emotions were raw. Fans flooded the Garden wearing Bruins jerseys and carrying American flags. Some players had written the words *Pray for Boston* on their skates. During a pregame ceremony, everyone paused for a moment of silence before a tribute video played overhead on the Jumbotron. The team had consulted with Marchese ahead of time about the tone of the video, knowing that young Henry would be watching the game from a luxury suite. The team opted not to show a photo of Martin Richard in the video out of respect to the family. Moments later, Rene Rancourt, a singer who had been belting out the national anthem at Bruins home games for thirty-five years, took the ice with microphone in hand. As he warmed up his voice in the hours before the game, Rancourt kept tearing up. *I don't know if I can get through this thing*, he thought.[65]

He began singing "The Star-Spangled Banner" just as he had done more than 1,400 times before, but this night was completely different. On this night, the anthem meant more to the city of Boston than it ever had. "O say can you see, by the dawn's early light," Rancourt crooned passionately. As he began the next verse, the Garden faithful joined in. "What so proudly we hailed, at the twilight's last gleaming." Rancourt dropped the microphone to his side and allowed the thousands of fans in attendance to finish the anthem. Fans and players wept as they sang, their harmonies rising high above the Garden ice into the building's rafters. "O'er the land of the free and the home of the brave."

The next morning Rancourt, a resident of Natick, Massachusetts, spoke to talk show hosts John Dennis and Gerry Callahan on WEEI radio. He said the Bruins had decided ahead of time to make that night's anthem a group sing-along. The decision was music to the singer's ears as he felt that he could not get through it alone. "I was very nervous, what if you stop singing and nothing happens? The sound was carrying me, lifting me up in the room. It was something that was indescribable."[66]

Meanwhile, the Celtics were playing their season finale in Toronto that night. Before tipoff at the Air Canada Centre, players from both teams gathered at center court. "Ladies and gentlemen, tonight we are all Boston fans," the public address announcer said. The night before in the Bronx, the New York Yankees set aside their heated rivalry with the Red Sox by playing Neil Diamond's classic tune "Sweet Caroline," which has long been a staple at Fenway Park, after the third inning.

On Saturday, April 20, the Red Sox held their first post-bombings game at Fenway Park. The Cathedral of Baseball, as it's been called, was perhaps the only "church" in the city big enough for thousands of Bostonians to pray and to heal. Taking a cue from their hockey cousins on Causeway Street, the Red Sox asked fans to sing the national anthem before the game. Boston police, state police, firefighters, and first responders stood on the field in salute with Commissioner Davis and also with Governor Patrick, who had postponed a trip to his retreat in the Berkshires to attend the game.

"This past week has been unlike any other in the history of Boston," the public address announcer told the crowd. "This week has also brought out the best in Boston. . . . We are one. We are Boston. We are Boston Strong."

These words drew loud cheers from the Fenway faithful. Photos of Martin Richard, Krystle Campbell, Lingzi Lu, and Sean Collier appeared on the Jumbotron. Fans then observed a moment of silence for the fallen and all those injured and still hospitalized. A massive American flag was unfurled along the Green Monster. A microphone was then handed to Red Sox star David Ortiz.

"Alright, alright Boston. This jersey that we wear today doesn't say Red Sox, it says Boston," Ortiz told the crowd. On behalf of the team, he thanked Mayor Menino, Governor Patrick, and members of the various police departments for their hard work. Once again, fans applauded in appreciation. The slugger paused for a moment. And no one in attendance or watching on television could have predicted what came next. Ortiz, like all Bostonians, was a jumble of raw nerves. He was heartbroken. He was angry. He was defiant.

"This is our fucking city!" Ortiz shouted into the microphone. "And no one's gonna dictate our freedom. Stay strong!"

The crowd, already on its feet, broke out into thunderous applause.

"I didn't know what I was going to say before I went out on the field," Ortiz wrote later in *Sports Illustrated*. "I wasn't trying to be that hero . . . I was looking for a hero to protect what was ours. Our city. Our marathon. Our way of life. When I said what I said and saw the look in people's eyes, I knew we would be alright."[67]

The Red Sox would continue to play a large part in the healing of the city throughout the 2013 season.

Following the game at Fenway, the governor got back on the Massachusetts Turnpike headed west toward the Berkshires. Everyone was running on fumes, including the state's chief executive. He arrived at his palatial country home surrounded by apple trees in the small town of Richmond, where he went for a quick swim. He was then driven to West Stockbridge for a bite to eat. His favorite restaurant in town was Rouge, known for its grilled Faroe Island salmon and braised free-range duck. Patrick loved the place because it was quiet and the owner, Maggie C. Merelle, always took good care of him. With his reading glasses and a biography of Deng Xiaoping on his iPad, the governor was led to a table in the back of the restaurant. Patrick looked haggard, and he was. He also had not eaten well over the past week, even missing out on his Thai food with his wife and daughter. Seeing this, Merelle—in quite motherly fashion—brought out dish after dish for the governor to nibble on. Patrick ordered duck confit, a bowl of soup, a plate of salad, and a stack of French fries. Each dish was accompanied by a glass of red wine.

"I had a little buzz," the governor remembers. "I felt mothered, not bothered."

When he went to pay the bill, Patrick reached for his wallet but quickly remembered he had left it at home. Sheepishly, he asked Maggie if he could stop by in a day or two to settle his tab. She said yes, and he made good on his promise soon after.

A week after the Boston Marathon Bombings, the city was slowly returning to some sense of normalcy, although it would never be the same. The wind quietly swirled in the eerie calm on Boylston Street, just feet away from where an innocent, gap-toothed eight-year-old boy and two beautiful young women lost their lives to terrorists' bombs. Boston firefighters, police officers, and EMTs, state troopers and National Guardsmen lined up along the sidewalk in front of the bombing scene and made an L shape across Boylston. Inside the L, Mayor Menino sat in his wheelchair, flanked by Commissioner Davis, US Attorney Carmen Ortiz, Suffolk County District Attorney Daniel F. Conley, FBI Special Agent in Charge Rick DesLauriers, and several top military commanders.

Menino, who had just days before checked himself out of Brigham and Women's Hospital where he was being treated for a broken tibia, sat solemnly, his eyes slightly squinted against the sun, which was now and again peeking through ominous clouds that only added to the somberness of the moment.

Just a week earlier, as Boylston Street prepared for the marathon, the street was its normal beehive of activity, the entire city blissfully unaware of the evil lurking in its shadows. Mothers pushed strollers. Business suit-clad men and women hustled to power lunches at hotspots like Abe & Louie's, Forum, Atlantic Fish Co., and Solas, texting as they walked. Tattooed bike messengers whipped in and out of traffic, racing to deliver documents to the Prudential Center and John Hancock Building. Cabs honked, pedicabs stalled traffic, delivery trucks double-parked, and tourists strolled the busy street, soaking in all the energy and vibrancy of a typical Boston spring day.

But on April 22, 2013 — seven days after two homemade pressure cooker bombs tore through life and limb, shattering Boston's peace and reminding the nation that terror lurks among us — Menino sat in his wheelchair in the middle of car-free Boylston Street in silence. An unnatural calm, accentuated by the dark, cold sky above, cast a pall over the stoic uniformed platoon of first responders.

The four-lane thoroughfare runs from Massachusetts Avenue to Boston Common and is the busiest street in the city on a normal day. But on this day, at this moment, the only sound were the boots and solemn directives from two police honor guard officers as they folded an American flag.

Menino gazed over the honor guard and beyond the line of public safety officers. High above them in the background were the terrible reminders of the tragedy that had taken place just a week earlier.

Windows at a LensCrafters store were blown out three stories high. The front windows of Marathon Sports were shattered and partially boarded up. Above Sugar Heaven—where just a week earlier, seconds before the bombs detonated, parents were taking their kids for treats—a banner cheering on marathon runners waved in tatters, partially torn by pellets packed into the explosives.

Behind the mayor and immediately outside the glass doors of the stately Boston Public Library, an American flag flittered at half-staff in honor of the dead and injured.

The honor guard's flag was folded in military burial fashion and was handed to Menino as he sat in his wheelchair, a final formality as the FBI officially turned the crime scene back over to the city so that the healing could truly begin. The flag given to the mayor was originally hoisted by race organizers at 6 a.m. on the morning of the bombings.

The lines of public safety officers broke into quiet applause. Carmen Ortiz leaned over and gave the venerable, seventy-year-old mayor a soft kiss on the cheek. Davis, DesLauriers, and Conley shook his hand. A military commander gave the mayor a pat on the back.

High above the scene, the clouds parted slightly and the sun shone through, casting rays upon some of the officials gathered below and spreading shadows across the sidewalk in front of the century-old library.

"Boston is the strongest city," Menino told the troops, his voice slightly cracking with a raw emotion that the city's longest-serving mayor rarely displayed. "Thank you."

"Boston was changed forever at 2:50 last Monday," he continued. "I'd shake all your hands, but I'm in this chair here."

The last comment drew a slight laugh. It was classic Menino: streetwise, humble, and self-deprecating, but always in charge. It's a natural trait he's used throughout his impressive political career, propelling him from backbencher on the City Council to the most powerful politician in Boston—and many argue, Massachusetts—for two decades.

Commissioner Davis stepped forward beside the mayor. He told the line of troops that President Obama had called him that morning, thanked him, and told him to be sure to thank all the officers and public safety personnel who dashed into action during and after the attacks.

"The cooperation and intense work that was done here, gives us a chance to put this city back together," Davis said. "I, too, thank you all."

"People will be back here walking up and down the street, and the terrorists will understand that they cannot keep us down," Davis added. "This area will be opened back up to businesses."

Davis pushed Menino in his wheelchair over to the blast site. A bouquet of flowers marked the spot where the first bomb went off. Sugar Heaven and Marathon Sports both still showed signs of the carnage. Tattered marathon banners hung from windows by race fans that day blew silently in the breeze.

"The blast went up at least thirty feet," Davis told the mayor, pointing up at the bombed-out LensCrafters windows.

Menino sat silently in his wheelchair. The mayor had been in the midst of national terrorist acts before, including on the morning of September 11, 2001, when two planes left Logan International Airport in his city, bound for suicide attacks in New York and beyond.

But these bombs ignited in *his* city, just blocks from *his* office at City Hall, killing *his* fellow citizens—a young boy, an international exchange student, and a young waitress, all precisely the kind of everyday people that Menino had battled for throughout his political career.

Within days of the bombings, Menino's focus was two-fold: ensuring victims and survivors got the aid they needed, and making sure Boylston Street and the surrounding neighborhoods got back to normal as quickly as possible.

"This city was knocked down but we stood right back up, on our feet quickly," Menino said, speaking to business leaders in a packed hotel conference room two weeks after the explosions. "That fateful afternoon, Boston Marathon volunteers rushed in to help their neighbors. . . . It's who we are."

"I have never been prouder of our city," he continued. "When the world turned its eyes to Boston . . . they saw greatness everywhere. They saw it in the skills of our police. They saw it in the speed of our first responders. They saw miracle after miracle. They saw it in our ambulances and our hospitals. They saw it in our city workers, putting a neighborhood back together. They saw it in our business community and its generosity. When the world looked, they saw greatness in a spontaneous memorial."

The mayor made reopening Boylston Street a priority in those first weeks. He worked closely with Councilor Mike Ross and business leaders in the neighborhood to help get the restaurants and stores back open. It was important to the mayor—for the image of the city—to have the main drag bustling once again.

Three days after Menino received the flag from the Feds, he returned to Boylston Street to have lunch at Solas, an Irish pub at the Lenox Hotel. He invited the media along in a show of strength to demonstrate that the neighborhood was back in business. Walking with crutches, he made his way from his black SUV to the outside patio, where he sat and enjoyed fish and chips. He took pictures with customers and wait staff alike. He was emotional.

"I reflect on what happened and I ask myself, 'Why?'" he said. "What kind of people would do this?"

Just across the street, Marathon Sports manager Shane O'Hare was equally reflective as he and his staff reopened the store.

"We're all pretty emotional," he said as lines of customers bought marathon-related gear. "There's a lot that went on that day. Everyone has their moments. . . . I hope it's a healing process."

The city sent grief counselors into the neighborhood to help traumatized workers—the waitresses, busboys, concierges, cashiers, and many others who witnessed the destruction and human toll of that dark day. Some left their jobs and didn't return. Others came back but clearly needed assistance.

"They're dealing with some really unfortunate things . . . and we're concerned about them," Sheila Dillon, head of Menino's Department of Neighborhood Development, said. "We want to make sure everybody gets the services they need."

O'Hare spent that day selling scores of Boston Strong T-shirts, hats, and bracelets. His eyes filled with tears as he talked about the outpouring of support.

"I hope it helps the victims," he said. "I'm walking and I'm moving. But they're still in hospitals and having surgeries. I feel bad for them."

Just down the street in Copley Square, symbols of remembrance piled up on the grass in front of Trinity Church. Since the day of the bombings, mourners had been leaving personal notes, flowers, teddy bears, and hundreds of running shoes, most of them personally inscribed with messages of loss and hope. White wooden crosses bearing the names and photos of Krystle Campbell, Lingzi Lu, Martin Richard, and Sean Collier were erected on the street and surrounded by bouquets of spring flowers. Equally drawn to the memorial were those who had breathed in the smoke from the bombs and those who were altogether spared the violence at the finish line. All had been part of the same community before April 15, but all were even closer now.

A smaller memorial, but one just as meaningful, had sprouted on the campus of MIT, where loved ones, friends, and total strangers came to say a final goodbye to Officer Sean Collier. Bagpipes wailed as an honor guard of Sean's fellow MIT police officers carried his flag-draped casket onto the field.

Fellow cops, numbering in the thousands and coming from as far away as Australia, filled rows of chairs across Briggs Field, where Collier was eulogized by his boss, MIT Police Chief John DiFava, and by US Vice President Joe Biden.

"What made Sean so good? There are many reasons," DiFava told the sea of mourners that included Sean's parents, brothers, and sisters. "I believe the most important is the fact that he was the same person in uniform that he was when he wasn't wearing the uniform. His caring and compassion was genuine, without duplicity, and because of this depth of character, he was able to achieve a level of trust with people of all backgrounds that was truly remarkable."

The vice president met with the Collier family privately and told them about losing his wife and one-year-old daughter in a car crash in 1972, and how he had learned to cope with the tragedy. He also offered them grieving strategies to get through the coming days and months with a pain so fresh. When Biden took the podium at Briggs Field, he shared personal stories about Collier told to him by the family and also used the service to explain the differences between Americans and those who target free people.

"On every frontier, terrorism as a weapon is losing," Biden said. "It is not gaining adherence. And what galls them the most is that America does remain that shining city on a hill."

[21]

SHARING THE BLAME

In early July 2013, Dzhokhar Tsarnaev made his first appearance in federal court, where he was arraigned on thirty charges stemming from the Boston Marathon bombings. Dressed in an orange prison jumpsuit and appearing sleepy-eyed and nonchalant, the nineteen-year-old terror suspect yawned during his brief eight-minute court appearance. He had a cast on his left arm and a wound that was still healing on the left side of his face. A group of MIT police officers, all wearing "Collier Strong" armbands, stood at attention outside the court house in South Boston in a show of solidarity for their fallen brother. Several marathon survivors attended the arraignment. They all wanted to get a closer look at one of the men who authorities say killed and maimed innocents in the name of Islam. Inside the courtroom, Tsarnaev said "not guilty" seven times before Judge Marianne Bowler. He also blew a kiss to both of his sisters, who were in attendance. They were not his only supporters. More than two dozen people stood outside the courthouse holding signs, some wearing T-shirts with his image.

Months later, United States Attorney General Eric Holder would announce that federal prosecutors would seek the death penalty against Tsarnaev. "The nature of the conduct at issue and the resultant harm compel this decision," Holder said in a statement.[68]

Death had already come to Tamerlan Tsarnaev, as well as his friend and accomplice in the Waltham murders, Ibragim Todashev. In late May 2013, investigators from the Massachusetts State Police and an agent with the

FBI tracked Todashev to Orlando, Florida, where they interviewed him for more than four and a half hours in his apartment. During the interrogation, the Chechen immigrant admitted his involvement in the gruesome September 11, 2011, murders of Brendan Mess, Erik Weissman, and Raphael Teken. Authorities then asked Todashev to write out his confession on a piece of paper. As the Chechen began to write, his mood quickly changed from one of cooperation to rage. This caused one Massachusetts state trooper to remove a decorative sword that was out in the open and hide it behind a shelf in the kitchen. The trooper then texted his state police colleague who had stepped briefly outside. The FBI agent had also taken his eyes off the murder suspect to review some notes taken on a legal pad. At that moment, Todashev lifted a coffee table he had been using to write on and threw it in the air at the federal agent, striking him in the head and knocking him to the floor. The Chechen ran into the kitchen as the FBI agent attempted to grab his ankles to slow his escape. The agent, now bleeding heavily from the blow to the head, could hear the rifling of drawers in the kitchen. The state trooper pulled his gun and raised it but quickly lowered it when he mistakenly thought Todashev was attempting to flee. Instead, the Chechen came right after him brandishing a long, javelin-like pole. Seeing Todashev running toward the trooper, the FBI agent fired as many as four shots at him. The Chechen was struck by several bullets, his body twisting as he dropped to his knees. Still breathing, Todashev lunged at the trooper again, this time getting cut down by four additional shots, including one through the skull. Ibragim Todashev was dead.[69]

His body was later claimed by his father and flown to Grozny, Chechnya, for burial at a Muslim cemetery. His father would maintain his son's innocence, as would the parents of Tamerlan and Dzhokhar Tsarnaev. In an interview with the Associated Press in Dagestan in late April 2013, Zubeidat Tsarnaev called the allegations against her sons "all lies and hypocrisy."[70]

The mother feigned outrage, but she refused to return to America to claim her eldest son's body, which remained at a Worcester, Massachusetts, funeral home for two weeks after he was killed. The simple reason was that no cemetery in the state would agree to accept it. Tamerlan's uncle Ruslan, who had called his nephews "losers," finally claimed the body and had it buried at a Muslim cemetery in Doswell, Virginia, unbeknownst to local officials who said they learned about it through the media.[71]

Reporters and members of Congress would keep this story white-hot for months to come.

During a trip to Russia in late May 2013, Massachusetts Congressman William Keating said that he had been shown specific information by members of the Russian Federal Security Service that Tamerlan Tsarnaev had planned to join the insurgency in Dagestan just one year before. US officials would later claim that the Russians had refused to provide additional information about Tamerlan to the FBI until after the bombings. During its initial investigation, the Feds believed that Tamerlan had posed a greater threat to Russia than he did to his adopted country. Yet, according to an April 2014 report filed by the Intelligence Community Inspector General, the CIA, the Department of Justice, and the Department of Homeland Security, there was plenty of blame to go around. In 2011, Russian officials warned the FBI that Tamerlan and his mother were adherents to radical Islam and that the son was preparing to travel to Russia to join "bandit underground groups."[72] The Russians also provided the FBI with the family's home address, phone number, and email addresses. The FBI agent assigned to the case made a few drive-bys of the Tsarnaev apartment on Norfolk Street in Cambridge and interviewed Tamerlan and both of his parents. What the agent failed to do was ask Tamerlan or his parents about plans to visit Russia. The agent also never visited or interviewed anyone at the Cambridge mosque where Tamerlan had made anti-American outbursts, and he never interviewed Tamerlan's wife, his former girlfriend, or any of his friends or associates. The agent never even alerted local police. Based on very little legwork, the FBI closed its investigation of Tamerlan Tsarnaev in June 2011, finding no link or nexus between him and terrorism.

When Tsarnaev made his travel plans to Russia in January 2012, a US Customs and Border Protection official alerted the FBI agent who had handled Tamerlan's case. The agent did not act upon the information, or he may not have gotten the information in the first place, as it might have simply gotten lost or misplaced: the federal agent often liked to communicate in an unreliable, low-tech way—by passing sticky notes.

As Tamerlan boarded an overseas flight from JFK International Airport in New York to Moscow on the evening of January 21, 2012, he was identified as a "potential subject of interest" by border patrol agents, but he was deemed a "low priority" compared to other passengers on the flight and therefore was not screened before he departed. When he arrived back in the United States on July 17, 2012, Tamerlan went unnoticed thanks to more miscommunication between border control personnel and the FBI agent. The report by the Inspector General concluded that "additional investigative steps would have resulted in a more thorough assessment" of Tamerlan Tsarnaev.[73]

Some have also called into question the FBI's decision against releasing photos of the Tsarnaev brothers on Wednesday, April 17, instead of a day later. The photos were shared by millions, including Sean Collier. Could the MIT police officer's execution have been prevented?

The man who made that decision, FBI Special Agent in Charge Rick Des-Lauriers, stepped down from his position in June 2013 and disappeared into the private sector. At just fifty-three years old, DesLauriers was only four years away from the mandatory retirement age for FBI agents.

Boston Police Commissioner Ed Davis, universally lauded for his work on the case, left the department in September 2013 for a position at Harvard University. He was succeeded by another Boston marathon hero, William Evans.

"I feel very positive about leaving at this time on my timeline," Davis said. "Knowing that I will be leaving having done my very best."

Mayor Tom Menino thanked the commissioner for protecting Bostonians during the city's most trying days. "On behalf of the entire city . . . I thank Commissioner Davis for his leadership and tireless commitment to improve the quality of life for the people of Boston."[74]

FIELD OF DREAMS

One key decision made in the hours following the bombings was to establish a sanctioned, primary charity to benefit survivors and the families of the victims. Both Governor Patrick and Mayor Menino had seen the chaos and corruption that had ensued after 9/11 when a number of phony charities popped up to separate well-intentioned donors from their hard-earned money. The name of the charity created by the two politicians was as simple as its mission. Instead of confusing the public with multiple charities, they would establish one fund. Officials quickly set up a 501(c)(3) nonprofit organization, and the call for donations to One Fund was announced on April 16.

The charity was a massive success. More than sixty-one million dollars was collected in the first seventy-five days. All the money went exactly where it was supposed to go — to the bombing survivors. People donated an additional twelve million dollars in the months to come. A portion of the money was generated during a special Boston Strong benefit concert at TD Garden in late May that featured Boston music icons Aerosmith, James Taylor, the J. Geils Band, Dropkick Murphys, and New Kids on the Block. Out-of-towners Carole King, Jimmy Buffet, and Jason Aldean also performed.

Many of the survivors, including Jeff Bauman and Carlos Arredondo, packed the Garden for the show. Boston's comic legends also took part, giving a grieving and healing city a chance to laugh.

"Boston Strong, I love that phrase," Lenny Clarke told the crowd. "You know what phrase I don't like? 'Shelter-in-place' . . . we were stuck in our homes for sixteen hours with our wife and kids. Twenty more minutes, we would've started killin' each other."

The New Kids joined Dropkicks for a thunderous chorus of the city's unofficial anthem "Shipping up to Boston" before taking over the stage with their early '90s pop hit "Hangin' Tough." There was a bit of everything for everyone.

"It's hard to even talk about Boston and everything that's happened without sounding cliché," said singer and actor Donnie Wahlberg as he waved a police shield given to him moments before by members of the MIT police department, Sean Collier's former colleagues. "There is just no way to ever thank all those who made the ultimate sacrifice, like your brother."

An hour or so later, all the performers gathered on stage with Steven Tyler, Joe Perry, and the rest of Aerosmith for a rousing rendition of "Come Together."

The city had come together like at no other point in its storied and patriotic history. But while many survivors found strength in groups, others fought their battles and attempted to heal out of the public eye.

In July, the Richard family traveled to one of their favorite places in the world, Lake Winnipesaukee in New Hampshire. It's a classic New England summer retreat where the family owns a home not far from where Larry and Nina Marchese live. The two families spend many summer weekends there, cooking out, swimming, boating, and playing games. The Richard family needed a break, especially little Jane, who had endured twelve surgeries and thirty-nine days in the intensive care unit at Children's Hospital. After that ordeal, she had been transferred to the Spaulding Rehabilitation Hospital a few miles away, where she would undergo long, arduous hours of physical therapy.

On the lake in New Hampshire, Bill and Larry took the kids out tubing. It was something Martin loved to do, and it killed Bill to be doing it without his son. Jane, despite her missing leg, tubed like all the other kids. But when some of the kids wanted to go knee-boarding, it was time to make a tough call.

The little girl is a spitfire and wasn't planning on letting a missing leg get in the way of her fun.

"I want to knee-board," she announced.

When she was told no, she protested, "Why? I have both knees."

It was child's logic that was equally heartwarming and heartbreaking. Throughout that first trip back to their New Hampshire house, Jane had played like the rest of the kids. She scooted on her behind around the floor of the cottage. All day long she swam out to a raft with the other children, climbed onto it, scooted across, and dove into the water.

But as inspiring as it was to see Jane recovering and just being a kid, it was devastating that Martin wasn't there. As they skimmed across the lake in the boat at sunset, Marchese's two boys — Casey, who was the same age as Martin, and Jackson, who is Henry's age — sat on the bow with Jane and Henry, their hair blowing in the late-afternoon wind.

Larry and Bill had seen this scene a dozen times before. But there were always five kids. In fact, the families have a favorite picture of all five children on the bow of the boat from the previous summer.

Now there were only four. Tears streamed down Bill's face beneath his sunglasses.

On another summer night, Henry slept over at the Marcheses with his best pal Jackson, as they had done many times before. Henry wanted to watch *Iron Man 2*, but Jackson told his dad, "Maybe we shouldn't. There are too many explosions."

Larry and his wife, Nina, told the boys no and tried to get them to watch something else. But Henry, smart like his sister and late brother, knew what was going on.

"I know why you don't want us to watch this," he said to the couple. "But it's OK."

He told Larry the explosions in the movie were fake.

"That's not what it's really like," he said.

Over the next several months, Heather Abbott spent countless hours in appointments with four different specialists: a surgeon who evaluated the limb and watched for infections; a physical therapist who helped her strengthen the limb and learn to walk on her new prosthetic leg; a rehabilitation therapist at Spaulding; and a prosthetic doctor in Warwick, Rhode Island, who regularly checked and adjusted fittings for the prosthetic.

In addition to her foot wound, a hole was blown in her eardrum. The hole has since healed but she never entirely regained her hearing, and she now wears hearing aids.

As the months have passed, Heather has had several different types of legs. Some cost as much as fifty thousand dollars or more, but Heather has had some donated to her. The One Fund has also helped defray costs.

In October 2013, she got a special prosthetic leg that allows her to wear a high heel. A cast was made of her leg and sent to England, to the same prosthesis company that made a cosmetic cover for Paul McCartney's ex-wife Heather Mills, who lost her leg in a car accident.

In June 2013, she suffered a scare when she fell getting out of bed. It's a common experience among amputees to forget at least once that they don't have their limb. For Heather, that day came when she was lying in bed, her mom in the living room. The doorbell rang and—momentarily forgetting that she only has one leg—she jumped out of the bed and fell down. Hard. She fell right on the limb, and it sent excruciating pain shooting through her body. She wasn't injured, but she was sore for a few days.

She hasn't forgotten again since that fall.

She also has a "water" leg that she can swim with. She received it in the summer of 2013 and was ecstatic to take her first shower standing up since before the bombings.

At a press conference after the bombings, Heather talked about how her injury wouldn't stop her and that she was planning to do a yoga paddleboarding class.

In August 2013, she made good on the pledge, strapping on her new water leg to go paddleboarding for the first time since she was injured. Several of her friends went with her that day at Newport's Third Beach.

Walking along the beach that day, Heather was self-conscious about how she looked in her bikini, with a plastic leg. She was not comfortable. The leg was also difficult to walk with, both on the sand and in the water, where the ground shifted beneath her—something she was not used to with her new prosthetic.

"Heather, it looks like you have a leg brace on. You can't even tell," one of her pals told her.

With her friends by her side, Heather waded out with her board, climbed on, and paddled out. She got to an area that was about shoulder deep. One of her friends held the board, and she stood up.

She was paddleboarding again. She smiled. It was exhilarating, even more so because she didn't fall.

In October 2013, Heather got a running leg with a blade foot that fits into a running shoe, much like the blades used by Olympian Oscar Pistorius. She started running with it on the treadmill at the gym. The limb gets sore from the pounding, so she keeps her runs short. It's frustrating for her, considering that before the bombing, it was routine for her to run three miles through the streets of Newport.

Something else that gets her somewhat discouraged is the pain she gets in her limb from standing on it for long periods of time at parties and social events—she can only remain standing for an hour or so at a time before she needs to sit down. It's frustrating for her and reminds her of what her life used to be like.

She is making progress on getting rid of her limp, with the help of the physical therapists at Spaulding. But she's self-conscious about a huge scar on her right leg, which is a reminder of the surgery that removed the vein in the attempt to save her foot.

Her mother stayed with her at her apartment for two months after she was released from the hospital, but Heather has since learned to live on her own again. At first, a simple task like bringing in groceries was a burden. Because her balance was off, she'd have to put the bags down to walk up the three steps to her front door.

Over time, her balance has improved, and she's now able to carry bags up the stairs. Small victories.

Before the bombings, she never worried about how far she might have to walk when she was making plans. But these days, it's the first thing on her mind. She'll sometimes plan her day based solely on how many steps might be involved. It's an annoying reality of being an amputee, but one that she hopes will one day stop being an issue as she gets more agile on her prosthetics.

"There are a lot of good things that have happened as a result of this, so I try to focus on those," she says.

She spends a lot of time with survivors Roseann Sdoia, Celeste Corcoran, and Jessica Downes. Jessica, a California native, and her husband, Patrick, a Boston College graduate, both sustained severe leg injuries in the bombing and each had a leg amputated below the knee.

Heather loves bonding with the women as they share intimate stories of their recoveries and vent their fears and frustrations. It's a group none of them ever wanted to be a part of, but here they are. And they're more than thankful to have each other.

"We're not all in the same place emotionally," Heather says. "One of my friends is very angry. She's like, 'My career has been taken away from me. Months of my life. I wanted to have children.' She's angry about it. I don't feel like that. I can still do my job. I wasn't planning to have a family. Maybe I would be more angry if it impacted my life more."

While many of those injured or maimed in the bombings have spouses or are in relationships that offer support, for Heather, it's been a stiff challenge to overcome her adversity on her own. She's also frustrated that she'll forever have to address the issue of her prosthetic leg with new people she meets.

"I have this whole new thing now that I have to explain," she says. "I don't know how to do that. I'm doing as much as I can to make it not an obvious thing. But there's going to be a point where I have to explain it."

She went back to work part-time at Raytheon in August 2013. Walking in the first day was overwhelming as she was welcomed back with hugs, cards, balloons, and gifts.

Heather works with 1,200 people and since she's been back, it seems every day one of those people wants to give her a hug, chat about how she's doing, or offer her some sort of help. She appreciates the outreach and support, but says sometimes it can be emotional. Other times, it can be an annoying reminder of the bombing when she's just trying to coast through a casual workday.

"It's weird to be walking down the hall to make a copy or do something normal and have people stop you," she says. "People mean well . . . but sometimes you just want to go to the bathroom or go back to your desk."

The post-bombing experience has been a whirlwind, to say the least. She met Michelle Obama a second time—at the First Lady's personal request—at a political fundraiser in Boston. She was on the cover of *People* magazine, along with Adrienne Haslet-Davis and Mery Daniel.

Mery Daniel spent six weeks in the hospital and at the Spaulding Rehabilitation Center. She had lost her left leg entirely, and she'd undergone countless surgeries to repair her right leg, the calf of which had been ripped off. She had only seen her daughter, Ciarra, three times since the bombing. She thought back to her own childhood, and the image came to mind of herself as a little girl wrapping duct tape around the legs of her dolls. She had always wanted to be a healer, and now she was forced to heal herself. Mery's medical board exams would have to wait until she was strong enough, both physically and mentally, to begin studying again.

And she still had miles to go in her recovery. As an amputee, she had received about $750,000 from the One Fund, but that money could only take her so far. Mery was facing a lifetime of medical treatments, a lifetime of new prosthetics. Other survivors had established personal crowdfunding charities, and Mery and her family eventually went that route, although fundraising was slow at first. By late May 2013, she had only raised a paltry sixteen thousand dollars to aid her recovery. Her pain was still fresh both from the wounds that were plain to see as well as from the psychological trauma caused by the bombing, which she relived every day in her mind. She suffered from phantom pains and a constant burning and itching feeling on the toes of her left foot that was no longer there. The rehabilitation itself was grueling, also—three hours of exercise each day that wore out her petite body. Yet Mery was determined to walk again, to live again. A month after the bombings, prosthetists created a plaster mold where her knee had once been on her left leg. The next step was to fit her with an artificial leg. United Prosthetics in Dorchester worked with Mery and helped her adjust to the device, which allowed her to stand for the first time since April 15—but she still walked funny. *Baby steps*, she told herself.

Soon her support system began to grow. In June, students at the William Seach Primary School in Weymouth, where Mery's father, Hary, drives a bus, organized a walkathon that raised another eight thousand dollars for her recovery.[75] The money allowed Mery and her husband, Richardson, to move into a new apartment in the South End, a first-floor unit that would be more manageable for her. She eventually returned to Boylston Street, to the exact spot where she almost lost her life—but also where she was reborn. Wearing a Boston Strong T-shirt, Mery found herself surrounded by well-wishers cheering her on. She was "Mery Strong."

By early fall, she was doing something she had never done before—she was training to ride as a member of the Spaulding Rehabilitation Hospital team during the local leg of a Massachusetts-to-Philadelphia charity cycling event. She took spin classes, which she loved, pedaling slowly but with great determination to the beat of eclectic African music—her favorite. Mery's strong will amazed everyone, even her caregivers.

"She just leaps. She's got the attitude 'Never say die. Never tell me I can't,'" said Mary Patstone, Director of Adaptive Sports for the Spaulding Rehabilitation Network.[76]

Using a hand-powered bike and every muscle in her strong upper body, Mery pedaled and pushed herself along the twenty-eight-mile course, completing the ride with her teammates. Everyday people and superstar athletes fed off the strength of this resilient marathon survivor. Mery was honored by the New England Patriots before a home game, and even took advantage of an opportunity to throw out the first pitch at Fenway Park to her Red Sox hero, David Ortiz.

As she tossed the ball from her wheelchair, the center field scoreboard lit up with a personal quote from Mery Daniel that read, "How we all came together that day, that's what's important to me. Not the evil part of it, but the best of us."

Following the marathon tragedy, the Boston Red Sox also discovered the best in themselves.

It had been a miserable two years for the Sox and their loyal fan base. They had one of their worst seasons on record in 2012, marked by the infamous chicken and beer scandal. Bloated, prima donna pitchers like Josh Beckett became the symbol of a team that had lost its Everyman soul.

Whereas the Sox in their mid-2000s World Series glory years had become famous for being a rogue band of knuckleheads who employed a hokey cowboy-up, never-give-up mentality, this batch of pampered superstars were failures and grotesque underachievers who not only crushed high expectations, but did so while brazenly admitting to scarfing down Pop-eye's fried chicken and swilling Bud Lite in the clubhouse during games. It was the antithesis of what Boston fans expected and demanded from their teams. It was the type of selfish behavior that the media, management, and all of Boston baseball fandom had always despised and railed against.

The damage done to the Sox brand by the chicken and beer crew was deep. The Red Sox's league-record run of sellout games came grinding to a halt as fans became disgusted with the product, on the field and off. Manager Bobby Valentine was the steward of a disgruntled, uninspired group of quitters who stood in stark contrast to the teams that won titles in 2004 and 2007. The 2012 Red Sox finished 69–93 — last in the American League East and the third worst record in the whole A.L. It was the team's first losing record in 15 years, its worst finish since 1965, and the first time the team had lost 90 games since LBJ was in office.

When the Sox took the field on the morning of April 15, 2013, they were a rag-tag bunch of rookies, cast-offs, and journeymen, with a few fading stars and quality holdovers from the World Series teams sprinkled in. They would soon grow into a bearded, brawny, gritty team that the city was once again proud of. The franchise's phoenix-like rise from the ashes began on Marathon Monday morning and unfolded daily over the subsequent weeks like a welcome diversion — and dose of inspiration — as the entire city of Boston rose from the depths of despair that followed the horrific bombings. Nothing could take away the pain of the tragedy at the finish line, but the Sox at least offered people something positive to think about as the city sought to begin the healing process.

It wasn't the first time Boston had turned its eyes to sports in the wake of dire tragedy. In 2001, after two planes left out of Boston's Logan International Airport and crashed into the World Trade Center, killing nearly three thousand people and changing our world forever, many in New England became enraptured with a handsome, young, unknown quarterback from San Mateo, California named Tom Brady, who was a welcome distraction from the painful realities of terrorism. Most of the passengers on those flights hailed from Boston, including former Bruins great Garnet "Ace" Bailey, who won two Stanley Cups with Bobby Orr and company in the late '60s and early '70s, and Boston University hockey star Mark Bavis. Most in New England knew someone, or knew someone who knew someone, who was on one of the planes or was in one of the Twin Towers. The wounds were deep and personal.

So when Tom Brady and his crew of underdogs went into New Orleans just a few months after the 9/11 attacks and upset the "Greatest Show on Turf"—Kurt Warner's high-scoring St. Louis Rams—in Super Bowl XXXVI, it provided a brief respite from the trauma and gave many a much-needed inspirational lift, if only for a moment. The fact that they were "the Patriots" was not lost on anyone. When accepting the Vince Lombardi Trophy in the Super Dome after Brady had orchestrated a miraculous last-minute victory, the team's venerable owner, Robert Kraft, famously referenced the attacks and the nation's grief and said, "Today, we are all Patriots."

By 2013, fears of terrorism, while never absent in Boston, had somewhat dissipated. And on the gorgeous, sun-splashed morning of April 15, concerns of an attack were as far from the minds of Bostonians as dreams of another World Series. That day, the Sox defeated the Tampa Bay Rays 3–2. But as quickly as the jubilant fans filed out of Fenway, baseball glory became a non-thought when the bombings rocked the city and reminded the nation of the lingering ideological war that knows no battlefield.

As Boylston Street became soaked in blood, the somber Sox boarded a plane for Cleveland. Their city was in pain, and the team took it to heart. They rallied and beat the Indians 7–2 the very next night.

The Sox and Indians wore black armbands to honor the victims, and a giant American flag at Cleveland's Progressive field flew at half-staff. There was a somber moment of silence prior to the first pitch. A young Indians fan presented the Sox with a sign he had written in red ink and adorned with hearts. The note, which was hung in Boston's dugout, read, "From our city to your city: Our hearts and prayers go out to you, Boston. Love, Cleveland." The Sox also hung in the dugout a jersey emblazoned with the number 617 (one of Boston's area codes) and bearing the name Boston

Strong. The jersey would stay with them for the rest of the season. The Sox continued to win and embarked on a torrid summer that saw them clinch the A.L. East on September 20. Along the way, they grew mountain man-style beards, played grind-it-out, blue-collar-style ball, and recaptured the city's heart.

"The one moment that really resonates with me is when we left here after the marathon bombing and when we stood on that line in Cleveland for the moment of silence," first-year manager John Farrell told a Comcast Sports New England reporter after the Sox had beaten the Toronto Blue Jays to clinch the division. "In the clubhouse that day there were some things that came out, some individual personalities. That was so clear to me that our guys really understood our place, not just in the city of Boston, but responding to a very hard situation. We got off to a good start in April. That moment resonated with me that this had a chance to be something special."[77]

Outfielder Jonny Gomes began to emerge as one of the team's most vocal leaders. During a double-header the Sunday after the terrorists were captured, Gomes used a bat with the words *Boston Strong* on it, as well as the names of the four people killed in the bombings and its aftermath. He later auctioned the bat off to benefit the One Fund.

Camaraderie with survivors like Mery Daniel and the victims' relatives started to grow. On May 7, Krystle Campbell's mother, Patricia, threw out the first pitch. Friends said it was the first time they had seen her smile since her daughter was killed in the explosion. A key day in Heather Abbott's recovery came on May 11, when she left Spaulding Rehabilitation Hospital. She was just days out of the surgery to remove the lower section of her leg, and the team invited her to Fenway to toss out the first pitch. Abbott's friends carried a banner and wore T-shirts that said "Heather Strong."

"I'm not the most athletic person," Heather told reporters before the ceremony. She had practiced throwing with her physical therapist and was determined not to use her wheelchair on the field. She hopped to the mound on crutches and tossed the first pitch to catcher Jarrod Saltalamacchia. They hugged, and then David Ortiz signed a ball for her.

The parade of survivors, first responders, and victims' relatives to Fenway would become a recurring theme throughout the season. The emotional tributes and the images of these amazing survivors walking out to the mound inspired the team. On May 28, Jeff Bauman and Carlos Arredondo did the honors.

By late summer, as the team continued to jockey for playoff position, the survivors struggled to regain control of their lives. On August 15, exactly four months after the bombing, little Jane Richard got a new prosthetic leg. A beaming picture of the little girl sporting the new limb was released to the media. In a statement accompanying the photo, the Richard family said:

> While she is getting more comfortable with it [the prosthetic leg], she is also limited with how much she can wear it at any one time. When she is able to have it on, she struts around on it with great pride and a total sense of accomplishment. Her strength, balance and comfort with the leg improve every day. Watching her dance with her new leg, which has her weight primarily on the other leg, is absolutely priceless.[78]

Before Game 2 of the American League Championship Series against the Detroit Tigers at Fenway, Jane strode proudly across the field on her new leg and wearing a Dustin Pedroia jersey. She was joined by the children's choir from St. Anne's Church in Dorchester, and together they sang the national anthem. The Sox went on to beat Detroit for the pennant, only to face the mighty St. Louis Cardinals in the World Series. By this time, the team and the survivors were one. Symbols of the marathon could be seen all over Fenway Park as the "B Strong" logo was shaved into the grass, stitched on uniforms, and emblazoned on the Green Monster.

The Sox took Game 1 of the World Series at Fenway by a score of 8–1, fueled by David Ortiz's second grand slam of the post-season. Each time he stepped up to the plate, fans could hear the words *This is our fucking city* echoing in their minds.

The Sox would lose the next two games but came roaring back in Game 4 after an inspirational speech by Ortiz in the dugout. "We better than this right here," he told his teammates. "Let's loosen up. Let's play the game the way we do."

The Red Sox would not lose again.

In Game 6, Boston found itself on the cusp of winning its third world championship in a decade and its first at Fenway Park since 1918. The city was electrified. Boston had rediscovered its passion through great pain, and on this night a wall of cheers would stem the steady flow of tears that had run through town like a river since Patriots' Day.

The game wasn't even close. The Sox got up on the Cardinals early and never looked back.

Fans were on their feet for the game's first pitch and never sat down. This was history. This was healing.

Ortiz was walked four times that night, three of them intentional. The Cardinals felt that he was simply too dangerous a player to allow him the chance to get wood on the ball. His teammates provided the power that night to fuel a 6–1 win. Still, he had provided enough post-season heroics to earn World Series MVP honors. As he did in April, Ortiz took the microphone on the field and spoke directly to the fans and the city of Boston.

"I wanna say this is for you, Boston, you guys deserve it," Ortiz said. "You've been through a lot this year and this is for all of you and all the families who struggled with the bombing earlier this year. This is for all of you."

The ballpark roared in appreciation.

"This is our BLEEP city," he added, replacing the infamous F-bomb and censoring himself for the national television audience.[79]

A few days later, as players, coaches, and front office personnel boarded twenty-five of Boston's famous amphibious duck boats for a rolling rally through the city, the 2013 world champions paid one last tribute to the fighters and the fallen of the Boston Marathon bombings. As the parade wound its way down Boylston Street, the convoy stopped at the marathon finish line. There, players Jonny Gomes and Jarrod Saltalamaccia joined staffers from Marathon Sports in placing the shining World Series trophy on the finish line. The trophy was then draped with a 617 Boston Strong Red Sox jersey. Noted tenor Ronan Tynan led thousands of parade-goers in singing "God Bless America."

[23]

THE DESERTED ISLAND

The holidays were a particularly difficult time for the survivors, especially for the families whose loved ones were no longer here.

For the Collier family, a trip to Florida was planned. Thanksgiving had always been Sean's favorite holiday, as it was an opportunity to bring all his brothers and sisters together at their mom's house for a great meal and great conversation. But this year, a change was needed as another gathering at mom's house would only remind Collier's loved ones of what they had lost. So the entire family hopped a plane to Florida where they could still be together, laugh a little bit, and remember the brother whose absence had brought them even closer over the past few months.

On Christmas Eve each year, the Richard family opens its Victorian home to friends and neighbors and they all sing "The Twelve Days of Christmas." But there would be no singing, no holiday cheer on the first Christmas since the bombing. Instead, Bill and Denise retreated to their safe haven—New Hampshire, where they booked the family into a quiet inn, turned off their phones, and tried to relax. Santa Claus would be visiting one less child this year, and the realization was crushing for Martin's parents, who had already been through so much.

Bill and Denise would continue to mourn, but they would also mobilize in memory of their son. A month later, the couple announced the formation of the Martin W. Richard Charitable Foundation with a mission to spread his message of "No More Hurting People" through educational, community, and athletic programs—including the Boston Marathon. In early February 2014, Bill Richard spoke publicly for the first time since the tragedy that took his son. "The Boston Marathon was always a special day for the family," Richard told a crowd gathered in Dorchester. "It became clear over these last few months that we would not run from the event, but embrace it to help us heal, to honor our son and his message and to pay it forward."

From more than 250 applicants, the family selected a group of seventy-two runners to represent Team MR8 in the 2014 marathon. The youngest runner was eighteen; the oldest was sixty-five years of age.

"While the pain of that day will forever be with us," Bill Richard said, "our hope is that this special event becomes a source of strength for our family and a means to make a difference in the world."

The Richards were not alone in their mission to pay it forward. Charitable donations continued to pour in from all over the world. But one Boston couple had a different idea. They wanted to bring the world to the marathon survivors. As Hank and Tricia Lewis watched from their home on the Boston waterfront while the horror unfolded on Boylston Street on that fateful April day, they were startled to see a familiar face captured in one of the photos that ran again and again on television.

"That's Carlos," Tricia pointed out to her husband. "He sailed with us just with us a few months ago."

As owners of Boston-based Vantage Deluxe World Travel, the Lewises had provided in late 2012 a free river ship cruise through Europe to Arredondo and other gold star families and wounded warriors. Arredondo, with his signature cowboy hat, had left an indelible mark on ship staffers through his tireless assistance to disabled veterans during the cruise. To Hank and Tricia Lewis, Carlos was family.

"How can we help Carlos and the survivors?" Tricia asked her husband. Together they came up with the answer. The couple would invite as many marathon survivors as they could, more than a hundred in all, for an all-inclusive river cruise through the south of France. The trip was planned for December and would cost Hank and Tricia Lewis about a half million dollars.

"We figured that by living in Boston, they were constantly surrounded by visual reminders of what they had gone through," Tricia Lewis recalls.

"We wanted to provide them with a chance to escape if just for a short while. We viewed the river ship as their deserted island." Vantage Travel staff members took to the project with great vigor and spent the next several months setting up the historic cruise.

When Michelle L'Heureux received her invitation, at first she thought it was a scam.

"No way could somebody be that generous," she said to her boyfriend, Brian. But she quickly learned that the offer was genuine and that everything, including airfare, would be provided by Vantage Travel. The Lewises also extended an invitation to Brian, as each survivor would be allowed to bring one guest.

Two weeks before Christmas, the survivors gathered at Boston's Logan International Airport for a flight to London and then Paris. From there they boarded the ship in Mâcon, a city of thirty-five thousand in central France that sits on the Saône River, a narrow, meandering waterway that feeds into the Rhône. On the first night aboard the *ms River Discovery II*, the travelers—some walking on crutches, some in wheelchairs, and others limping slightly from shrapnel wounds— milled about, sipping cocktails and making small talk. They were uncertain of what to say, whom to sit with, and whether it was even OK to smile and laugh. Michelle recognized some of the survivors she had met either at the hospital or later in support groups. Other faces she had not seen since the bombings. "I'm not sure, but I think she was standing close to me in front of Marathon Sports," she whispered to Brian as another woman passed by. Many survivors were ambivalent about taking the trip, fearful of spending eleven days aboard a small cruise ship surrounded by constant reminders of the bombings. There was also fear that traveling in such a large group of marathon survivors would provide terrorists with an opportunity to "finish the job." Some victims chose not to go for that very reason.

The grieving parents of Lingzi Lu did make the trip. They felt they had to. Jun Lu wanted to better understand what had happened to his beloved daughter on Boylston Street. He came in search of answers, but what he found was something different. Jun Lu did not speak English, and the translator who accompanied him and his wife on the trip did not fare much better. Without the ability to bond with other passengers, the Lus withdrew deep within themselves, walking the ship and eating alone. The pain was vivid in Jun Lu's eyes and on his shoulders, which carried the tremendous burden of losing their only child. Passengers smiled at the Lus, not knowing how else to communicate. Lingzi's parents could hardly muster a smile or even a nod in response.

Carlos Arredondo took the cruise with his wife, Melida, and Jeff Bauman and his fiancée, Erin Hurley. He noticed Jun Lu picking at his food and recognized the look on the man's face. It was a look he's seen every day in the mirror since the deaths of his sons, Alex and Brian.

If there was one thing Carlos knew, it was loss. He walked across the room and reached out. He smiled. He took the man's hand. Carlos is charismatic and persistent, a natural healer, and as he stuck with Jun Lu, a relationship began to form. The men came to speak as friends, as mourning fathers. "Sometimes I don't need to say anything to him," Carlos said on the cruise. "I give him a hug, or touch his shoulders, or shake hands. We sit on the bus together. Hopefully that makes him feel comfort."

Five days into the cruise, Carlos and his wife, Melida, accompanied Lu to a concert performed by two violinists and a cellist in the lounge. Lu told them with pride that his daughter played the cello. This was the very reason, however, that his wife remained in their cabin. The music would be too painful a reminder for her. As the trio's instruments filled the room with harmony, the father closed his eyes. "My daughter's happiness was her music," he told Carlos. "This makes me feel close to her." Afterward, he was finally able to smile at the memory of Lingzi.

As the ship sailed down the river, the self-consciousness fell away, and survivors began to share seafood, steaks, and fine French wines in the ship's dining room. They swapped marathon survival stories, sometimes trying to find answers, other times seeking to provide some. "So, which bombing were you at?" was a common question. And the answer often revealed a grim serendipity: Most of them had been just steps from one another.

Alan Starr is an audio engineer who came to the 2013 marathon—the first Boston Marathon he'd ever attended—to watch a friend run. He was standing about twenty-five feet away when the first bomb exploded in front of Marathon Sports. Starr felt the impact as he was blown back into the crowd. He was dazed, confused—his mind in a fog. He stood there as people started to run. His ears were ringing terribly, but he could hear the faint sound of someone say, "Help, she's bleeding."

He looked to his right and saw two young women leaning against a doorway. One teenage girl was bleeding from the leg. Starr ran to help another first responder apply pressure to the girl's gaping wound. He then took his jacket off and wrapped it around her leg. He tried keeping her calm. Moments later, someone else yelled, "You have to get out of here, there could be more bombs!" Starr grabbed the girl by her legs, lifted her up, and carried her to safety in the medical tent. He placed her down on a stretcher and returned to help others.

Alan Starr shared his story during dinner on the ship.

"I never saw the girl again," he told fellow passengers. "I don't know who she was. Her face was covered by debris."

Sarah Girouard, a student at Northeastern University, sat across from Starr, listening intently as he spoke. Sarah had been hurt at the bombing. A piece of metal had ripped through her right leg below the knee, fracturing her tibia before exiting the other side. Another piece of metal had lodged in her ankle. After dinner, Sarah approached Starr in the lounge and asked him a few questions. He answered.

"That was me you saved," she told him. "Thank you."

Another passenger, Jillian Boynton, looked around the ship at all the survivors bearing different types of physical scars—and she felt guilty.

"My friend pulled me away from Boylston Street," she said. "I should have stayed. I should have helped people."

But Boynton, a sales representative from Nashua, New Hampshire, was in need of help herself. She went to the hospital hours after the bombing and collapsed after doctors told her she had suffered a damaged eardrum. She also suffers from post-traumatic stress disorder and was forced to shift from an outside sales position to an inside sales job because she cannot be around a lot of people. This cruise would be a challenge for her—one of both highs and lows.

Linda Witt also suffered hearing loss and had to undergo reconstructive dental surgery. A resident of Neenah, Wisconsin, Witt had visited Boston to watch her son, Bill Tanguay, run the marathon to raise money for the Animal Rescue League. She had also come to celebrate her birthday. Witt was enjoying a cup of coffee outside Forum when the second explosion lifted her off the ground and thrust her forward six to eight feet. She lost her hearing immediately, and she also lost her sense of taste and smell. Witt's son, Bill, accompanied her on the cruise to France.

"Living in the Midwest, I feel detached from it all," she said. "I came here to find my 'marathon family' and to bond with them. No one else understands what we've all gone through." Over the next several days, Linda Witt found the bond she was looking for.

After dinner in Mâcon, Michelle L'Heureux set out to explore the city with some of the others. The night was cool and foggy, and the group took turns pointing out the city's ancient architecture, which in some places dates back to the tenth century. They settled into a pub called La Traboule hidden away in a brick alley, and as Michelle grew more comfortable with her new companions, she opened up.

"See this?" she said, pulling her yoga pants tight around her knee and upper thigh. A deep indentation appeared in the back of her leg. "All the fatty tissue behind my knee—it was all blown off."

Sitting next to her at La Traboule was Sabrina Dello Russo. The two had not met before the trip, but they got acquainted at dinner and became instant friends, sharing cigarettes, champagne, and stories. Sabrina, a native of Boston's Italian North End, was at the finish line, enjoying a cocktail with a group of friends on the patio of Forum, when the second bomb detonated. The blast knocked her to the ground, leaving her dazed. It blew her cell phone out of her hand. Her ears rang. She didn't know exactly what had happened, but she did know people were dead. As she looked around, she saw limbs strewn about.

Sabrina suffered hearing loss and a traumatic brain injury. She is also racked by survivor's guilt, knowing how much worse her injuries could have been. Since the bombings, she has undergone gone countless hours of therapy. She had to leave her job at Liberty Mutual for a few months, and has cut her workload in half. She cries more than she used to. Like Michelle, she has nightmares. Sabrina has looked at lots of pictures from the bombings. One in particular, taken before the explosions, haunts her. In it, she stands just feet away from Roseann Sdoia, Martin Richard, and the suspected bomber, Dzhokhar Tsarnaev.

"I look at it every day," she said.

When the group returned to the ship, Michelle noticed Jeff Bauman chatting with friends by the piano bar inside the lounge. She was standing right next to Bauman on Boylston Street—she knows this because she's seen pictures of the two of them standing together—just seconds before the blasts, and, gruesomely, after. That evening on the ship, she met him in passing a few times, but could not muster the courage to go over and have a quiet conversation. The hours passed. The back of Michelle's left leg got sore. She began massaging her scar gently, but the pain did not go away. At around 3 a.m. she stood, using her good leg for support, and walked over to Jeff, who was now spinning in his wheelchair on the dance floor. They embraced. Michelle, who generally does not let anyone touch the scar, held her breath as Jeff's hand instinctively began rubbing her wound. His touch startled her, but she did not move away.

"If I could've taken the blast for everyone, I would have," he whispered.

"You went through enough, Jeff," she replied.

He looked up at Michelle and smiled. "Keep working on those legs," he said. "You're gonna be all right."

She couldn't speak. Instead, Michelle moved in and hugged Jeff tightly. After a few seconds, she let go and, without a word, walked out of the lounge, fighting back tears. Moments later, she was back in her cabin, weeping uncontrollably.

Jeff Bauman is used to these sorts of interactions. They have become as much a part of his life as his daily efforts to walk on his titanium legs. On the cruise, he felt loose and happy. So much so that on one night, he and a friend commandeered the piano player's microphone and began rapping freestyle while a small crowd of younger survivors gathered on the dance floor, watching, dancing, and smiling.

"I know I'm a symbol of the bombings for everyone," he said later. "Still, I feel lucky. I only had to undergo three surgeries after I was hit. So many people here are in for the long haul."

In Saône-et-Loire, Sabrina and Michelle continued to bond at Cluny Abbey, which was established by Benedictine monks in 910. The Catholic day of prayer for the dead, All Souls' Day, was first established here—something that was not lost on the two women and the rest of their group.

The imposing church is made up of several large rooms, each separated by a heavy wooden door. When a door closed abruptly during the tour, the loud noise startled many survivors, who were visibly shaken by the sound. Some sat on benches and focused on their breathing while others exchanged knowing glances, composed themselves, and turned their attention back to the tour guide and the soaring architecture.

"Ever since the bombing, I can't take loud noises," Michelle said. "Thunderstorms and fireworks are too much for me."

Yet, there was much to celebrate on the cruise. Jeff Bauman announced to some friends that he and Erin were expecting their first baby. Another couple, Colton Kilgore and his wife, Kimberly, survivors of the first bomb blast, announced that they, too, were expecting.

In Lyon, France, where Christmas lights lined the streets, James "Bim" Costello and his girlfriend, Krista D'Agostino, rode a giant Ferris wheel in Place Bellecour, just yards away from a magnificent statue of King Louis XIV mounted on a horse.

Costello became one of the public faces of the bombings when a photo of him wandering out of the carnage in a daze, his clothes singed and tattered, went global. He suffered shrapnel wounds and severe burns, and spent two weeks recovering in Spaulding Rehabilitation Hospital. There he met D'Agostino, a nurse. They started dating. By the time they flew to France, they'd been together for seven months.

Atop the Ferris wheel, Costello proposed. D'Agostino gleefully accepted. He then slipped onto her finger a diamond ring that J. P. and Paul Norden, two brothers who each lost a leg in the bombings, helped him smuggle onto the trip without her knowing. She held the diamond up against the glittering lights of the Ferris wheel. Costello snapped a photo with his iPhone and posted it on Facebook. The couple returned to the ship and retired for the night. The next morning, they awoke to buzzing smartphones. Their photo had gone viral. Media outlets from Boston to Paris had picked up their story, and the couple was overwhelmed with interview requests. That evening at dinner, the crew brought out a cake with a huge sparkler candle for them, and everyone cheered their engagement. They kept mostly to themselves over the next couple of days, walking the chilly streets of the small villages and cities hand in hand, until they cut their trip short to travel to New York for an appearance on the *Today* show.

In Lyon, Michelle and Sabrina found a darkened lounge where they sat with friends, sipping mojitos, taking selfies, laughing, and swapping stories about, yes, the marathon, but about other things, too. They felt good. They wanted to dance. They asked the bartender if he could recommend a place.

"There's a club called Boston Café," he told them.

Silence.

But there was no question they would go. They walked the three or four blocks to the bar, located in the opulent Place des Terreaux. It's a familiar Irish pub–type setting, with twentysomethings drinking cheap beer and listening to Michael Jackson's "Beat It." It was packed, and hot—not unlike Faneuil Hall pubs back home in Boston. Michelle, who struggles with large crowds, began to feel anxious and quickly hustled to a corner where she could sit, breathe, relax, and have a cold drink. Some of the others danced.

Someone asked the manager about the name. Are the owners from Boston? No, he says, they "just love Boston-style pubs." The manager asked why the travelers were in Lyon. They told him.

"Hold on," he said, hurrying away. He returned a few minutes later with an armful of souvenirs—a few sweatshirts and several hats, all with the Boston Café logo. The group tried to give him some money, but he refused, waving them away with a smile.

"You are our guests," he said. "Thank you for coming in."

Down the river, in Viviers, Jeff Bauman decided it was time for him to get off the ship for a while. He called for Carlos, and his friend pushed him down the gangplank and along the town's cobblestone streets. They moved in the shadow of rows of leafless plane trees, similar to sycamores, that were planted by Napoleon's army throughout France. A few others went along, and the group ducked into a tiny café just as the owner was about to close to run a few errands.

This, Carlos determined, would not stand. He charmed the owner, smilingly convincing the man that the café would be in good hands while he was gone, and promised to pay for each drink they took. The owner, who spoke little English, obliged, and nodded to the only French regular in the place to keep an eye on things. He then pointed to a cooler where a few twelve-packs of Heineken were being chilled and gave a thumbs-up to Carlos, who took over bartending duties. Members of the group hoisted their bottles in a toast to him. He returned the salute. "This is what this trip is supposed to be all about," Carlos said. "People—survivors—getting to know one another, helping each other out, having fun." He gave Jeff a pat on the back and handed him a Heineken.

The other survivors marveled at the relationship between Carlos and Jeff, at how Carlos took the younger man under his wing as a surrogate son of sorts, after saving his life. Every time Jeff left the ship, it was with Carlos pushing him. When Jeff went to bed, Carlos helped him. They ate every meal together. They were inseparable. They have even traveled to Costa Rica, and are frequently at events together back in Boston.

But it's not just Jeff. The entire group owed a debt to Carlos. During the long trip, he acted as their shield when they needed protection. He was usually the first one to step up to the microphones to give the media the sound bites they needed so that the others would not have to. When they needed to talk, he listened intently and looked them deep in the eyes, often holding their hands or putting an arm around their shoulders. Because of his heroism that day, they felt safe around him. He gave them comfort. And in return, they gave *him* comfort.

The trip provided many of them with that rarest of opportunities: a chance to talk openly and freely about what has been haunting them for months. There was no judgment aboard the ship. No filters. Just catharsis. Just relief. And Carlos was an agent of this.

"Now we can talk to each other like we've known each other a long time," he said. "There's been a few moments where I shared my experience with some of them, and they help me out, to get it off my chest. And I've been listening to a few stories myself. I hope I help out as well. Like family. Like an old friend. It's amazing how this works."

Survivors also found strength in another man, seventy-one-year-old Bill White of Bolton, Massachusetts, who traveled on the cruise with his wife, Mary-Jo. The couple had attended the Boston Marathon in 2013 on a whim. They had taken an MBTA train into the city where they watched much of the race at the finish line before making their way to the Arlington Street Green Line station for the trip back to Bolton. They were just a few feet away from Tamerlan Tsarnaev's bomb-laden backpack when it exploded. Mary-Jo suffered a broken wrist and shrapnel injuries, but her husband was hurt badly. Bill, a Vietnam veteran, suffered catastrophic wounds to his right leg—a leg doctors could not save. Fitted with a prosthetic and crutches, the elderly man had to learn to walk again. White refused any assistance during a number of exhaustive treks through the French countryside. Stoically, he would lift himself off the bus as the large group explored quaint villages such as Chateauneuf-du-Pape, where Pope John XXII, a noted wine lover, had erected a castle to keep a better watch on his grapes during the Avignon Papacy.

"I look at this darling man and I say to myself, 'If he can do it, so can I,'" Michelle said of White. As she was with Jeff Bauman, Michelle was nervous about approaching Bill White, whom she had remembered from the hospital. She finally introduced herself after the trip, and the two now chat regularly.

The trip ended in Tarascon, but before everyone parted, one of the French tour guides addressed the group. "This has been the most memorable cruise we've ever been a part of," she told them. "It has been such a sobering experience for our staff. We look at each of you and we see tremendous strength. Your strength has lifted each other, and it has lifted us as well."

Examples of that strength abounded throughout the journey.

Rebekah Gregory, a twenty-six-year-old Texas mom who has had fifteen surgeries to repair severe damage to her leg and ankle, walked on crutches and in a cast from her latest surgery as she toured medieval castles and ancient churches with relatives, several of whom were also injured in the first explosion.

Michelle shrugged off the chafing and stinging of her skin grafts as they rubbed against the fabric of her clothes while she toured King Louis II of Anjou's castle in Tarascon.

Victoria McGrath, a twenty-year-old Northeastern student originally from France who has had several surgeries to repair major leg injuries, had sometimes been forced to use a wheelchair, but in France, she embarked on daily walking excursions, hiking steep streets without aid and touring wine country with her friends.

In Viviers, Eric and Ann Whalley, a British couple in their mid-60s whose stroll from their home in Charlestown to the finish line on Marathon Monday landed them in the hospital with excruciating leg injuries and more than a dozen surgeries between them, carefully negotiated dirt paths and stone walkways to reach the top of a scenic plateau. There, the couple stood holding hands, gazing down over the countryside below.

Michelle L'Heureux and Sabrina Dello Russo hugged as they prepared to board separate buses to Marseille airport for their flights home. They pledged to get together in Boston, and they have, becoming close friends. Alan Starr, Carlos and Jeff, the Whites, and the Whalleys all said heartfelt goodbyes. Phone numbers and email addresses were exchanged; plans were made.

Jun Lu and his wife returned to China, alone. They did not get the answers they were looking for. No one on board could recall seeing their daughter at the finish line that day. But before they left the ship, Lu and his new friend Carlos embraced once more. "Please come visit us," Lu said. "Please come to China." Carlos accepted the offer without hesitation.

[24]

THE NEW NORMAL

Dzhokhar Tsarnaev sits in isolation in a small prison cell at the Federal Medical Center in Devens, Massachusetts, forty miles from the finish line on Boylston Street. He is cut off from the outside world. Communicating with other prisoners is strictly forbidden. Sunlight is rare. His only visitors are his sisters, a psychiatrist, and members of his legal team, which includes five attorneys, a team of paralegals, and two investigators.[80] His lawyers are trying to keep him alive and away from lethal injection if and when he is found guilty. Their plan is to argue that he was seduced and manipulated by his older brother, Tamerlan, and that he acted under his "domination and control."[81] It is a defense the victims find laughable. To muddy the waters even more, his lawyers claim that the FBI had encouraged Tamerlan to become an informant to provide the Bureau with intelligence on Boston's Chechen and Muslim communities.[82] Dzhokhar's lawyers argue that the alleged pressure from the FBI toward Tamerlan to get him to rat on his fellow Muslims may have added to his "increased paranoia and distress."[83]

Federal prosecutors are looking to expose a different side of Dzhokhar. He was not a manipulated man-child, they argue, but a cold-blooded killer. Prosecutors claim that Tsarnaev has made "detrimental" statements during jailhouse visits with his sisters. This legal Ping-Pong game will continue to go back and forth through his trial. Meanwhile, Dzhokhar sits in his cell, living off meals of chicken and rice and allowed to make only one phone call, write only one letter each week. This is the life of an American teenager—an American teenager accused of killing and maiming his fellow citizens, including a young boy who should be enjoying the fourth grade.

Dzhokhar Tsarnaev is caged, but his victims are free—free to resume their lives in new and different ways. In January, Jeff Bauman and Carlos Arredondo were invited to attend President Obama's State of the Union Address as special guests of the First Lady. A week later, they were asked to deliver the commencement address at Fisher College in Boston. Such opportunities could not have been imagined before April 15, 2013. The survivors had sacrificed their bodies and their minds, but they had also discovered a new strength in the well of their souls. Through their healing, they reclaimed their lives, tackled new challenges, and savored new experiences. Mery Daniel, Heather Abbott, and Adrienne Haslet-Davis found themselves backstage at a Beyoncé concert taking photos with the singing star. Members of the Collier family, the Richard family, and others were invited to Fenway Park for the 2014 home opener, where they presented World Series rings to the Red Sox. Survivors Colton Kilgore and Sabrina Dello Russo began training for their first Boston Marathon.

Michelle L'Heureux returned to the ski slopes, a place she feared she would never be able to return to. She was nervous but dug deep, thinking to herself that it was time to get back to some of the things she loved. But when the day arrived, she worried about her quad muscles in her injured leg, which hadn't yet returned to full strength. Would they be strong enough to handle the turns and stops?

Michelle met her best friend Sare Largay at Blue Hills in Milton, Massachusetts. They entered the small lodge, got bundled up, and Michelle strapped into her ski boots for the first time since before she was injured. Ski boots are always stiff the first time you put them on at the beginning of a season, but for Michelle, the feeling was especially foreign—and a bit scary.

Carrying their skis, they walked to the lift line, put down their skis, and Michelle snapped in. It was something she'd done literally thousands of times in her life, but this time, it felt really good. She smiled, albeit a bit anxiously.

Overcoming her fears is a personal goal. And skiing this night was one of them.

Getting onto the chairlift is as natural as tying shoes to Michelle. But on this night, she was afraid. She couldn't bring herself to get onto the chair. Partly she was afraid about her leg, but she was also scared of getting on the rickety, old, metal chairlift. She feared an accident.

It was the same fear she felt in Lyon, France, a month earlier when she got on a Ferris wheel with other survivors. She thought about the Ferris wheel and how she was scared then, too.

Nothing happened on the Ferris wheel. Nothing is going to happen now, she told herself.

Sare sensed her apprehension and asked the lift operator to slow it down for them. The chair slowly pulled up behind them, Michelle grabbed the rail, sat down, and they were off toward the top of the hill.

Nearing the top, Michelle was afraid to raise the bar, so Sare grabbed her arm, held it tight, and raised the bar.

They skied down the small off-ramp and onto the snow. Michelle stood at the top for a solid five minutes. She was terrified. *Have I made a mistake? What if my leg gives out? What if I fall?* Her mind was racing.

Michelle started to slide down the hill and made her first turn. It felt awkward, but she had done it hundreds of times before. *I can do this*, she thought.

She was shaky, but she made each turn, keeping her speed down. She gained confidence along the way. Her leg was definitely feeling weak, so she stopped about halfway down.

She rested a minute and then started up again. As she got toward the end of the short intermediate trail, she started picking up a bit too much speed, her weakened leg resisting her efforts to slow her body down.

She pulled it together, though, and slowed herself down, regaining control. She made it to the bottom. She smiled.

They did six runs that night, and it got easier each time. Her turns got sharper and she skied a bit more freely each time. But by the final run, Michelle's leg was sore.

The friends snapped out of their skis and called it a night. Michelle was exhausted but was also exhilarated that she had returned to doing something she loved. It was another milestone for her as she resumed her "new normal."

Since that first time back skiing, Michelle realized that she needed to pick up the work on rebuilding her quad muscles. She started doing wall sits, in which she crouches down with her back against a wall and her knees bent at a right angle. She also started doing more weight exercises with her legs at the gym—for she had in mind a promise she'd made to her Marathon Day "heroes" that she would run a 5K road race with them the day before the 2014 Boston Marathon.

Michelle, like many survivors, regularly gets together with her heroes. For Michelle, those are Andrew Daly, Joe McMenamy, and Lauren Blanda. All three are friends with a manager at Marathon Sports and were there the day of the bombing to watch the race.

Joe worked at Marathon Sports, while Lauren worked at nearby City Sports. Andrew, a running specialist for Adidas, sells to Marathon Sports. Lauren and Andrew have been dating for years and got engaged in January 2014.

Michelle credits the three with saving her life that day. As she lay on the floor of Marathon Sports, the three kept her calm while they tore T-shirts off the racks and made tourniquets to stop the bleeding from her gaping wounds.

After EMTs evacuated Michelle, Joe walked away from Marathon Sports covered in her blood. His pants were soaked with it. He, like most there that day, was in shock.

He called his mom and told her the whole experience had changed him. He now wanted to become a firefighter or an EMT. In February 2014, he took the exam to become a Boston firefighter.

One afternoon in January, Michelle was at the gym walking on the treadmill as usual. She was feeling unusually strong this day and, with her heroes in mind, she decided to try and run for the first time since the bombings.

OK, *let's see what I can do*, she said to herself, increasing the speed.

She started to trot. Then she started to jog.

I'm running, she thought to herself.

It wasn't easy, but she felt good. Her goal was to do a mile. Around the seventh-tenths mile mark, she started feeling weak. Her knee was aching from the pounding, and her wound was chafing. She wanted to quit.

She was getting annoyed with herself.

A year ago, you could have run a mile, but you just didn't choose to, she thought to herself. Her anger rising, her thoughts turned to the terrorists.

You have to finish this mile.

She pictured the faces of Dzhokhar and Tamerlan Tsarnaev. It's something she does regularly, whenever her arm or leg injury is becoming an obstacle. It gives her motivation to finish.

If I finish this mile, I win, she told herself. She then mentally addressed the terrorists directly: *You're not going to win this. You did this to my leg, but I'm going to prove you wrong and I'm going to finish.*

She finished the mile. She let out a sigh of exhaustion, turned off the treadmill, and headed for the locker room. She was sore, but she was satisfied.

She won.

She went home, took some Motrin, and iced her knee. Surprisingly, she woke up the next morning with no pain. That day, she went back to the gym and ran one and a half miles.

Two weeks later, she and her boyfriend, Brian, who is training to run the marathon again, went to the gym together.

They ran side-by-side on treadmills. After a mile, Michelle told him, "One mile." She wanted to stop.

"Keep going," Brian encouraged her.

She got to a mile and a half.

"Keep going," he said.

Her goal was to make it to two miles. She made it.

"Woo-hoo!" she said, letting out a small yell. People working out turned around and looked at her awkwardly.

She didn't care. She was another step closer toward being able to run the 5K race with her heroes.

FROM FINISH LINE TO FINISH LINE

Jun Lu and his wife stood in front of Forum one year to the day after losing their daughter, Lingzi. Boylston Street was quiet. Jun Lu stared down at the sidewalk and must have wondered, as all parents would, whether his child had experienced pain as she was dying or whether the end had come quickly, mercifully. The Lus were joined on this dreary morning, April 15, 2014, by Bill and Denise Richard and their children, Jane and Henry, as well as the family of Krystle Campbell. They nodded their heads as Cardinal Sean O'Malley offered a short prayer. Bill Richard wiped away tears as Jane and Henry joined Boston's new mayor, Marty Walsh, in placing a wreath at the site. Another wreath was laid a block down Boylston Street in front of Marathon Sports. An honor guard made up of Boston police, Boston firefighters, Watertown police, and state troopers stood at attention next to the wreaths while bagpipes solemnly wailed "Amazing Grace."

Later that morning, the families gathered inside the John B. Hynes Veterans Memorial Convention Center near the finish line, where hundreds attended an emotional memorial service to remember Martin Richard, Lingzi Lu, Krystle Campbell, and Sean Collier, and to honor all those injured that day. Sean Collier's parents, brothers, and sisters were present, as was Michelle L'Heureux, accompanied by her dad. Some of the survivors, including Adrienne Haslet-Davis, spoke. "The city has stood by us, supported us, and helped us heal," she said. "It is up to us to make sure that every single second after counts, because believe me, they do."

Governor Deval Patrick told all those gathered about the photo of Martin Richard carrying his campaign sign. "We're not strangers. We are in the end, one community," he said. "We are all connected to each other, to events beyond our control, to a common destiny."

In the audience, an exhausted Jane Richard was asleep in her mother's arms. Mayor Marty Walsh, a neighbor of the Richard family, spoke about Jane's courage and noted that the little girl had recently returned to playing church-league basketball on her prosthetic leg. Recently, she had been fitted for her first "Cheetah" running leg, a gift from an organization called Wiggle Your Toes.

Vice President Joe Biden, who spoke the year before at Sean Collier's memorial service, reminded those gathered that Boston was not alone. He called the attack at the marathon an attack on America.

"We will never yield, we will never cower. America will never ever, ever stand down," Biden said. "We are Boston. We are America. We respond, we endure, we overcome, and we own the finish line!"

But it was former mayor Tom Menino who made the greatest impact that day. A month before the bombing anniversary, the newly retired mayor announced that he was being treated for an advanced stage of cancer that had spread to his liver and lymph nodes. Looking frail and aided by a cane, Menino took the podium to a standing ovation from the crowd.

"This day will always be hard. It will never be easy to gather so close to that finish line. It will never be easy to be so close to that place where our lives broke apart," he said. "We long to be anywhere but here."

He then paraphrased a line from Ernest Hemingway's classic novel *The Sun Also Rises*. "You are strong at this broken place."

Menino told the survivors that the city would bear responsibility for their welfare in the years to come. "When the lights are dim and cameras go away, know our support for you will never waiver."

Following the service, the former mayor, Governor Patrick, Vice President Biden, and other dignitaries led survivors down Boylston Street through driving rain to the finish line where they, along with thousands of people watching on television, observed a moment of silence just before 3 p.m.—at the exact time of the first explosion one year before.

Michelle L'Heureux managed to hold it together for the ceremony, but the moment of silence struck a chord deep inside her. Standing on Boylston Street with so many other survivors, in complete silence except for the tolling church bells, she began to cry.

Mery Daniel chose to observe the anniversary at home. She expressed her feelings throughout the day with status updates on her Facebook page, where she wrote, "As I laid on the ground, the only contact I had with reality was the smell. It was the same as the love that awakened me three days later."

On that deeply personal anniversary, she took to Facebook once again with these thoughts:

> Today marks 1 year anniversary of my Rebirth . . . Happy Birthday to me . . . 1 year ago I woke up and heard the unspeakable . . . much to my surprise, it wasn't the long incomprehensible speech that I remember rather my reaction to it . . . I was as calm, serene and peaceful as I have never been . . . like a mother who has been in labor for years . . . it was a safe and happy delivery. I cherish the Day for what I thought it meant. I crossed the desert. . . .

That night, a young art student with a history of mental illness set the city on edge when he was caught on video parading down Boylston Street clad in black with two fake pressure cooker bombs. Police seized them and charged the man with possession of a hoax device and other offenses. The man claimed it was a prank, but the stunt didn't sit well with cops, first responders, or the survivors.

The following Saturday—just two days before the 2014 Boston Marathon—the city organized a 5K race on Boston Common. Dozens of survivors ran in the event, including Michelle, who had put aside her fears and wore a "4.15 Strong" shirt for the occasion. She ran with her boyfriend, her best friend, and her four heroes—the four who worked on her that day inside Marathon Sports. The group stayed together and ran at Michelle's pace—clocking 11.5-minute miles.

"It looked the same as Marathon Day, so that part was a little weird," she said of the route. "But running down that road with them all around me felt really good."

When she crossed the finish line, tears came to her eyes. She squinted hard and blocked out the dark thoughts of that horrible day. Today, she had taken back control.

She posted a picture of herself crossing the finish line on Facebook with these words: "You tried to terrorize us, but you actually united us!! Strong city & strong people!! And I finished a 5k—holy sh*t!!"

Two days later, her words were echoed by Bill Poole as he stood on the familiar ground of Lexington Green where, once again, he would recite the words delivered hundreds of years before by Captain John Parker. Five thousand indomitable Bostonians awoke during the pre-dawn hours to attend the reenactment of the Battle of Lexington on April 21, 2014—Patriots' Day.

"We remember those who lost their lives in the Boston Marathon bombing one year ago," Reverend Peter Boulatta said during his invocation before the reenactment, "those who bear the scars of that thankless act of violence—injuries to the body and soul."

Moments later, mock shots were fired, reenactors fell on cue, and musket smoke filled the air. Bill Poole surveyed the large crowd and saw a look of reverence and determination in their eyes.

"This is our day, not the terrorists' day," he said. "The bombings were an attempt to turn our attention away from our society and our freedoms. The terrorists did not succeed."

Still, the town of Lexington took precautions, beefing up security for the first time in years. This time, spectators were ordered to keep their belongings in clear or mesh backpacks, and ladders, often used to see over crowds, were outlawed. Police also kept a close eye out for any unattended bags.

There was truly a price to be paid for freedom, and this meant tighter security in Lexington and, of course, at the Boston Marathon, where 36,000 people had registered to run in 2014, a near record. The number of anticipated spectators topped one million, which was twice as many as in 2013. It seemed that everyone wanted to be a part of this historic day for the city of Boston.

Danny Keeler spent the morning of the big race doing what he had done for years: helping to finalize the security plan. This year, there were more than 3,500 cops along the route. The finish line was a fortress patrolled by dozens of bomb-sniffing dogs, uniformed officers, and undercover cops. There were several new video cameras installed in the area. Boston police had also consulted heavily with counterparts in New York City and London to learn how they kept the cities safe for New Year's Eve in Times Square and the 2012 Summer Olympics. Still, in a free society, the odds favored the terrorists—and they always would.

"We have to get this right 110 percent of the time," said Keiran Ramsey of the FBI. "The bad guys only have to get lucky once."

The Boston Police Department changed its patrol strategy for 2014. In prior years, cops would line Boylston Street and look into the crowds toward buildings and the sidewalk. This year, because of the bombings, cops were positioned along the buildings and on the sidewalks and trained to look out at the crowds and toward the street.

It was a tactical move Keeler thought would help cops see the crowds better. As he had done the previous year before the bombings, Keeler spent the morning going over security plans, deploying officers, and patrolling Boylston himself.

Boston cop Javier Pagan was back on duty for the marathon and was assigned to the Back Bay. He wasn't at his usual post near the finish line; instead, he was assigned to patrol at the corner of Newbury and Dartmouth streets. It was some distance from the finish line, but it was still close enough that throughout the day Javier thought about the horror he had witnessed that day a year earlier. This day, his captain told him and his fellow officers to beware of copycats or people looking to grab the spotlight with a dangerous prank.

"I liked the fact that I wasn't at the finish line," he said. "Even though I was just up the street from it, it was more relaxed. Still, we were all on high alert."

Police had set up security checkpoints at the top and bottom of Boylston Street and at every side street in between. Bags were checked and given a yellow sticker that read: *Inspected*.

After the murder of Martin Richard and the injuries to his sister, Jane, many wondered if parents would keep their children away from the race—and even whether the marathon would be a family-friendly event ever again. Those concerns were alleviated by the site of throngs of moms and dads pushing strollers and holding hands with their young children along the finish line. Danny Keeler smiled as he watched the parade of families go by. *Pure Americana*, he thought to himself.

"It completely reinforces the resilience of the city," Keeler said. "Let's get back to what it was always about: a family day celebrating these athletes."

Although runners must normally qualify in a previous race in order to run Boston, survivors of the bombings were offered bibs to run in the 2014 Boston Marathon, even if they had never run a marathon before.

Survivor Sabrina Dello Russo—Roseann Sdoia's best friend—ran her first marathon in her friend's honor. She raised more than fifty thousand dollars toward Roseann's recovery fund.

Also running his first marathon was survivor Colton Kilgore, the North Carolina man who celebrated his wife Kimberly's pregnancy on the trip to France. They were among those injured in the bombings. Nine family members cheered Colton on as he ran, including his five-year-old nephew, Noah, who a year ago had been struck by shrapnel that tore a hole in his leg. Also seriously injured was Colton's sister-in-law, Rebekah Gregory. Rebekah was among those on the France trip. She had had sixteen surgeries before the trip and walked on crutches and in a cast from her latest procedure throughout the cruise. In June 2014, Rebekah faced the agonizing decision of whether to have her injured leg amputated. At that point, she couldn't put weight on the limb, and she was in constant pain. Doctors have told her that the leg will likely never heal properly, and as of August 2014, she was still considering amputation.

Colton ran the race to honor his relatives who were more severely injured than he was. It was his way of paying homage to them. When he crossed the finish line, he wore a broad smile through his trademark thick beard and raised his hands in victory.

"It was nice because now I have this as a memory," Colton said. "Now, when I think of the Boston Marathon, this will be the first thing I think about—I ran the Boston Marathon."

Michelle L'Heureux decided to skip the marathon that day. Instead, she spent it at her Quincy home with a close friend, and they watched the race on TV. Her boyfriend, Brian, ran it once again, but Michelle just didn't want to deal with the anxiety of returning to the finish-line crowds.

But around 4 p.m., after Brian finished the race, she decided to head into Harvard Gardens, a pub near Beacon Hill, to meet up with Brian and some of his runner friends to celebrate their finish. Michelle was supposed to meet the same group at Harvard Gardens the previous year, but she never got there—instead, she was fighting for her life at Faulkner Hospital.

"I didn't get to go last year," she said. "I got to celebrate with them like I didn't last year. I got to celebrate the marathon. . . . I felt really happy to be in that place that got taken away from me."

They had dinner and champagne. Just two weeks after the anniversary, Michelle went back to the hospital to have surgery on her ruptured eardrum. And in the summer, she had another reconstructive surgery on her scarred left arm.

Tracy Munro had been weeping sporadically since the bombing anniversary the week before. Her nerves were frayed, but she went down to the race with her boyfriend and watched from Coolidge Corner, a few miles from the finish line.

"There were some tense moments when I grabbed on to Bryan's arm in a wave of sheer fear that something bad was going to happen," she said. "But it didn't."

Munro watched as members of Team MR8 passed by on their way to the finish line. Each of the runners received huge cheers along the route in memory of young Martin Richard. An elderly man wearing a New York Yankees jacket and cap, normally considered a sin in the heart of Boston, got a free pass at the finish line because he also wore a necklace with a framed photo of the eight year-old Dorchester boy around his neck with a caption that read: *My Hero*.

The only loud noise coming from the sidewalk in front of Marathon Sports on this day in 2014 was the thunderous sound of applause as Meb Keflezighi of San Diego took his long final strides down Boylston Street.

"My God, here comes the American," shouted a voice in the crowd. Spectators could hardly believe their eyes as no American had won the men's race in more than thirty years.

Thousands of race fans craned their necks to catch a glimpse of Keflezighi as he crossed the finish line. The crowd started chanting, "U.S.A.! U.S.A.! U.S.A.!"

Keflezighi himself had been a face in the Boston Marathon crowd in 2013. He had watched the race but had left about five minutes before the bombs went off.

"When the bomb exploded, every day since I wanted to come back and win it," he said afterward. "I wanted to win it for the people of Boston. It's beyond words."[84]

Keflezighi dedicated his marathon win to the victims. He pointed to his racing bib. Written along the corners in magic marker were the names Martin, Krystle, Sean, and Lingzi.

AUTHORS' NOTE

CASEY SHERMAN

As an author, you're only as good as the stories you write, and the stories we learned about and included in our book will continue to inspire us for years to come. We spent a year working on this book and thousands of hours researching the details and facts surrounding the Boston Marathon bombings. Most of the information we share was told to us firsthand by the men and women who lived it. This book could not have been done without the tremendous courage of Mery Daniel, Michelle L'Heureux, Heather Abbott, Jeff Bauman, Carlos and Melida Arredondo, Alan Starr, Tracy Munro, Bill White, Linda Witt, Colton Kilgore, John Mixon, Jillian Boynton, Sabrina Dello Russo, the Richard family, and so many others.

To the family of Sean Collier, thank you so much for introducing us to your beloved brother and son. I hope we did you proud.

I would also like to thank Governor Deval Patrick for his honesty and leadership, Mayor Tom Menino for his valor, and former Boston Police Commissioner Ed Davis for his guidance. Thanks also go out to Danny Keeler—a true Boston cop if there ever was one—along with Officer Javier Pagan, Larry and Nina Marchese, Bill Poole, and District Attorney Dan Conley.

Thanks to John Dennis and Gerry Callahan for suggesting this project.

A special thanks also goes to Richard Pult, Roger Williams, Dorothy Aufiero, Paul Tamasy, Eric Johnson, George Regan, Tom Cunningham, Corly Cunningham, Lisa Doucet-Albert, B. J. Finnell, John McNeill, and Fisher College, whose students Delia Brimmer, Victoria Guay, and Kaleigh Cordeira worked tirelessly with us on the research for this book. I'd also like to thank Hank and Tricia Lewis and Vantage Deluxe World Travel for a trip that was life changing and life affirming. More information on its great Vantage Heroes Cruise program can be found at vantagetravel.com.

And of course I'd like to thank Laura, Bella, Mia, my mother Diane Dodd, brother Todd F. Sherman, and uncle Jim Sherman.

Please donate to One Fund Boston Inc. at PO Box 990009, Boston, MA 02199.

DAVE WEDGE

I would like to recognize and thank (in no particular order) the following people for their hard work, assistance, support, friendship, and kindness: Dot Joyce, Bonnie McGilpin, Governor Deval Patrick, Mayor Thomas M. Menino, Doug "VB" Goudie, Bill Hemmer, Nicole Dow at CNN, Nicole Kieser at Fox 25, Danny Keeler, former Boston Police Commissioner Ed Davis, Boston Police Commissioner Bill Evans, Mayor Marty Walsh, Larry Marchese, Seth Gitell, Suffolk District Attorney Dan Conley, Boston Police Department Officers Andrew Crosby and Javier Pagan, Watertown Police Chief Ed Deveau, The Collier family, Sabrina Dello Russo, Michelle L'Heureux, Phillip Connolly, Brian Chartier, Carlos and Melida Arredondo, Heather Abbott, Jeff Bauman, Krystara Brassard, Colton Kilgore and family, Elaine Driscoll, Bianca De La Garza, Coach Willie Maye, John Cotter, Jamie Orsino, John Cetrino, Boston Fire Commissioner John Hasson, Boston Fire Chief Joe Finn, my many esteemed and hard-working Boston Herald colleagues, Doug Rubin, Megan Johnson, Gayle Fee, Lauren and Dave Falcone, Emma Ratliff, Graham Wilson, Jeff Lawrence, Kerry and Jim Stanton, Delia Brimmer, the Carvalho family, Christopher Cassara, Kevin Hickey, Matthew McMahon, Robert Hynes, J.P. Plunkett, Brian Bennett, retired New York Police Department Officer Christopher Hunt for wisdom and inspiration, and my family: Jessica, Jackson and Danielle, Dad, Nancy, Allyson and the entire Wedge and Cornelius families. Dave also dedicates this book to the memories of Grace Virginia Wedge, Arlene Grace Wedge, Christopher Reagan, and James Earnest Procaccini. Miss you all every day.

NOTES

[2] MURDER IN WALTHAM

1. Bob Hohler, "Waltham Victim's Girlfriend Says Tsarnaev Visited," *Boston Globe*, May 25, 2013.

2. Ibid.

3. David Filipov, Sally Jacobs, and Patricia Wen, "The Fall of the House of Tsarnaev," *Boston Globe*, December 15, 2013.

4. Alan Cullison, "A Family Terror," *Wall Street Journal*, December 13, 2013.

5. John Blosser and Michael Glynn, "Hate Torn Mom Ordered Boston Bombing," *National Enquirer*, May 13, 2013.

[3] EASY MONEY

6. Donovan Slack, "Snelgrove Panel Rips Police," *Boston Globe*, May 26, 2005.

7. Ibid.

[4] SAFE HAVEN

8. Erik Ortiz, "Zubeidat Tsarnaeva, Mom of Alleged Boston Bombers, Became Increasingly Stricter in Islamic Faith," *New York Daily News*, April 23, 2013.

9. Evan Allen, "State: Marathon Bomb Suspects' Family Received Welfare, Food Stamps," *Boston Globe*, April 26, 2013.

10. Simon Shuster, "A Dead Militant in Dagestan: Did This Slain Jihadi Meet Tamerlan Tsarnaev?" *Time*, May 1, 2013.

[6] DAGESTAN

11. Simon Shuster, "The Boston-Bomber Trail: Fresh Clues in Rural Dagestan," *Time*, April 29, 2013.

12. Howard Koplowitz, "Tamerlan Tsarnaev Had Contact with Mahmud Mansur Nidal, Dagestani Islamic Militant, During Russia Trip," *International Business Times*, April 30, 2013.

13. Anton Troianovski, "Lost Son," *Wall Street Journal*, May 24, 2013.

14. Ibid.

15. Stewart Bell, "Canadian Jihadist's Disturbing Video Shows Fanaticism of Rebels Who May Have Inspired Boston Bomber," *National Post*, May 1, 2013.

16. Tom Parfitt, "Boston Bombs: The Canadian Boxer and the Terror Recruiter Who 'Led Tsarnaev on a Path to Jihad,'" *The Telegraph*, April 28, 2013.

17. Simon Shuster, "Exclusive: Dagestani Relative of Tamerlan Tsarnaev Is a Prominent Islamist," *Time*, May 8, 2013.

18. Cord Jefferson, "Here's the Jihadist Magazine That Taught the Boston Bombers How to Kill," *Gawker* (blog), April 23, 2013, http://gawker.com/heres-the -jihadist-magazine-that-taught-the-boston-bom-478605581.

19. Janet Reitman, "Jahar's World," *Rolling Stone*, July 17, 2013.

[8] TERROR STRIKES

20. United States v Dzhokhar Tsarnaev, Case 1:13-cr-10200-GAO, Document 319 *Government's Opposition to Defendant's Motion to Suppress Statements*, May 21, 2014, http://cbsboston.files.wordpress.com/2014/05/usa-oppostion-to-suppress -statements-05-21-2014.pdf.

[11] SAVING LIVES

21. Elson F. Monteiro, report to Boston Fire Department, May 9, 2013.

22. Phillip Skrabut, report to Boston Fire Department, February 20, 2014.

23. Douglas P. Menard, report to Boston Fire Department, February 20, 2014.

24. Ibid.

25. Mike Foley, report to Boston Fire Department, February 20, 2014.

26. Adalberto Rodriguez, report to Boston Fire Department, February 20, 2014.

27. James Plourde, report to Boston Fire Department, February 20, 2014.

28. David Finkel, "A Father Transformed by Anguish: Scars Define the Man Who Burned Himself After Son's Death in Iraq," *Washington Post*, January 16, 2005.

29. Ibid.

30. Shannon Casas, "Georgia Doctor Aided Victims of Boston Bombing," *Athens Banner-Herald*, April 21, 2013.

[13] KEELER'S GHOSTS

31. Laurel J. Sweet, "Cop Rips Gutless Jurors: Family Rages as Teen's Accused Killer Freed," *Boston Herald*, April 30, 2004.

32. Ibid.

33. Ralph Ranalli, "Judge Accepts Manslaughter Plea in Decapitation of E. Boston Man," *Boston Globe*, February 9, 2005.

34. Boston Globe Staff, "102 Hours in Pursuit of Marathon Suspects," *Boston Globe*, April 28, 2013.

35. Peter Gelzinis, "Cop Watched Over Victims Like a Father," *Boston Herald*, April 11, 2014.

36. Ann MacMillan Bankson, "Remembering a Chance Meeting with Officer Sean Collier," *MIT News*, April 4, 2014.

[15] CITIZEN SOLDIERS

37. Morgan Rousseau, "Boston Marathon Runners Return to Collect Bags, Surprised by Medals," *Boston Metro*, April 17, 2013.

38. Bill Richard, "Statement from Bill Richard Regarding the Bombing Attack on Boston," *Richard Family Updates* (blog), April 16, 2013, http://richardfamilyboston.tumblr.com/post/49044312649/4-16-2013-statement-from-bill-richard-regarding-the.

39. Paige Buckley, "Thousands Attend Vigil for Richard Family, Marathon Victims at Garvey Park," *Dorchester Reporter*, April 16, 2013.

40. M. Alex Johnson and Bill Dedman, "Second Boston Marathon Victim Identified as 29-Year-Old Woman," NBC News, April 16, 2013, http://usnews.nbcnews.com/_news/2013/04/16/17781262-second-boston-marathon-bombing-victim-identified-as-29-year-old-woman?lite.

41. Anthony Everett, "Exclusive: Aunt of Marathon Victim Lu Lingzi Speaks about Loss, Moving Forward," *WCVB Chronicle*, April 7, 2014.

42. Family of Lu Lingzi, "Letter from the Family of Lu Lingzi," *BU Today*, April 17, 2013.

43. Everett, "Exclusive: Aunt of Marathon Victim Lu Lingzi Speaks about Loss, Moving Forward," *WCVB Chronicle*, April 7, 2014.

44. United States v Khairullozhon Matanov, Case 1:14-cr-10159-WGY, Document 1 *Indictment*, May 30, 2014, http://www.mad.uscourts.gov/training/pdf/14-10159INDI.pdf.

45. Molly Hennessey-Fiske, "Owner: Bombing Suspect Demanded His Car Back from Shop on Tuesday," *Los Angeles Times*, April 19, 2013.

46. JuJu Chang and Anthony Castellano, "Dzhokhar Tsarnaev 'Acted Like Nothing Happened' Day After Marathon, Friend Says," *ABC NEWS Nightline*, April 20, 2013, http://abcnews.go.com/US/umass-dartmouth-friend-dzhokhar-tsarnaev-acted-happened-day/story?id=19005157.

47. Miranda Leitsinger, "Classmates of Suspected Bomber Dzhokar Tsarnaev Suggest 'Brainwashing' by Older Brother," *NBC News*, April 21, 2013, http://usnews.nbcnews.com/_news/2013/04/21/17851546-classmates-of-suspected-bomber-dzhokar-tsarnaev-suggest-brainwashing-by-older-brother?lite.

48. New York Post Staff, "Bag Men: Feds Seek These Two Pictured at Boston Marathon," *New York Post*, April 18, 2013.

[17] TRAITORS

49. Eric Moscowitz, "Carjack Victim Recounts Harrowing Night," *Boston Globe*, April 26, 2013.

[19] THE LOCKDOWN

50. John Miller, "Officer in Firefight with Boston Suspects Recalls Moment He Was Shot," *CBS NEWS*, May 14, 2013, http://www.cbsnews.com/news/officer-in -firefight-with-boston-suspects-recalls-moment-he-was-shot/.

51. Richard Weir, "Bomb Suspect Died of Bullet Wounds, Trauma to Head," *Boston Herald*, May 3, 2013.

52. Divina Grossman, "UMass Dartmouth, Message from Chancellor Divina Grossman," *Claire T. Carney Library News* (blog), April 19, 2013, http://www.lib .umassd.edu.

53. Denise Lavoie, "Prosecutor: Tsarnaev Said Martyrs Go to Heaven," *Washington Times*, July 7, 2014.

54. Ibid.

55. Boston Globe Staff, "Dzhokar Tsarnaev, Azamat Tazhayakov at UMASS Dartmouth Day After Bombings," *Boston Globe*, July 15, 2014.

56. United States v Dias Kadyrbayev and Azamat Tazhayakov, Case 1:13-mj-02161-MBB, Document 1 *Criminal Complaint*, May 1, 2013, http://www.scribd.com /doc/138928442/Criminal-Complaint-Against-Dias-Kadyrbayev-And-Azamat -Tazhayakov.

57. Patricia Wen, "Tsarnaev's Roommate Found Friends' Visit Odd," *Boston Globe*, July 8, 2014.

58. United States v Dias Kadyrbayev and Azamat Tazhayakov, Case 1:13-mj-02161-MBB, Document 1 *Criminal Complaint*, May 1, 2013, http://www.scribd.com /doc/138928442/Criminal-Complaint-Against-Dias-Kadyrbayev-And-Azamat -Tazhayakov.

59. United States v Khairullozhon Matanov, Case 1:14-cr-10159-WGY, Document 1 *Indictment*, May 30, 2014, http://www.mad.uscourts.gov/training /pdf/14-10159INDI.pdf.

60. Ibid.

61. Patricia Wen and Milton Valencia, "Pistol in Gun Charge Case Similar to One That Killed MIT Police Officer," *Boston Globe*, July 22, 2014.

62. United States v Dzhokhar Tsarnaev, Case 1:13-cr-10200-GAO, Document 319 *Government's Opposition to Defendant's Motion to Suppress Statements*, May 21, 2014,

http://cbsboston.files.wordpress.com/2014/05/usa-oppostion-to-suppress
-statements-05-21-2014.pdf.

63. Laurel J. Sweet and O'Ryan Johnson, "Feds: Dzhokhar Tsarnaev
Emailed Mom Saying He Would See Her Again in Afterlife," *Boston Herald*,
June 3, 2014.

[20] CAPTURED

64. Heidi Evans and Larry McShane, "What Have We Done?" *New York Daily
News*, April 25, 2013.

65. *The Dennis & Callahan Morning Show*, WEEI Sports Radio Network (Boston,
MA: WEEI, April 19, 2013).

66. Ibid.

67. David Ortiz, "A Year After Marathon, Boston Is Even Stronger," *Sports
Illustrated*, April 21, 2014.

[21] SHARING THE BLAME

68. Adam Goldman and Sari Horwitz, "U.S. to Seek Death Penalty in Boston
Bombing Case," *Washington Post*, January 30, 2014.

69. Florida Ninth Circuit State Attorney Jeffrey L. Ashton, letter to FBI Director
James Comey, March 25, 2014.

70. Associated Press, "Zubeidat Tsarnaeva, Mother of Boston Bomb Suspects,
Insists Sons are Innocent," *New York Daily News*, April 29, 2013.

71. Wesley Lowery and Matt Viser, "Virginia County Officials Say They're
Trying to Determine If Laws Broken in Marathon Bombing Suspect's Secret
Burial," *Boston Globe*, May 10, 2013.

72. Office of the Director of National Intelligence, "Unclassified Summary of
Information Handling and Sharing Prior to the April 15, 2013 Boston Marathon
Bombings," April 10, 2014, http://www.dni.gov/index.php/newsroom/reports
-and-publications/204-reports-publications-2014/1042-unclassified-summary
-of-information-handling-and-sharing-prior-to-the-april-15,-2013-boston
-marathon-bombings.

73. Ibid.

74. Garrett Quinn, "Ed Davis Steps Down as Police Commissioner," September
23, 2013, http://www.masslive.com/news/boston/index.ssf/2013/09/ed_davis
_steps_down_as_boston.html.

[22] FIELD OF DREAMS

75. Associated Press, "Step by Step, Boston Marathon Amputee Reinvents Her
Life," *Boston Herald*, October 15, 2013.

76. Eric Moskowitz, "Living Stronger by the Day, Marathon Victim Aims for Big Ride," *Boston Globe*, November 30, 2013.

77. Comcast Sports New England, September 20, 2013.

78. Bill Richard, "Richard Family Update Four Months After Bombing," *Richard Family Updates* (blog), August 15, 2013, http://richardfamilyboston.tumblr.com /post/58348686890/august-15-2013-richard-family-update-four-months.

79. Anthony DiComo, "Most Valuable Papi: Ortiz Outstanding," October 31, 2013, http://mlb.mlb.com/news/article/mlb/most-valuable-papi-david-ortiz -outstanding?ymd=20131030&content_id=63544092&vkey=news_mlb.

[24] THE NEW NORMAL

80. Michael Wines and Serge F. Kovaleski, "Marathon Bombing Suspect Waits in Isolation," *New York Times*, April 14, 2014.

81. United States v Dzhokhar Tsarnaev, Case 1:13-cr-10200-GAO, Document 319 *Government's Opposition to Defendant's Motion to Suppress Statements*, May 21, 2014, http://cbsboston.files.wordpress.com/2014/05/usa-oppostion-to-suppress -statements-05-21-2014.pdf.

82. Ibid.

83. Ibid.

[25] FROM FINISH LINE TO FINISH LINE

84. Kelly Whiteside, "Meb Keflezighi Carries Victims in His Heart During Boston Marathon Win," *USA Today*, April 21, 2014.